Guide to Software Systems Development

Clive Rosen

Guide to Software Systems Development

Connecting Novel Theory and Current Practice

 Springer

Clive Rosen
Passerelle Systems
Newcastle-under-Lyme, Staffordshire, UK

ISBN 978-3-030-39732-6   ISBN 978-3-030-39730-2   (eBook)
https://doi.org/10.1007/978-3-030-39730-2

This Springer imprint is published by the registered company Springer Nature Switzerland AG
The registered company address is: Gewerbestrasse 11, 6330 Cham, Switzerland

Dedicated to: Sally, my wife, without whose love and support there would have been no chance this book would have ever seen the light of day.

Preface

Why Software Systems Development?

Just over 50 years ago, the NATO conference on software development [4] proposed, almost apologetically, that software development needed to become more like engineering and adopt a more disciplined approach. The term "software engineering" stuck, first as a metaphor, then as a paradigm, originally as a challenge, later as a doctrine.

It should be recognised that, in the 1960s, many software systems were unreliable. Prior to 1968, it was not only the software that was unreliable, but the hardware could also break without warning. But then it was new, state-of-the-art technology. People were astonished at what computers could achieve. It was 10 years prior to the BBC Horizon programme "Now the Chips are Down" [3] when the UK (and possibly the world) woke up to the digital revolution as it is now known. In 1968, people were more prepared to put up with computers going wrong,[1] but even so, computers were beginning to earn a reputation for promising greatness and delivering mediocrity.

At that time, the type of system being developed was very different. Computers were mainly physically large, and expensive mainframe computers and the systems being produced were primarily big infrastructure products used for stock control, payroll or scientific purposes.

Since 1968, the world has been transformed by technology.[2] The technology that sits in a watch would have more than filled a shed the size of a football field. Software development projects were concerned largely with developing operating systems or batch control processes. Today, new software is more likely to be a web-based utility, app or game. Yet large systems developments are still highly

---

[1]It was not until 1981 when Detective Jim Bergerac (played by John Nettles in the TV detective series "Bergerac") was shown throwing a VDU screen through a window in frustration with his computer.

[2]The Summit supercomputing machine unveiled in June 2018 is approximately 10^{12} times as fast as "supercomputers" in 1968.

prevalent, and one thing has not changed. Whilst hardware has become more and more reliable, software reliability has improved little. Brooks, noting the differences between software and hardware in his seminal paper "No Silver Bullet" [1], predicted this. Agile methodologies that have had some success on smaller projects, do not seem well adapted to larger ones [2, 5], and traditional methodologies have a poor track record.

Why is This?

One reason, according to the software engineering community, is that project management teams lack sufficient discipline to ensure that processes and procedures are followed and that standards are maintained throughout the development process. Yet a great many project managers have received training on project tools such as Prince II and are well aware of the processes and procedures that should be used, but the tools and the methodologies they implement just do not seem to work too well.

A second reason offered is that insufficient time and effort are spent gathering and understanding requirements. There is some evidence to support this assertion. This begs the question as to why the requirement acquisition activity is curtailed. Is it simply because during this consultation period, little apparent progress seems to be being made and project managers get itchy feet? Is it rather that no amount of time collecting requirements seems to be enough so developers may as well just get on with the job?

Software systems development takes a broader view. Software systems development starts with the premise that the development process is part of an open system, and as such is subjected to factors beyond the capability of a project manager to control. The product being developed will also be part of a system when implemented, and that system will interact with the software system in multiple and unpredictable ways. Looking at software systems development in this way helps to recognise the tensions inherent in the process that make software systems development a truly challenging endeavour.

There is however one further factor that makes software systems development unique. It is that software systems possess a combination of factors not found in any other human artefact. Firstly, as Brooks identified, software is intangible (and complex). Software is not the only product that has this combination of attributes, but it is the only human artefact that is also determinant. It has a fixed form. Software is exact and precise, a logical algorithm that cannot be changed or respond in real time to changes in its external environment. As such, it is, and has to be, predefined. The problem for software systems development is compounded by the fact that the environment in which it operates is in constant flux, but the software system itself is absolutely rigid. No amount of procedure and formality can square this circle as the software engineering paradigm tries to do. After more than 50 years of trying, it is the contention of this book that it is about time the computing and IT community looked for an alternative.

That alternative lies in investigating the true nature of software systems. This book lays out the argument in support of that alternative. Whilst it does not offer solutions to the problem, it does suggest some practices based on a deep analysis of the problem that could be employed to mitigate the difficulties.

This book explains why the software engineering paradigm has run its course and offers an alternative based on open systems theory. It recognises that software systems development is, at its heart, a problem-solving endeavour and that there are real problems that need to be solved in the present. A purely theoretical approach might provide some answers in the long term, but would not provide solutions to today's problems. On the other hand, just trying to stumble across fixes to those problems on a day-to-day basis fails to advance knowledge on what works, why it works and when it works. Practical proposals have to be based on a theoretical framework so that the limits of the propositions can be tested. This book aims to both provide a theoretical foundation and draw some practical conclusions from it that project managers will find helpful on a day-to-day basis. That is not to say that the project managers will necessarily find the conclusions drawn very comfortably. Change rarely is, but madness is repeating the same thing and expecting the result to change.

The software engineering approach is analogous to continuously tightening the bolts on a rusting machine only to find one or two more drop off every year never to be found again. It is not necessary to throw the whole engine out, but it is about time to start replacing some of the parts and perhaps repurposing the machine for the challenges ahead. It is hoped that this book shines some light on how to do this.

Newcastle-under-Lyme, UK   Clive Rosen

References

[1] Brooks FJ (1987) No silver bullet: essence and accidents of software engineering. Computer
[2] Dingsøyr T et al (2018) Exploring software development at the very large-scale: a revelatory case study and research agenda for agile method adaptation. Empirical Softw Eng 23 (1):490–520
[3] Goldwyn E (1978) Horizon. Now the Chips are Down. BBC. on British Broadcasting Corporation.   https://www.bbc.co.uk/iplayer/episode/p01z4rrj/horizon-19771978-now-the-chips-are-down
[4] Naur P, Randell B (1968) Conference report of NATO science committee. NATO, Garmish, Germany
[5] Rolland K et al (2016) Problematizing agile in the large: alternative assumptions for large-scale agile development. In: 37th International conference on information systems (ICIS 2016). Cork Open Research Archive, Dublin, Ireland

Contents

Chapter 1
A New Approach to Software Systems Development

1.1 Introduction

Open a text book on software engineering (SE) and you will almost certainly find, somewhere near the beginning, a diagram of the software development life cycle (SDLC) (sometimes called "the systems development life cycle" or simply the "software life cycle"). This diagram purports to show the phases through which software development progresses. Ignore for the moment the differences in the naming of these phases between texts, the important point is that one phases follows another in a more or less clockwise fashion until a project is completed. The process is then repeated with another iteration of the product. The actual mechanism of progression will differ depending on the methodology adopted by the project team, but essentially the argument is that the software development process is a continuous process of contiguous phases. If the correct disciplines are applied, this process will deliver a successful software product at the end [16, 22]. To paraphrase the conventional argument, the fact that so many software projects fail, [5, 6, 31] is not due to the limitations of the model, but because software developers fail to comply with the rigours of the methodology that operationalised the model (Fig. 1.1).

This book questions this assertion and the theoretical assumptions on which it is based. An alternative socio-technical paradigm is proposed, but before doing so, some definitions are required. This minor detour is required to provide a solid foundation for the arguments that follow and because the confusion in the use of terminology has hampered better understanding of the software development process. Software Engineering texts often confuse the terms "model", "methodology" and "method". It may appear to be a little pedantic for a practical companion to software systems development (SSD) to engage in esoteric definition, and perhaps not the most engaging way to start this book, but the misuse of these three terms has led to a failure to address the real problems of SSD. The detour will take in:-

(a)   clarifying what a model is
(b)   why models are important

© Springer Nature Switzerland AG 2020
C. Rosen, *Guide to Software Systems Development*,
https://doi.org/10.1007/978-3-030-39730-2_1

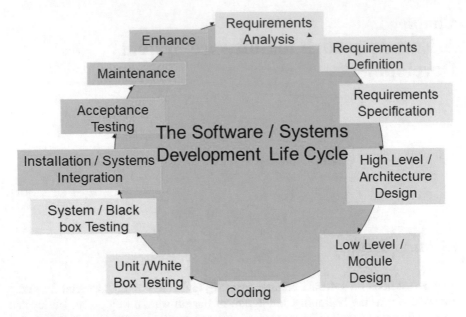

Fig. 1.1 The software development life cycle

(c) defining "methodology" and "method" in the context of the definition of "model".

It is perhaps unfortunate to have to start with such an abstruse discussion when the objective is to provide practical pointers, but getting it over with quickly might prove to be a blessing in disguise. Once having described the terms it will be shown how their inappropriate use has caused such mischief to the understanding of the SSD process.

1.2 "Models", "Methodologies" and "Methods"

In the software engineering literature, the three terms "Models", "Methodologies" and "Methods" are used interchangeably. This has led to some unfortunate misunderstandings.

1.2.1 Models

The term "model" can be used in a number of contexts such as a "mathematical model", "physical model", a "theoretical model" and so on.[1] All models have two things in common;

(a) They aim to represent an aspect of the real world,
(b) They are limited by what they choose to include in the representation.

So, for example, a wooden model of a ship may be accurate in most details as a representation, but it would most likely be smaller than the real thing, and, depending upon the purpose for which the model was made, it may exclude many of the component parts. Similarly, a mathematical model might not include all the factors that might affect a system in the real world. A mathematical model, or any model, only needs to be good enough to demonstrate the aims of the model. It need not, indeed it cannot be 100% accurate and/or precise.

Models can however be invaluable in testing out aspects of a system which would be impractical to do on the real thing. Theoretical models[2] may, or may not have been tested against real world observations. Their purpose might be simply to provide better understanding of how a system works. Alternative models might offer different explanations. Some academic disciplines have an abundance of theoretical models; management theory is composed of them, psychology is defined by them, economics is divided by them. This is not true of software systems development. In software systems development, there is just one, SDLC. Although many texts describe this as a "framework", it is indeed a model as it purports to show the progression of processes required for developing software.

1.2.2 The SDLC Model

A great deal of typescript has been used to give credence to methodologies based on SDLC. The confusion between the model and these methodologies has misdirected academic and business attention towards developing better methodologies when the real problem has been with the reliability of the model. There are a number of methodologies that are claimed, in error, to be models. This confusion between models and methodologies has hampered the development of SSD as a science and led to the misplaced assignment of problems in the field. Disentangling models, methodologies and methods is therefore a necessary starting point.

---

[1] See Mellor [19] for a more detailed discussion.

[2] A theoretical or abstract model is a model based on a theory. Whilst there is a semantic difference between the theoretical and abstract models, in most cases the terms can be interchanged when the model is a theoretical model. (A theoretical model is always abstract, but an abstract model is not always theoretical.)

One of the main purposes of an abstract model is to help to understand a phenomenon. A model cannot be a precise representation of a phenomenon because it cannot include all the factors that might affect that phenomenon. One common use of a model is to help to predict the future. E.g. models of climate change or economic models. This is not the only use of an abstract model as will be seen, but many models do serve this function. The success or otherwise of such a model depends on the extent to which it can help to predict probable outcomes. Within a discipline such models are often hotly contested. Economic models for example may not be very precise. This is usually the result of factors the model failed to take into account. In these circumstances, some will say that the model is wrong, but others might argue that the model just lacks precision, but shows the correct trend. A good model may be judged on how well it enlightens the understanding of the system as well as its accuracy.

SDLC is limited in both these regards.

Firstly, when considering SDLC as a model of the of the systems development process it fails to offer any predictive value. This is because it provides no discrimination between types of software development. All software development inevitably follows the SDLC. The lone whiz kid developing a program for her own use in her garage has to identify why she wants the program and what it is trying to achieve (requirements). She will sketch out a design (either in her head or on paper), then code it up and check to see if it works. This approach differs only in the level of formality and the quantity of documentation produced from say a rigorous Prince II governmental infrastructure project, but the process (and hence the model of the process is the same). Which procedures and standards are imposed before the project can progress from one phase to the next is not an attribute of the model. That is a matter of methodology and is discussed further below. So, SDLC is a model of limited value because, as it is a model of all SSD it has no capability of discriminating between large and small, formal or informal, "good" or "bad" software development projects. SDLC just is. There are two questions however that can be asked of it.

1. Is it helpful?
2. Is it accurate?

Helpfulness is partially determined by accuracy, but not necessarily. If the model presents a way of understanding something it can still be useful even if it is more metaphorical than actual. Accuracy is about the limitations and/or the boundaries of the model. When and where does it stop representing the concept it is intended to represent. Helpfulness is almost entirely subjective for most models (mathematical models may be the exception in this regard) so it is difficult to hold a rational conversation regarding a models helpfulness. The limitations and boundaries of a model however should be as clearly understood as possible. The accuracy of SDLC will now be considered.

SDLC should be considered to be a "process model" as it is intended to describe the phases through which software development passes. It is described as a process model in which one phase follows the next in an organised and clear progression. The Latin phrase for this is "ad seriatim". However, when one looks at the empirical evidence for this ad seriatim process, the findings are disappointing. In reality, almost no software development project progresses this smoothly. Methodologies such as "waterfall" and "spiral" may attempt to manage the progress and restrict deviation from the model by imposing procedures and standards on progression between phases, but the necessity for such procedures only underlines the flaws in the model. The reality of software systems development (SSD) is that during for example the design phase, it is normal to have to revisit the requirements. However meticulously the requirements process has been, inevitable ambiguities arise that need to be resolved. In fact, when we look at requirements definition in detail, it becomes obvious that requirements can rarely be frozen as the software engineering paradigm demands. This will be discussed later in this chapter. The consequence is that there is a continuous interaction between the design and the requirements stages. Agile methods attempt to resolve this problem by eschewing the methods of more traditional methodologies, but such an approach is not always appropriate, and it does not change the reality of the model.

The problem at the coding stage is similar to that at the design stage. Problems arise that may require the programmer to revisit the design stage, or even go back to the requirements stage. In reality, it is possible that during any stage in the SDLC, it can be, and often is, necessary to revisit any previous stage in the life cycle. Thus the SSD process is actually better illustrated by Fig. 1.2 than the traditional SDLC. (Pfleeger suggested something similar [21, p. 51] but considered it to be avoidable rather than an inherent property of the process.)

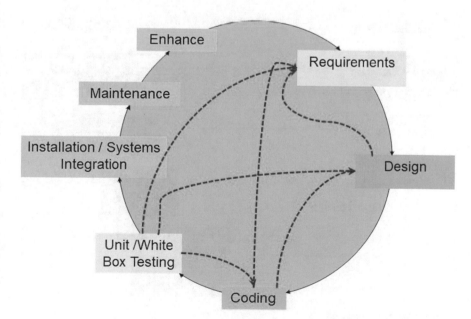

Fig. 1.2 Software systems development actual stage progression process

Previous descriptions of the SDLC as an ad seriatim process are therefore inaccurate. SDLC is better described as a "state" model rather than a process model. In other words, it might be possible to identify what stage or state the development is in at any particular time, design, coding etc., but the model does not provide any predictive value regarding what stage will follow. It may well be a subsequent stage, but it could equally be any of the preceding states. The implications for project planning are evident, and may well account for the failure of many projects to meet their timescales. SDLC cannot be used as a model upon which to base project costs or plans. As a state model SDLC can support decision making regarding what might be required within a state, such as which methods are most appropriate, but offers little in the way of enlightenment regarding progression between states. New models are required for this purpose. This limits the value of SDLC as a basis for designing methodologies as will be shown.

Before moving on to discuss methodology or alternative models, and in apparent contradiction to what has been previously stated, there is one other model applicable to SSD regularly quoted in the literature. It is known as the "V-model" Fig. 1.3. This model looks different from SDLC, but is conceptually very similar. Rather than illustrate the SSD process as a cycle, the V-model portrays it as a hierarchical series of linked pairs. It is still an ad seriatim process model, but each integration phase process is paired with a design phase process by a relationship between fault discovery and fault injection. Rook [24] suggests there is a relationship between processes on the left hand side of the model and processes on the right.

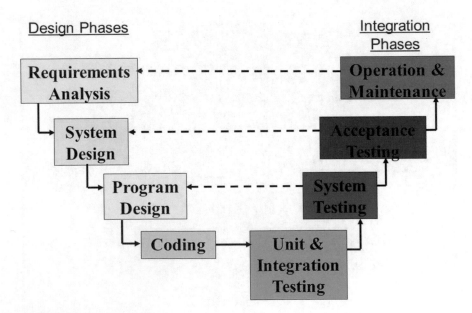

Fig. 1.3 The "V" model [24]

Each integration phase is verified against the corresponding design or specification baseline on the other side of the diagram. (ibid. p. 10)

In other words, faults found in stages on the right hand side of the diagram could be attributed to being introduced during the corresponding phase on the left hand side. Boehm [3] identified the cost of discovering the fault as increasing exponentially as the development progressed through the stages. This finding was verified by Westland [32]. This research led to a great deal of attention in trying to eliminate faults before the project progresses beyond the current phase. Royce [25] to whom the Waterfall Model has been attributed (although Royce himself did not use the term "waterfall") recognised that some rework was likely to be required at each stage. He also recognised that it was likely that developers might need to revisit a previous stage although his aspiration was to limit regression to one previous stage. This was to be achieved by conducting reviews before a project should be allowed to progress to the subsequent stage. Fagan [10] suggested the use of formal "inspections" to identify errors before allowing further progress. Boehm [4] proposed using risk analysis, whilst Beck [1] suggests that this problem is eliminated when using "extreme programming" (ibid. p. 23).

All these proposals are examples of "methods". Whether or not they are effective methods cannot be determined without defining the context in which they are applied and identifying the factors affecting success. Neither the V-Model nor SDLC offer much insight into defining context or identifying success factors. The research provides an example of seeking solutions before a theoretical model of error generation has been developed. The "V" model offers potential insights into the development process in regards to the role faults play in the cost and timescales of a project, but not how to avoid faults.

The V-Model is effectively a redrawn version of SDLC and offers little additional insight with regards to the process itself. Consequently, from a theoretical perspective, SSD is left with a single, flawed model of limited insightfulness. This conclusion would be disputed by those that claim the "Waterfall model" and the "Spiral model" for example are models. In reality these "models" are methodologies based on SDLC because they suggest ways to execute the model and not (partial) descriptions of the world.

1.2.3 Methodologies

A methodology can be described as a systematised approach to the management of a model [15]. It was stated above that there are, within the SE community, a number of approaches that describe themselves as models ("the Waterfall Model" Pfleeger [21, pp. 48–50], Ghezzi et al. [13, pp. 402–405], Sommerville [28, pp. 29–32], "the Spiral Model" [4, 19] etc.) that are not in fact models, but methodologies; they suggest ways in which a model (SDLC) can be operationalised. A model aims to illustrate some aspect of the real world whereas a methodology (in this context) is a systematised approach to implementing or operationalising the model. This is important because the success of a methodology is wholly dependent on the accuracy of the model upon which they are based. The methodology may allow adjustments to be made for exceptions that arise from the limitations of the model, but if, as has been suggested, the model is flawed, the methodology on which it is based will be clunky at best and may even generate additional problems. In software engineering nearly all methodologies, (Waterfall, Spiral, iterative and evolutionary) are effectively based on SDLC. Each, in their own way, attempt to manage the limitations of the SDLC model, but are still constrained by it. The problem is not that this makes these methodologies unviable, but that when problems start to occur in the project, project personnel are blamed for the difficulties, not the underlying process failure. The methodology is used as a defensive shield which obfuscates the real problem that the model fails to address. Software systems development is itself a dynamic process not a static one. SDLC cannot provide the confidence required for project planning and cost modelling. Methodologies based on SDLC fight an uphill battle to maintain control over the process.

The "Agile" community has long believed this [1, 7], but attempts to define an alternative methodology such as DSDM [29] have, not offered an alternative model of the process. Instead they have provided a collections of methods. Methods are useful, but cannot provide insight into the process. They may help to get the job done, but offer no description of what that job is.

1.2.4   Methods

"Methods" are tools or techniques that can be used during the process. Methods include prototyping, pair programming, programming languages, modelling tools, risk analysis and a host of other activities and techniques that have been suggested to support the development process. Methods have the attribute that they need not be exclusive to any particular methodology. The "Daily Scrum" meeting for example is typically associated with the Scrum approach [30], but there is nothing inherent in daily scrum meetings that preclude them from say being used in a Waterfall project. Risk assessment is most commonly associated with the Spiral methodology (nee model); design inspections with Waterfall, but either could equally be useful in an incremental approach.

The distinction between methodology and method is important because it means that project managers have a much larger palate of tools from which to choose than is often suggested by orthodox descriptions of a given methodology. Methodologies are usually accompanied by their own preferred methods. Distinguishing between methods and methodologies liberates the individual methods from application to any given methodology. Daily Scrum meeting could be used during an incremental development. Although Scrum is often described as a methodology, its lack of formal systematisation suggests it would be better described as a collection of methods. Scrum's methods such as pair programming for example, are not restricted to Scrum.

Cockburn, in his original discourse on the Agile approach [8, p. 121] comes close to implying this. Cockburn's description of Agile is actually a meta-methodology; a project manager should choose the most appropriate methods at the appropriate time for the appropriate problem. Cockburn even provides a model for doing this (ibid. p. 116). Unfortunately, whilst Cockburn's proposals might have merit in theory, in practices it appears to have been a bit too radical for the software development industry. In practice industry adopters' of Agile have largely chosen one particular collection of methods, SCRUM.

1.2.5 Consequences of Confusing Models, Methodologies and Methods

Confusion between models, methodologies and methods is symptomatic of a lack of intellectual rigour when it comes to the understanding of the software systems development process. Solutions are proposed, and often widely adopted, before having some basic theory upon which to base an understanding of the conditions in which they might work. This means that the limitations, assumptions and precon ditions upon which they are based cannot be evaluated. A recent example of this is Fitzgerald and Stol [11], who propose "lean" approaches to SSD. This may, or may not be a good idea, but for whom? Under what circumstances would it be a good idea and which potentially catastrophic? The principle behind the "lean" approach seems to come from analogy with manufacturing processes, but unless there is some understanding of the differences between manufacturing and SSD it is difficult to assess whether the analogy is applicable or otherwise.

Models provide a template against which to test a proposition. Empirical evidence, when held up against a model may result in modifications being made to the model. This is the scientific method. Unfortunately, because of the confusion between models, methodologies and methods, the SDLC model has not been challenged sufficiently. Effort has gone instead into proposing methodologies or designing methods. Claiming that methodologies are in fact models obscures the fact that the model has been subject to little critical scrutiny. SDLC may well offer useful insight as a state model. It may be possible to develop models of the transitions from one state to the next, but this has not occurred in SSD because the software engineering paradigm has deflected research interest from the model towards (primarily) method generation. This has not served the subject area well. Alternative models are required if new insight is to be achieved.

Theory does not have to be 'correct' before it can be applied. A good theoretical model however does provide a benchmark against which observed reality can be measured and empirical evidence collected. Kurt Lewin is attributed with the saying "there is nothing so practical as a good theory". Models can be tested, refined, improved or abandoned in the light of new evidence. They provide a basis upon which to advance understanding. Confusing methodology with models provides no basis

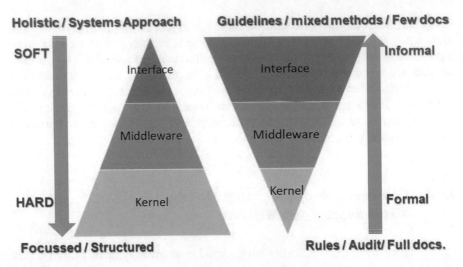

Fig. 1.4 A model for choosing a methodology based on Beynon-Davis [2])

upon which to assess the benefit derived from a methodology or when this benefit is likely to be greatest or of little use. How can one reasonably choose whether to adopt a formal methodology such as PMBok [22] or one of the Agile approaches?

1.2.6 A Model for Choosing a Methodology

Whilst not a model of the SSD process Benyon-Davis' three level software architecture model [2] (Fig. 1.4) is an example of a model that could help to choose an SSD methodology. This model suggests that the decision is dependent on the type of project. Most projects can be considered to contain three levels of software; a kernel or infrastructure part, a middleware (transitional) component and an interface component. Projects that require major infrastructure development upon which the middleware and interface are dependent, are likely to require a more formal methodology, more rigid disciplines and a greater level of development documentation. This is because timescales are likely to be greater, the number of people and groups larger and the system more complex. Making changes to the kernel in this situation are likely to be costly due to the repercussions for dependent middleware.[3]

Consider for example a major infrastructure project to manage tax revenues, and the management of goods and services across a newly constructed national boarder with an expected product life of 50 years. What might this product architecture look like? Probably some foundation software developed for the government based on innovative technologies such as block chain, mass data collection and advanced data

---

[3] Although object orientation and code encapsulation is intended to minimise inter-module dependency, this cannot always be avoided at the systems level.

analysis techniques. The security requirements of such a system would probably be paramount, so access to this infrastructure would need to be restricted to fully validated and authorised APIs (Application Programming Interfaces), possibly written by third party suppliers. The APIs in this case would provide the bulk of the middleware. End user transactions from say companies registering freight movements would be required to interface with the APIs. Such a system may well look like the left hand pyramid depicted in Fig. 1.4. It is difficult to see how one might complete this development using an emergent design approach such as XP.

The reverse is true for developments that are composed mainly of interface development such as a new web site, requiring little middleware or kernel. These are provided by web browsers and the World Wide Web. The infrastructure already exists in the form of the World Wide Web and interface changes can be quickly and relatively cheaply made independently of each other. Scrum or XP might be ideally suited for this type of project.[4]

At the beginning of this chapter it was shown that SDLC did not discriminate between informal casual projects and highly formal mission or safety critical projects. SDLC describes all projects regardless of their formality. The Beynon-Davis model helps to fill that void.

Methodologies can be applied in a "hard" or a "soft" manner. A "hard" implementation would infer the rigorous application of procedures such as inspections and change control management. This would be appropriate for safety and mission critical applications. Maintaining strict control over project costs would require focus on contractually agreed requirements. Project organisation would be more formally structured. A "soft" approach would be the reverse; less formal, more flexible organisational structures, and procedures; guidelines rather than standards and rules.

This is a relatively crude model that nevertheless could support significant decision making on the project. Furthermore an organisation might choose to refine it for its own purposes and circumstances and thus deriving its own methodology as suggested by Cockburn [7, 8]. For any given project this might be a pragmatic approach to choosing a methodology which is more likely to achieve better results than picking any pre-defined methodology off the shelf. However, organisations tend to look for packaged solutions (methodologies) possibly because they are easier to apply and they appear to offer greater credibility and therefore security than a pick and mix approach. Generalised methodologies must be based on credible models. SDLC as a state model rather than a process model fails to offer insight into the process so cannot provide general guidance on an appropriate methodology.

---

[4]It is quite possible for a project to contain developments at all three architectural levels. It may therefore be appropriate to choose a different methodology for each part of the project. This is something a manager might consider.

1.3   The Appeal of Software Engineering

SDLC is based on the software engineering paradigm; the idea that the software development process is analogous to engineering development processes. This paradigm emerged from the NATO conference on software development [20] attempting to improve the success rate of SSD projects. The concept of software engineering was proposed very tentatively. Since then it has become the preeminent paradigm.

There is very little doubt that the software engineering approach has great appeal. It offers a systematic, methodical predictability that contrasts with the unpredictability of craft industries and undisciplined code hacking. In the 1960s when programming was emerging as a major commercial opportunity, providers were looking for a methodology that would convince investors that software developers knew what they were doing. Software engineering provided a convincing narrative. Whilst there have been notable failures, the ubiquity of software intensive systems suggests that there has been sufficient success to allow the software engineering paradigm to endure. However this has parallels with the shaman's promise of a cure. If most people would survive anyway, those few that don't can be disregarded as not following the remedy closely enough. Sometimes the belief in the cure is, in itself, sufficient to encourage the recovery of the patient. Sometimes fixing the "accidental" issues as Brooks might say, that is the hygiene problems, will promote improvement. If however, there is little fundamental theory that can be empirically tested, then it becomes impossible to say that this treatment was responsible for the observed effect. Software engineering methodologies are similar. They are based on the principle that something is better than nothing, and if discipline works for engineers, it should work for software developers. This reasoning fails to appreciate the fundamental differences between software systems and engineered systems that are elucidated in the next two chapters.

The analysis that follows suggests that the engineering metaphor, first tenuously presented 50 years ago by Naur and Randell (ibid.) as a way forward, is not a suitable paradigm. Whilst it may be appealing as it offers the prospect of the predictability of engineering, it cannot deliver on that promise. A different approach based on the true nature of software systems is required. This takes the form of SSD as a socio-technical process based on social interaction, interpersonal and intergroup communications that must be resolved into a determinant artefact.

Whilst many methodologies recognise the importance of communications in software systems development projects, none have located communications at the heart of the process. Doing so changes the nature of the debate and provides a new perspective on the challenges faced by SSD. Understanding these challenges offers the prospects of more effective solutions being found.

1.4   A New Model?

Having made the distinction between models, methodologies and methods, it becomes apparent that there are an abundance of methodologies and methods, but a that can sparsity of models that can offer deeper understanding of the process. Methodologies and methods are the tools of the practitioner, models are the tools of the theorist. SSD started life as a practical activity; as a tool to solve a very real problem. It did have a theoretical basis in mathematics and logic, but digital computers soon became a potential solution looking for a much broader swathe of problems than the confined, and well defined military challenges that nurtured their initial development. Breaking out of those confines resulted in mathematics alone becoming insufficient for providing theoretical support for the new uses to which computers were being put. In particular, as the 1968 NATO conference recognised, there was a lack of understanding of the software development process hence the proposal for a software engineering paradigm. However, the software engineering paradigm should not be the end to the search for theoretical models. The seductiveness of the paradigm seems to have led to its becoming a fetish. Confusing models and methodologies has obscured the critical evaluation of the model. If greater clarity is to be achieved, new models have to be developed.

This is not the first call for further development of theory in computing. A call emerged from the International Conference on Software Engineering 2000 [9]. Sommerville [27] made a similar plea. Glass in a series of articles [14] appeared to endorse this call. McBride [18] suggested the need for such theory. Mäkelä and Mutanen called for a new research domain of "Software Business" in 2005 [17]. This particular call was roundly dismissed by Rönkkö et al. [23] on the grounds that Mäkelä and Mutanen had failed to make the case that the software business was sufficiently different from any other business milieu to warrant it being a new research domain. In terms of business, this may well be the case. Rönkkö et al. (ibid.) lay out the criteria for justifying a new research domain.

> To constitute a discipline, research on software business would need to define its paradigm including research subjects, sets of topics, and theories. Additionally, if a new paradigm for software (business)[5] were to succeed, it should demonstrate superior explanation when compared to the current paradigms in for example economics and sociology (ibid. p. 207)

This is a tough challenge, and not one likely to be met in total. This book does however

1. Aim to differentiate SSD from other artefact production and development activities
2. Aim to offer a new paradigm without claiming that this is the only possible perspective.
3. Offer a coherent theoretical basis for the new paradigm in relation to other academic disciplines.

---

[5]Brackets added by author.

The full ontology called for by Rönkkö et al. is well beyond the scope of this book, but it is hoped that this book will set a compass in that direction.

SSD however, as has been pointed out, emerged as a result of searching for a practical solution to a real problem. Even if one considers computing's origins from the Jacquard loom, the focus was on the capabilities of the machine, not the digitisation of the patterns. That came later. In this spirit of practical problem solving, the practical implications of the theories presented here will be explored in the context of the everyday realities for software systems developers and project managers.

Experienced project managers often feel misunderstood and misrepresented, particularly when things go wrong. The press and other technology commentators are keen to highlight software system failures [5, 6, 12, 26]. The blame, and certainly the responsibility is often placed at the manager's door. The clear implication is that they have they failed to follow the processes, procedures and standards so clearly laid down in the quality manuals. SSD project managers must be less capable than project managers in other fields. Little is said about the practical limitations of those processes, procedures and standards. If failure is so prevalent, then perhaps the theory behind the processes, procedures and standards is flawed. This is the contention of this book. As a result of the practical orientation of SSD, an alternative theory is offered together with an exploration of the practical implications for software systems development. This book argues that SSD is inherently more challenging than other production and development environments. This may come as a relief for project managers even if they are less keen on the implications for their practice. There are however a number of suggested ideas on how some of the difficulties can be mitigated.

Theory that is undermined by empirical evidence needs to be challenged. Theory that does not inform practice might be of academic interest, but, at least in the short term, is of limited value. But practice in the absence of sound theory provides no basis for understanding and therefore no prospect for improving practice. Theory informs practice and practice should evince new theory. This book aims to challenge the existing theory of software engineering, offer an alternative theoretical approach and explore the implications for practice. The current paradigm has passed its 50th birthday. It is due to be challenged.

1.5 Discussion Questions

1. How closely do project managers adhere to any of the development methodologies available?
2. Is software failure as common or as serious as it is portrayed?
3. How important is it to distinguish between models, methodologies and methods? Is this distinction useful?
4. Are there other models of software systems development that might be considered helpful?
5. Is software engineering a reality, an aspiration or an oxymoron?

6. Who is to blame for SSD failures?
7. Is it true that there is very little theory in SSD and if so, does it matter?
8. What would a model of transition between states of the SDLC look like?

References

1. Beck K (2000) Extreme programming explained. Addison-Wesley, Boston
2. Beynon-Davies P (2002) Information systems: an introduction to informatics in organisations. Palgrave, Basingstoke
3. Boehm BW (1981) Software engineering economics. Prentice-Hall, Englewood Cliffs, New Jersey
4. Boehm BW (1988) A spiral model for software development and enhancement. Computer 21(5):61–72
5. Charette R (2005) Why software fails. IEEE Spectr 2005(September):36–43
6. Charette RN (2005) Why software fails. IEEE Spectr 42(9):42–49
7. Cockburn A (2000) Balancing lightness with sufficiency. Cutter IT J 13(11):26–33
8. Cockburn A (2002) Agile software development. Addison-Wesley, Boston, Massachusetts
9. Easterbrook S et al (2000) Beg borrow and steal workshop. In: International conference on software engineering, Limerick
10. Fagan ME (1976) Design and code inspections to reduce errors in program development. IBM Syst J 15(3):182–211
11. Fitzgerald B, Stol K-J (2017) Continuous software engineering: a roadmap and agenda. J Syst Softw 123:176–189
12. Flowers S (1996) Software failure—management failure. Wiley, Chichester
13. Ghezzi C et al (2003) Fundamentals of software engineering, 2nd edn. Prentice Hall, Upper Saddle River, New Jersey
14. Glass RL (1998–2009) Loyal opposition. IEEE Softw
15. Gonzalez-Perez C, Henderson-Sellers B (2008) Metamodelling for software engineering. Wiley, Chichester, UK
16. Iso ISO et al (2017) Systems and software engineering—software life cycle processes. ISO/IEC, Switzerland, p 12207
17. Mäkelä MM, Mutanen O (2005) Research in software business: implications of the special qualities of software as a good. In: Proceedings. 2005 IEEE international engineering management conference, vol 2. IEEE, pp 780–783
18. McBride N (2007) Letter to the professors. Retrieved 20/05/2007, 2007
19. Mellor P (1998) A model of the problem or a problem with the model. Comput Control Eng J 8–18
20. Naur P, Randell B (1968) Conference report of NATO science committee. NATO, Garmish, Germany
21. Pfleeger S (2001) Software engineering theory and practice, 2nd edn. Prentice Hall, Upper Saddle River, New Jersey
22. Project Management Institute (2000) A guide to the project management body of knowledge. The Project Management Institute, Pennsylvania, USA
23. Rönkkö M et al (2010) The case for software business as a research discipline. In: Tyrväinen P, Jansen S, Cusumano MA (eds) International conference of software business (ICSOB). Springer, Jyväskylä, Finland, pp 205–210
24. Rook P (1986) Controlling software products. Softw Eng J 1(1):7–16
25. Royce WW (1970) Managing the development of large software systems: concepts and techniques. WESCON, Los Angeles

26. Sardjono W, Retnowardhani A (2019) Analysis of failure factors in information systems project for software implementation at the organization. In: International conference on information management and technology (ICIMTech). IEEE, Jakarta & Bali, Indonesia, pp 141–145
27. Sommerville I (2003) Key note. Empirical assessment of software engineering. Keele University, Keele, Saffs, UK
28. Sommerville I (2011) Software engineering, 9th edn. Pearson/Addision Wesley, Boston, Massachusetts
29. Stapleton J (1997) DSDM dynamic systems development method. Addidon-Wesley, Harlow, UK
30. Sutherland J, Schwaber K (2017) The scrum guide. The definitive guide to scrum: the rules of the game. ScrumGuides.org
31. The Standish Group International (2015) The Chaos Report 2015. The Standish Group, Boston, Massachusetts
32. Westland JC (2002) The cost of errors in software development: evidence from industry. J Syst Softw 62(1):1–9

Chapter 2
The Nature of the Beast

2.1 Introduction

Since the 1960s the accepted conceptual model adopted for software systems development (SSD) has been the software engineering paradigm. This approach draws an analogy between SSD and engineering development arguing that the disciplines used to develop engineering products are applicable to software systems products. This analogy has (as was noted in Chap. 1) been appealing, but it has its limitations. The model presented based on the software engineering paradigm is the software development life cycle, and in Chap. 1 this was shown to be flawed in both helpfulness and accuracy. This is the result of a failure to appreciate the limitations of the comparison with engineering. The most significant of these is tangibility. Engineered products are tangible, software systems products are not. This has an impact on requirements definition, users, developers, communications between users and developers and communications between developers within the development team. The implication of the analysis of these points leads to a new communications model of software systems development based on a socio-technical paradigm. This chapter will explore each of these issues in turn to demonstrate the need to move on from software engineering and look towards developing new models and methodologies.

2.2 The Nature of Software

Fred Brooks in his seminal work on the nature and characteristics of software "No Silver Bullet" [3, 4] differentiates "accident" and "essence" in the software development process. Brooks identifies four essential characteristics of software; "complexity", "conformity", "changeability" and "invisibility".

© Springer Nature Switzerland AG 2020
C. Rosen, *Guide to Software Systems Development*,
https://doi.org/10.1007/978-3-030-39730-2_2

Complexity is, perhaps, the best understood or at least most well researched[1] of these properties. Although made up of only three very simple constructs (sequence, iteration and selection) interactions and combinations of these constructs soon become highly complex. Small programs are relatively easy to follow, but the complexity seems to increase almost exponentially with size.

In Brooks' discussion of conformity, he suggests that software systems must conform to real world systems as, essentially software attempts to model aspects of the real world, be it a stock control system or a tax collection system. (Obviously games software can escape this particular characteristic as it generates its own world!)

Brooks' third characteristic, "changeability", refers to the ease with which software can be changed. This he considered to be a problem because each time a program is changed, it suffers from entropy, that is a (very slight) degradation from its original integrity. Eventually, when a sufficient number of changes have been made, the program becomes unsupportable. Object orientation (code encapsulation) is intended to protect against this particular eventuality, however OO addresses functionality rather better than it addresses quality requirements.)

The fourth characteristic Brooks identifies, "invisibility", has perhaps the most profound impact on software systems. Software cannot be seen. It runs in a virtual environment that composed of electronic signals passing between digital components. Software systems can be represented in various diagrammatic forms and the software itself is represented by the coding language constructs. These are abstract representations of the binary pulses that execute the actual algorithms. The artefact itself only exists in digital form which is essentially invisible. The code may be a precise representation of the software, but it only shows sequence, not timing.

In fact, software is not only invisible, it is intangible. That is, it cannot be heard, felt, tasted or smelt.[2] Software is one of very few human artefacts that have this particular property.

Intangibility makes a cognitive difference to appreciation of an artefact. It is possible to visualise something that is tangible and develop physical models. Intangible products can only be modelled abstractly. Physical properties also make common understanding easier. Software doesn't have this luxury. This is a major difference between software systems and engineering systems.

There are other intangible products, financial services and education amongst them. However, Dijkstra, in his advocacy of formal methods pointed out that software is also determinant, that is, it has a fixed form [7]. Software is a mathematical formula, a set of algorithms, precise, and for a given version of the code, unchanging. This property, of determinacy, when combined with intangibility made software a unique human artefact. Other intangible products such as financial products lack the precision of software. Tangible products can more readily be modelled physically,

---

[1] A brief search of IEEE Xplore reveals that more than 25,000 articles on the subject have appeared in the last 50 years.

[2] The user interface clearly has physical characteristics and can be represented in a variety of forms, but it represents only a part of the code. The code invoked by the interface has the same characteristics as all other code.

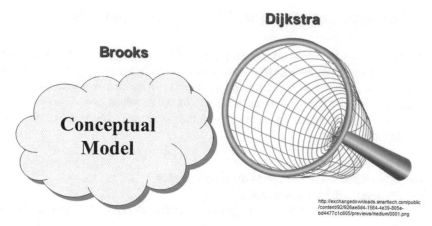

Fig. 2.1 The objective of software systems development

software cannot. So software is both conceptually abstract and determinant. In other words software systems development is like trying to contain a misty cloud in a butterfly net. Furthermore, as will be shown later, the cloud is constantly changing shape, size and density (Fig. 2.1).

Dijkstra's advocacy of formal methods has failed to achieve traction in the real world largely because it is predicated on the need to develop formal specifications. Formal specifications require at least four conditions;

1. A clear and definitive understanding of the requirements.
2. An ability to freeze those requirements.
3. Stakeholder agreement on the requirements.
4. Measurable outcomes.

However, particularly in large systems development projects (excluding perhaps system control programs), at least three of these conditions cannot be met (1, 2 and 4), and the fourth is unlikely. Point 1 is discussed below. The inability to achieve Points 2 and 3 are the inevitable consequence of the discussion on point one. Point 4 is discussed in detail in Chap. 6.

The combination however of Dijkstra's determinacy and Brooks' intangibility result in software systems being a unique type of artefact. The software systems development process is therefore worthy of specialist study on these grounds. The engineering metaphor cannot be appropriated in its entirety without critical evaluation of all its implications. An alternative paradigm however needs to pass Rönkkö et al.'s [17] test referred to in Chap. 1. This challenge has to show what is so extraordinary about software systems development and to offer an alternative model to support the paradigm. What follows aims to meet this challenge.

2.3   The Nature of a Software System's Requirements

Text books on requirements engineering generally act as works manuals on how
to collect software systems requirements. Tools and techniques are very useful, but
they avoid the practical problems of requirements elicitation. A number of these
difficulties arise from the number and diversity of stakeholders, and others from the
nature of the product. When all are taken together, they result in the uncomfortable
conclusion that

- Requirements are always incomplete
- New requirements will emerge as projects progress
- Requirements will be misconstrued
- Requirements elicitation is a socio-political activity as much as it is a technical
  one.

Van Lamsweerde [18] identifies 11 desirable qualities of requirements:

- Completeness
- Consistency
- Adequacy
- Unambiguity
- Measurability
- Pertinence
- Feasibility
- Comprehensibility
- Good structuring applied to documentation[3]
- Modifiability
- Traceability (ibid. pp. 35–36).

Unfortunately, the top seven are unachievable as will be shown below. The consequence is that requirements are emergent, cannot be frozen and that tensions will
always exist between competing versions of the requirements.

2.3.1   The Ambiguity of Natural Language

Van Lamsweerde (ibid. p. 120) identifies six problems in using natural language to
define requirements

- Ambiguity
- Noise
- Forward referencing
- Remorse

---

[3]This point applies to documenting the requirements rather than the requirements per se.

- Unmeasurable statements
- Opacity (ibid. 120).

He proposes applying local rules to minimising the impact of these flaws, but prefers to use a "semi-formal" (ibid, p. 127) specification language to supplement natural language. This is a standard approach to the problem of recording requirements.

This approach however does not eliminate the risk of using natural language alone. It also adds to the problems by losing some of the richness of natural language and, by adding a layer of interpretation to the original, creating greater potential for misinterpreting the original requirement.

People's use of language is both unique to them and context specific. In other words, the requirement analyst must understand both the person and the situation of the person. To achieve this, she/he needs to develop a positive relationship with the stakeholder so that misconceptions and ambiguities can be minimised. This can only be done in the language of the stakeholder. How the analyst uses the data is a second order problem.

2.3.2 Non-functional Requirements (NFR)

It is probably fair to say that when most systems developments fail, it is not because the system doesn't do what it is supposed to do, but because it doesn't do it well enough.

There are two types of requirements; functional and non-functional (also known as quality[4]) requirements. A functional requirement is one that does something; you can either add a name to a database or you cannot. That function is either part of the system or it is not. A binary decision has to be taken as to whether to include a function or to omit it. Functional requirements often reflect processes in the real world. So, providing one has a clear definition of the process, it is possible to implement the function. It is of course possible to fail to register a particular functional requirement in the requirements specification for many reasons such as failing to speak to the right person, failing to ask the right questions or failing to apportion the correct significance to an event. One might argue that this results from an inadequate requirements elicitation process, but, as will be shown, there are other potential causes. Functional requirements lend themselves to encapsulation and object oriented implementation. Developers are generally quite adept at providing functionality when they know it is required.

Non-functional requirements are much more difficult. They do not address what the system does, but how well it does it. NFRs have a range of values from good to bad, high to low. They are much more difficult to identify, specify, design a system

---

[4]Kotonya and Sommerville [13] include other types of requirement and constraint other than quality requirements such as process requirements and external requirements amongst the non-functional requirements. Here, no distinction is made between NFRs and quality requirements; they are used interchangeably.

to meet, measure or test to see if the system is satisfactory. NFRs define the quality of the system; such things as reliability, portability, usability and security.[5] From the user perspective there is often little consistency regarding how good a system is or should be. Take for example a travel advice system.[6] It is relatively straightforward to provide a function to implement say a query on whether a traveller needs a certificate of vaccination for yellow fever to enter a particular country from some other country. However, if one asks how long a user might be prepared to wait for a web page to load with the information, there is no definitive answer. One client sitting at home, planning a world trip might be prepared to wait a couple of minutes or longer. After all there is no particular rush. For someone sitting in a passenger terminal, desperate to book the last seat on a plane to Cameroon with a dodgy internet connection and the battery on their laptop running low, 10 s might seem an eternity. Performance is one of the quality attributes that is relatively easy to specify as it has units of measurements against which it can be evaluated. Most quality requirements do not. Take for example security. One might be able to say that a particular system is "not very secure" or "has known vulnerabilities", but what is the measure of "very secure"? It is quite possible, by adopting secure development strategies, to enhance the probability of producing a secure system, but assessment is risk based and largely subjective [12]. Determining the goal/requirement of the quality attribute beforehand remains difficult. Bass et al. [1] suggest using "quality attribute scenarios". Scenarios are a useful method of eliciting all forms of requirements and their proposal offers a structured approach that leads to a metric based on the systems response to a stimulus. Van Landuyt and Joosen's study on this approach [19] suggests that its success is dependent on the assumptions made about the requirements during the requirement gathering process and these can have both positive and negative effects.

It is both difficult to identify measures of quality criteria, and to evaluate the relative importance of NFRs. This is problematic because quality criteria can conflict with each other. Take for example usability and security. These two criteria are, almost by definition, diametrically opposed. Any security measure introduced into the system will make the system harder to use. Passwords are a classic example. How frustrating is it when one cannot remember a password when all one wanted to do was check a flight time? Security might also compromise performance and even maintainability. Having relatively few valid metrics for NFRs results in problematic design decisions. Evaluating trade-offs between one quality criterion and another is problematic when the decision depends on ones point of view. The criterion cannot be measured effectively particularly as the relationship between the objective of the requirement and the design decision is, in any case, tenuous due to the problems associated with designing in quality.[7] IEEE 1061-1998 (R2009) and IEEE 1061-1992 [10, 11] identify a process for doing this, but provides little guidance on how to implement the design decision.

---

[5]NFRs are discussed in more detail in Chap. 6.

[6]This example is returned to later when discussing end users.

[7]See Chap. 6.

NFRs manifest themselves at the systems level. Their impact only becomes evident when the whole system is implemented. So the effect of a design decision made at the module level, may not become apparent until the whole system has been integrated. This provides a strong incentive to make minimal changes to the system at any one time when this is possible so that the system level effect of the change can be assessed. When one is developing a new system, the kernel of the system has to be developed before any functionality can be delivered.[8] It may not be viable to test components of the infrastructure for its quality attributes before other components are also ready. Testing small units of code may not be viable in this situation.

As non-functional requirements are analogue in nature, being precise about the standard the system needs to achieve is difficult, and, as discussed above, the standard might be context sensitive. As NFRs are a function of the system as a whole, it is difficult to methodically design a product that satisfies the standard set. Often, it is only when the system is installed in its working environment that the quality criteria can be effectively assessed. At this point, fixing problems can become very expensive. In the case of, for example, security, it may not be known whether the systems is secure enough until the system has been breached. Even if one were able to establish an appropriate standard at the start of a project, the dynamic nature of the real world could result in that standard being insufficient by the time the product is delivered. A rival product may have changed user expectations; a new, more invasive virus might have been released; a government regulation might have changed. These types of problem are not restricted to software systems developments, but the intangible nature of software can make them harder to track and implement.

The idealised view that requirements should be frozen gives insufficient recognition to NFRs and their nature. The consequence has been that rather than developing models of how and under what circumstances NFR volatility grows, software engineers have proposed "get arounds" such as XP and Scrum. Abandoning methodology for a set of methods may provide a quick fix in some circumstances, but does not help better understanding of the process.

Stakeholders are not a single homogenous group of like-minded people who all think the same way and want the same things. Different groups, with different requirements and objectives, will stress different aspirations, even contradicting each other. Often non-functional requirements are taken for granted. For example, it may seem obvious to a stakeholder that the system should present an identical interface whatever platform it runs on, so there is no need to even mention it. A developer may not appreciate that even "minor" differences to accommodate different technologies are unacceptable to some users because they constantly have to switch between platforms and might find differences confusing. Other users may prefer an "optimised" solution because this takes advantage of features available on different platforms. If the user representative is from the latter group, they may not appreciate the difficulty it might cause to the former group. When the members of the first user group eventually see what has been done, fixing the "error" may be very costly. Obviously, identifying this type of omission early in the development process is desirable, but

---

[8] See Chap. 1.

not always possible. It is the sort of problem that leads developers to ask the question 'when did the requirement change?'. The answer being that it never did, but no one knew.

2.3.3   Emergent Requirements

Requirements volatility is the bane of the software developer's life. Having coded up a particular function, she/he is told it is no longer needed or that it needs to be modified and, "by the way, can you shove this in as well?".

However frustrating this is, it is also inevitable. It is the consequence and analogue of "over simplification syndrome".[9] As users and developers learn more about how a system works, or has to work, the more complex it becomes and the more anomalies and omissions that have to be dealt with.

SSD is particularly prone to this syndrome because of the complexity in the processes it tries to model and because of the inherent difficulty of processes definition.[10] As the development progresses, it becomes evident that a particular task had not been identified, or that it was not done the way that had been assumed, or that it was not the only task that needed to be performed.

Possibly, if more time had been take in the requirements acquisition phase, these omissions might have been identified, but requirements gathering has to be terminated at some point. Usually this it an arbitrary decision as no process currently exists for determining when requirements collection should be ended.

Agile methodologies have taken the view "that's fine; we'll include it in the next iteration", but when the requirement is part of an infrastructure component, this may not be appropriate. The inevitability of emergent requirements means that methodologies need to learn how to handle them (and volatile requirements; see Sect. 2.3.6) or new methodologies must be developed in the future.

2.3.4   Tacit Knowledge

Developer have to produce a determinant product where each process identified in the requirements analysis has to be converted into a predefined process composed of sequences of data manipulation. Understanding the stakeholders themselves adds an order of magnitude to developer's problem. When one bears in mind the intangible nature of the product being developed this adds yet another order of magnitude

---

[9]"Oversimplification syndrome" is the tendency people have to minimise the difficulties when they are not in possession of sufficient data. The less people know about a subject, the simpler it seems to be. The converse is also true; the more one knows about something the more one appreciates the complexity of it. "A little knowledge is a dangerous thing" because of "oversimplification syndrome".

[10]See Chap. 3.

to her/his difficulties. Stakeholders live in their own bubble that can be called "the Application Domain". In this world, they are the experts. They have their own knowledge and understanding of how that world works, an expertise that they have built up over the time they have worked in that world. As they develop their expertise, they move from a rules based understanding to an intuitive awareness of how things operate. The rules cannot explain or account for every eventuality. The more complex that world, the more likely there are to be exceptions occurring to the rules. The process of becoming an expert is a process of internalising how to deal with the exceptions. This expertise becomes tacit knowledge that only emerges when it is needed. It is expertise that even the holder does not know they possess until they need it. It is difficult for a novice (such as a requirements analyst) to recognise.

One requirements elicitation techniques used is that of observing "an actor" as they do their work. The actor is then asked why they took a certain action during an observed event. The actor will often provide an explanation. This explanation is actually a post hoc rationalisation of something they will have done without thinking. It will, almost certainly be a simplification of what was actually going through their mind. This means that much of what application domain experts describe to developers is imprecise and omits potentially valuable information. If the stakeholder doesn't know they possess the knowledge, they cannot pass it on to the requirements analyst. Systems theory, discussed in Chap. 3 suggests that this is unavoidable. Generally speaking, trying to identify information that is missing is much harder than identifying incorrect information, particularly when the explanation provided is plausible. This lack of detail often results in the need to clarify what happens in a particular situation later in the development. Sometimes it can result in a complete failure to handle a particular factor or condition.

2.3.5 Exceptions/Anomalies to the Process

Amongst the most catastrophic failures that occur in systems are those that are caused by exceptions to the normal operation. That is, those situations that occur rarely or have never previously occurred. As has been noted above, in systems that have been operational for some time, users develop expertise to handle anomalous events. This is often referred to as a sixth sense. A new system needs to handle exceptions to the process in a safe way, and so must pre-empt them. This requires capturing the expertise of the user.

It is advisable therefore that, during the elicitation process, time is dedicated to identifying potential exception scenarios and documenting them. This might be achieved by "war gaming" situations for example to identify potential anomalies. How common this is at present is hard to know. Gaming, or something similar would be a useful addition to most requirements elicitation methodologies to help to identify anomalies and handle volatile requirements.

2.3.6   Volatility of Requirements

Chapter 3 discusses the proposition that software systems have to model the real world. The real world, by its very nature is constantly changing. It is inevitable therefore that some of these changes will affect the software system as it is being developed. Sometimes failing to incorporate a change will render the system obsolete or unviable before it is even commissioned. How volatile the environment is will be reflected in how often requirements are likely to change during the SSD project. If the environment in which the software system is expected to operate is volatile, it will increase the risk to the project and to the project's timescales. This should be assessed as part of the project's risk evaluation exercise. The probability is that an environmental change will affect the system's design at some point and the development process needs to be capable of managing this (as was identified regarding emergent requirements and exception handling.) This change management process needs to be a standard part of the development process rather than treated as an exception to that process. It might prove difficult to estimate the cost of change management, but, as has been argued above, it is inevitable that change will be required during the development and need to be accommodated within the development process.

2.3.7   Summarising Requirements

Summarising the argument above, it can be seen that software system requirements are prone to change, will emerge over time, are hard to identify and often oversimplified. Non-functional requirements in particular pose challenges for developers. Most of these problems are rarely given the attention they deserve, because they are assumed to be "frozen" before the real process of development begins. In any moderately large software systems development it is very unlikely that requirements can actually be frozen.

Understanding requirements from the stakeholders' perspective is challenging but necessary. It requires a deep awareness of, one might even say empathy, with the stakeholder. This is a social skill, not a technical one. Evaluating trade-offs between different stakeholders and their requirements requires organisational sensitivity, political judgement as well as an understanding of how these decisions will affect the system design. This is a socio-political skill as well as requiring technical knowledge. Despite this being common knowledge in the industry the engineering paradigm offers little insight into solving these socio-technical questions and has attracted relatively little research interest.

Given the centrality and the complexity of the task, it is concerning that the role of specialist requirements analyst in the software systems development process (SSDP) is so undervalued [9]. Requirements elicitation is too often considered to be something that happens before the real job of developing the system begins, when not only is it critical to the whole enterprise, it runs parallel to the other activities in the development process and occasionally gives them a kick just to prove it.

Requirements elicitation demands a great deal more attention from a theoretical and a practical perspective, but it also requires much greater regard for the demanding role it plays in the development process and the sophisticated skills it requires to conduct it well.

Yet understanding the nature of software system requirements is only one side of the challenge. It is people who generate those requirements, and it is also essential that the requirements elicitation process recognises the characteristics of the people involved. The next section explores this phenomenon.

2.4 The Nature of a Software System's Users

A stakeholder is any person or group that has either a direct or indirect interest in the system, and they are highly diverse. There are basically three categories of stakeholder, commissioners, end users and system administrators. In addition there are people who will be affected by the new system who are not directly involved with it. The characteristics of each of these roles is discussed below.

A distinction will be made in the next section between the application domain and the development domain. The application domain is where the system will be used. This is not a geographic location, but a group of people (stakeholders) who will have access to the system in one capacity or another. In contrast the development domain, self evidently is where the system is developed. Again this refers to the developers, not their location. Both these domains are populated with groups of people, stakeholders in the application domain and developers in the development domain. The rest of this chapter will be devoted to exploring the two domains and the relationship between the two domains.

2.4.1 Categories of Stakeholder

2.4.1.1 Commissioners

Generally speaking the most prominent stakeholder, and the one who, for obvious reasons, receives the most attention is the "commissioner" or sponsor; the person or group who initiates the project and bank roles it. It is the commissioner(s) who identify the aims and objectives of the system and who carry great influence regarding what is to be done, and often, how it is to be done. Their requirements are obviously very important. They are often treated as the most important requirements and given the most attention. This can be a problem. As a product, SSD shares a characteristic with baby food and nappies. The purchasers of these products are rarely the actual consumers of the product. Commissioners may never actually come into contact with the system and are probably not expert in how it should work. Commissioners generally want to keep development costs and timescales to a minimum but also like to know how much investment they are committing to the project. Commonly they are not the real users of the system, and their aims and objectives may well conflict with other stakeholders. Consider, for example, an automation project that is likely to make current workers redundant, or a tax and benefit system that may reduce system management costs, but will result in benefit claimants incurring additional costs to register.

Requirements are usually generated by commissioners or their representatives. Their detailed knowledge of the system is often more theoretical than practical. It is the way the system is supposed to work rather than the way it actually does work. Their perspective is one of business goals rather than detailed systems knowledge and expertise. After all, it is not so important what work arounds or add-ons that have been introduced, provided the system (however it works) meets the needs of the organisation. Commissioner's representatives will often be mistaken for systems experts when this may well not be the case. They may also be the only stakeholders actually consulted about the requirements. This can, and often does lead to problems later on in the development.

2.4.1.2 End Users

The actual users of the system can be highly diverse.

Returning to the example, of the travel advice and booking system. One might need to take account of visa regulations, travel bans, location safety, local taxes, airline flight schedules and perhaps a dozen other functions. Users might include seasoned travellers, backpackers, silver surfers looking for their first cruise. Users can also include contributors to the system, travel companies, visa management companies, health officials and hosts of others. In addition there are the representatives of the organisation who are providing the service. They may require information on how the system is being used, processes for charging other users, means of moderating contributions and so on.

Each group will have their own requirements and expectation, ways of interrogating the system and so on. Identifying the range of users might be difficult in itself requiring the contribution of travel advice experts, foreign exchange consultants and holiday representatives as well as members of the provider organisation.

Each group will have a particular way of seeing the world which could affect the way they interact with the system.

End users are the real experts regarding the system. They hold the tacit knowledge, knowledge of the exceptions, (they may, in some cases be responsible for generating the exception) and the operational quality requirements. They are also subjected to changes from existing systems to the new system. Their understanding of the system is critical. Generally though they have lower status than commissioners of the system. Some may not be consulted at all when projects are planned. The representatives of the commissioners may be mistaken in some instances for end users. End user stakeholders are likely to be many and varied (as in this example) so it is difficult and costly to consult them all. Sometimes end users are considered to be collateral damage as when, for example a person's job role is downgraded or when the commissioner's plans change. If end users see themselves as victims of systems change, they are likely to be uncooperative. As they hold expert knowledge, this can be detrimental to the elicitation process.

Elicitation methodologies and methods are often directed at end users, but, if they are not consulted, or insufficiently consulted, the elicitation techniques are of limited value. If the system is to be successful, developers and commissioners must consider access to, the cost of and the time to be allocated to consulting end users. Commissioners also need to consider how much end users will be involved during the development and post-delivery phases.

2.4.1.3   Administrators

A third category of stakeholder that needs to be considered are the systems' operators and administrators. Their perspective is entirely different to both commissioners and end users. Amongst their concerns are maintainability, reliability and the identification and correction of problems when they do arise. The consequences of failure to take sufficient care of their concerns and expertise is well illustrated by the systems migration project undertaken by TSB, a UK high street retail bank, in April 2018. This was an £18 m project that went badly wrong, locking customers out of their accounts and exposing some accounts to other, unauthorised customers. The project has reportedly cost TSB £200 m and may result in additional multimillion pound fines being imposed by the Financial Conduct Authority. System administrators are considered to be low status stakeholders lacking specialist expertise. They are often left out of consultations on requirements, but, as can be observed from this example, this can be a costly error.

2.4.1.4   Indirect Stakeholders

Indirectly affected stakeholders are least likely to be considered by changes to a system. They may be, for example, customers or suppliers of an organisation, and will be expected to conform to the new processes. Should this result in losing the customer or supplier, this would have a detrimental effect on the organisation. Indirect stakeholders might be hard to identify, but during the requirements acquisition phase, at least some consideration should be given to who they might be and what impact the new system might have on them. Losing one's customers because, for example, the new system unnecessarily requires additional information from them, would be unfortunate, and possibly avoidable.

2.4.2   Conflict of Interest

The conventional approach to requirements acquisition is to talk to the commissioners and the commissioner's representative experts, identify the processes to be included in the system, specify the functional requirements with a nod towards some quality requirements, produce a requirements specification and hand it over to the developers to implement.[11] In this scenario, there is limited scope for conflict of interest between stakeholders as user representatives are generally aligned to the objectives of the commissioner. There may be some disagreement about priorities and the importance of quality attributes between different sectional interests that is often resolved by decisions made by the commissioner's representatives.

When end users and administrators are included in the requirements elicitation process and greater consideration is given to the NFRs, there is much greater scope for stakeholder disagreement.

Each stakeholder group will have a unique perspectives on what the system should do and how well it should do it. Each user group will also have some vested interests. In the case of the organisation's employees, these interests will reflect the internal politics of the organisation, and are likely to result in conflicting requirements for the system. These are real issues. They are not manufactured by soliciting a more diverse range of views. They present a problem for the system's designers earlier in the development process than if only a small group of stakeholders is consulted. Conflicts of interest must be resolved at some point. Sooner is better than later as the longer the conflict of interest lies undiscovered, the more rework that is likely to be required.

The issues raised by different stakeholder groups are likely to be as much socio-political as they are to be technical. This does not mean that they are unimportant with regards to the system design. Differences will reflect stakeholder groups' perspective on what the system should be (is) for as well as what it should do. Their perspective affects users' expectations of the system. If these expectations are unfulfilled it will impact the users' acceptance of the system.

Resolving socio-political conflicts within the client's organisation may seem to be outside the developer's remit, but as far as they affect the system design, they are very much the designer's concern. Resolution depends on diplomatic sensitivity and political adroitness as much as technical expertise. These are not normally skills associated with requirements engineers, but, seen from this perspective, they are necessary if a viable system is going to be delivered.

2.4.3   Status of Stakeholders

Heavily affecting the resolution of conflict in a new systems development is the status of stakeholders. Different stakeholder groups have different status within an

---

[11] A caricature certainly, but often not too far from the truth.

organisation, even if the stakeholder is from outside an organisation.[12] This can be totally unrelated to their interaction with the system. As has been previously observed, commissioners generally have the highest status among stakeholders, and the greatest influence over the system's design, but may never have to make direct use of it, and may not know much about what it should do at an operational level.

Low status groups (potentially including the system's administrators) are rarely consulted about their requirements. Their views are likely to be ignored even if they have been consulted. It might actually be difficult to even speak to them (see Sect. 2.5).

Requirements analysts need to be aware, and take account of how status relationships are likely to affect the determination of what the system does and it operates, adding further to the skill set they require.

2.4.4 Conclusions Regarding Stakeholders

The potential diversity of stakeholders' interests, perspective, world view and status makes it difficult to "capture" a complete set of requirements. Tools help. Kotonya and Sommerville [13] suggest "viewpoint analysis" for recording stakeholder perspectives. Identifying stakeholders, evaluating their input and then integrating it into a coherent set of requirements is the difficult part [16]. The problem is though that even when this has been done, requirements will continue to change. Minimal changes in relationships between stakeholders can result in radical changes in requirements as the socio-political currents change. Such subtle changes are often hard to detect. If the requirements capture process has been completed (or at least considered to be so) the focus of interest will be on technical accomplishment of those requirements, not on how the requirements are changing. If one acknowledges that requirements are in constant flux, then it is development process that needs to change to accommodate that reality. If one accepts the socio-political nature of requirements, then it becomes essential to employ people who have the skill to interpret the socio-political currents and explain how they impact the system requirements.

2.5 The Nature of Communications Between Users and Developers

2.5.1 Access

Curtis [5, 6] observed that organisational problems interfere with developers being able to communicate with stakeholders. He argued that behavioural change was

---

[12] A large, valued customer will hold greater sway than an occasional purchaser.

required as well as better tools. A number of those tools such as conferencing software, email, blogs etcetera are now available that make it at least technically possible for people to communicate effectively over a distance. Yet it is still rare for regular contact to be made between the two groups, even when such contact is a prescribed part of the development methodology as it is in Agile development.

The reason for this is that contact is a socio-political problem, not a technical one. The hierarchy of organisational structure is not simply for organisational efficiency, it reflects power and authority within an organisation. Maintaining the hierarchy involves maintaining authority over communications both within the organisation, but particularly between the organisation and external bodies. In other words, it is in the general interest of the organisation to control communications between stakeholders and the development domain. Similarly the development domain will also have its own power structures and even if the organisational structure is looser, it will have vested interests in controlling external communications.

It is unsurprising therefore that communications between the application domain and the development domain will be restricted. Overcoming these particular barriers depends upon the cultural norms of the application domain and the development domain organisations. This is a socio-political issue, not a technical one.

2.5.2 *Language and Culture*

Stakeholders live in a world of their own which can be described as the "Application Domain". Application domain inhabitants have their own specialist jargon for sharing ideas in their world; commonly used phrases, short cuts, and common assumptions. For example in the financial world people talk about "hedging", "hair cuts", "dead cat bounces", "bulls" and "bears". Every application domain will be replete with similarly obscure terms. Some terms will define specific concepts, others will be context specific. The systems development domain has some concepts that have different meaning to different groups. For example beta testing within an in-house development team might mean the second phase of testing, black box testing or systems testing. For an application developer beta testing might mean allowing public access to the software in order for them to discover errors. During requirements elicitation, it is not only essential to know the language, but also to be able to interpret it correctly. The language often provides pointers to the cultural values of an organisation. Organisational and personal values are not normally considered important in software development. They do however influence the stakeholder acceptability of systems changes. They also influence the worth requirements engineers give to a particular contribution because the organisation's values predispose the requirement engineer to who is, and who is not legitimately allowed to express a particular point of view.

2.6   The Nature of the Problem

This chapter began with a discussion on the nature of software and the observation that software is intangible. This means that when expressing what they want, stakeholders will describe an abstract concept of what they imagine the system will look like. As software is intangible, it lacks physical representation, so the image will remain purely conceptual, existing only in the mind of each individual stakeholder. The concept will be phenomenological, that is uniquely construed by each person from their world view. It will include some conception of the processes involved and some of the hopes and expectation they have for how the system will work.

It will be incomplete and constantly changing. It will be incomplete because, as noted above, much expert knowledge is tacit and only accessible when required. It will be changing because, as the person changes their perceptual angle on the system, their conceptualisation of the system shifts.

In an artefact with physical properties, the conceptualisation can be written down, drawn or modelled which helps to stabilise the concept. This is not possible in software systems, so the conceptualisation remains abstract, conceptually incomplete, variable and unique. This is the same for every stakeholder, so the system to be produced can be represented by Fig. 2.2.

All these requirements, hopes and expectations constitute an ethereal cloud of abstract thoughts that the stakeholder expects the new system to satisfy (conceptual models 1 6); When these are brought together they form an abstract conceptual model, the Abstract Conceptual System (ACS). This ACS will similarly be both incomplete and volatile.

The ACS is incomplete because of the limitations of requirements elicitation, because it is not possible to elicit requirements from all stakeholder groups and because each stakeholder's conceptualisation will be incomplete. The ACS will be compromised further due to their lack of status of some of the stakeholders in the application domain, political considerations such as not wanting certain groups to know about the development or logistical reasons. Some groups may be protective of their expertise. Other groups may not wish to cooperate in the requirements capture

Fig. 2.2 The requirements capture process illustrated

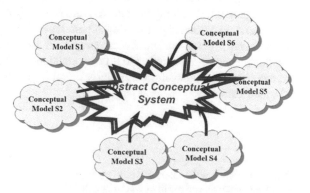

process. In the real world, it is rarely possible to speak openly and freely to all stakeholder groups. This Abstract Conceptual System now has to be handed over to developers for implementation.

Stakeholders live in the Application Domain in which enculturation has grown common(ish) concepts, language and ways of viewing the world. Developers inhabit a different world, "the Development Domain". Developers too have their own jargon; O-O, C#, encapsulation, recursion. Each term means something to another developer, but may mean nothing at all to someone unfamiliar with developing software. Some terms such as "artificial intelligence" seem to mean something to the lay person, but have multiple layers of complexity to the expert. Developers of course have their own expertise and specialisms and a particular (some might say peculiar) way of seeing the world. This expertise is not that of the application domain, and it is a very rare individual who has expertise in both. These differences cause an hiatus between application and development domains. Attempts at interdisciplinary approaches to overcome this problem have largely failed because of this breakdown in communications [2].

A software system, being a determinant model of the application domain, needs to capture as much of the expertise of the application domain as possible to replicate and presumably enhance the model. In fields other than SSD, product developers are probably expert in the domain[13] in which they are developing. They also have the advantage of being able to produce physical models of that product before embarking on full scale production. These physical models facilitate communication between developers and other stakeholders and so can minimise the chances of misunderstanding through miscommunication. The intangibility of software makes this impossible for the software developer. Systems developers have produced various diagrammatic representational forms of the systems design, but these are abstract representations and often require expertise to interpret. By definition being models of the system, they are incomplete. Such modelling tools have generally been designed to help developers do their work rather than facilitate communication with stakeholders. Each role within the software development process has its own way of viewing the system and, to some extent, its own culture and language. Consequently system architects might have one understanding of the ACS, designers, coders, testers and documenters might have very different understandings.

Managers of the development process are generally one step removed from access to the detailed knowledge that developers have. They may well be expert in the development process and possess management and leadership skills, but it would constitute a superhuman effort to hold an equal level of expertise of the detail of the product as well. Managers, particularly on large projects, need to manage through delegated authority.

---

[13]This is not always the case. Advertising creatives may not be experts in the product they are advertising, but they can readily demonstrate their ideas with mock ups or story boards.

2.7 A Model of the Problem

The problem of communicating requirements exists not only between the application domain and the development domain, but between developers within the development domain and between developers and their managers. So from a communications perspective, the SSD process looks like Fig. 2.3.

Stakeholders in the application domain and developers in the development domain will each have their own, unique understanding of the ACS. Being an abstraction, it will be incomplete with little awareness of where the gaps are and therefore how significant these gaps might be. As a conceptual model it will be reconstrued each and every time any person thinks about it. The ACS therefore is constantly changing. The success of an SSD project therefore is a function of three factors:

1. The extent to which stakeholders and all developers hold a shared vision of the ACS, its consistency.
2. How much of each person's vision is included in the ACS, its completeness.
3. How much and how quickly the ACS is changing, its volatility.

The conclusion to be drawn from this argument is that understanding the factors that affect these three issues, is more relevant to the success of an SSD project than the development process used to develop it.

Requirements analysts with specialist expertise in communication skills might be considered ideally placed to oversee this process. Yet as Herrmann observed [9] specialist requirements analysts are a rare breed in the software systems development process (SSDP). This may be one reason why SSDP has the poor reputation for success that it has.

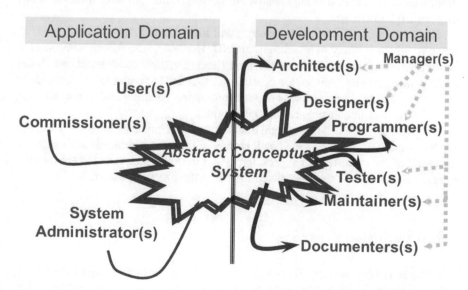

Fig. 2.3 A communications model of the software systems development process

2.8 A Paradigm for the Problem

Figure 2.2 suggests that each stakeholder creates an apperception of what they want from the system and what they perceive to be in the ACS. This is construed from their personal understanding of the system, their previous experiences plus their attitudes, values and expectations. Requirements therefore consist of both technical and social attributes [2].

The elicitation process requires the communications of each stakeholder's apperception of the ACS with each developer who must evolve their own apperception. This is also socio-technical in nature [8].

Developers need to communicate with each other. Whilst diagrammatic tools have been developed to support this process, due to the intangible nature of software systems, these are abstract representations. They require expertise to interpret and transition into some other form of abstract representation, such as lines if code. There is much room for differences in interpretation which can only be resolved by intra-team communication [2]. So the systems development process itself includes socio-technical processes.

Finally, the system itself becomes a representation of real world processes and interacts with its external environment. This, unless it is a fully embedded system, will require some human engagement. Hence, the output from these processes should be considered from a socio-technical perspective.

Given that so much of the software systems development process at least contains socio-technical components, it must be worth considering what can be learnt from other academic domains, research and practice about how they address their problems. One should of course bear in mind the differences determinacy and intangibility make, but only looking towards one school of thought must limit the scope of potential knowledge.

There is already considerable research and theory into socio-technical systems, much of which is likely to be relevant to SSD. However, new theory is required to better understand the nexus of a product being both intangible and determinant. Better understanding of this combination of attributes may lead to better tools for handling it. Methodologies must be capable of accommodating volatility and incompleteness as well as miscommunication and misperception.

It is possible that a better paradigm than the socio-technical paradigm and a better model than the ACS can be developed. However, the tools techniques and cognitive approach of the socio-technical paradigm seem to offer some new insight into the problem that is SSD. This is expanded further in the following chapters.

2.9 Conclusion

Over the last fifty years since the term "Software Engineering" was first coined [15], software engineers have worked to constrain the impact of the factors that affect the SSDP using a flawed process model (SDLC). The methodologies based upon

SDLC have struggled to return consistent and effective results. The socio-technical factors identified here are, as Brooks might have said [3] the "essence" of SSD, not "accidents" of the development process. The software engineering approach has had some success as can be seen from the ubiquity of working software systems in use today, but it has also had many notable failures. Some have put this down to the inconsistent use of process. The argument presented here is that the process needs to be redefined.

The software engineering approach has constrained the ways of thinking about the unique nature of software and how this affects the process of developing software systems. It is only through a better understanding of the actual process that it will be possible to develop more consistently effective methods of working.

This chapter suggests that one fruitful view might be to consider the ongoing relevance of communications in the development process. This view sees SSD as a socio-technical process rather than a purely technical one. Such a view enables the adoption of theory from non-technical fields to inform how software systems should best be developed. Some may regard this as a retrograde step, but if a more broadminded approach achieves better results, it has to be worth considering.

This socio-technical approach to SSD is not new having originated with Mumford [14]. It has attained some brief moments in the limelight, but failed to achieve ongoing acceptability. The software engineering mentality tends towards seeking tools and methodologies to alleviate the inherent difficulties. Socio-technical systems design (ibid.) and socio-technical systems engineering [2] have sought this route, but this may not be the best approach, at least in the first instance. The cognitive gap between the application domain and the development domain can only be closed by people with the requisite comprehension and communication skills. The uncomfortable conclusion is that developing sufficient people with these skills is the real challenge of software systems development.

2.10 Discussion Questions

1. Do Agile methodologies provide the only means of managing volatile requirements?
2. What mechanisms are there for ensuring software systems satisfy stakeholder quality requirements?
3. How can software systems designers balance competing stakeholder requirements?
4. Is there anything that can be learnt from the design of other non-determinant products or services?
5. How can communications between developers and stakeholders be improved and what has to change to enable this?
6. Is oversimplification syndrome a real phenomenon and if so what can be done to tackle it?

7. If the arguments presented in this chapter are correct, how is it that so much software is produced successfully?
8. Is the software systems development community ready for a new paradigm?

References

1. Bass L et al (2003) Software architecture in practice, 2nd edn. Addison-Wesley, Boston, USA
2. Baxter G, Sommerville I (2011) Socio-technical systems: from design to systems engineering. Interact Comput 23(1):4–17
3. Brooks FJ (1987) No silver bullet: essence and accidents of software engineering. Computer
4. Brooks FJ (1995) No silver bullet refired. In: Brooks FJ Jr (ed) The mythical man-month. Addison-Wesley, Reading, Massachusetts, pp 205–226. 20th Anniversary Edition
5. Curtis B (1989) Three problems overcome with behavioral models of the software development process. In: 11th international conference on software management. ACM
6. Curtis B et al (1988) A field study the software design process for large systems. Commun ACM 31(11):1268–1287
7. Dijkstra EW (1989) On the cruelty of really teaching computer science. Commun ACM 32(12):1398–1404
8. Guinan P et al (1998) Enabling software development team performance during requirements definition: a behavioral versus technical approach. Info Syst Res 9(2):101–125
9. Herrmann A (2013) Requirements engineering in practice: there is no requirements engineer position. In: Fraunhofer JD, Opdahl AL (eds) REFSQ'13 proceedings of the 19th international conference on requirements engineering: foundation for software quality. Springer-Verlag, Essen, Germany, pp 347–361
10. IEEE (1993) IEEE Std 1061–1 992 IEEE standard for a software quality metrics methodology. Institute of Electrical and Electronics Engineers Inc, New York USA
11. IEEE (2009). IEEE Std 1061-1998 (R2009) IEEE standard for a software quality metrics methodology. The Institute of Electrical and Electronics Engineers, Inc., New York USA, 1061-1998 (R2009)
12. Katt B, Prasher N (2018) Quantitative security assurance metrics—REST API case studies. In: 12th European conference on software architecture: companion proceedings (ECSA '18). ACM, Madrid, Spain
13. Kotonya G, Sommerville I (1992) Viewpoints for requirements definition. Softw Eng J 7(6):375–387
14. Mumford E (2006) The story of socio-technical design: reflections on its successes, failures and potential. J Inf Syst 16(4):317–342
15. Naur P, Randell B (1968) Conference report of NATO science committee. NATO, Garmish, Germany
16. Nuseibeh B et al (1994) A framework for expressing the relationships between multiple views in requirements specification. IEEE Trans Softw Eng 20(10):760–773
17. Rönkkö M et al (2010) The case for software business as a research discipline. In: Tyrväinen P, Jansen S, Cusumano MA (eds) International conference of software business (ICSOB). Springer, Jyväskylä, Finland, pp 205–210
18. Van Lamsweerde A (2009) Requireents engineering from system goals to UML models to software specification. Wiley, Chichester, UK
19. Van Landuyt D, Joosen W (2015) On the role of early architectural assumptions in quality attribute scenarios a qualitative and quantitative study. In: 2015 IEEE/ACM 5th international workshop on the twin peaks of requirements and architecture. IEEE, Florence, Italy

Chapter 3
Software Systems Development:
An Open Systems Perspective

3.1 Introduction

Chapter 2 looked at the basic software engineering assumption that software systems requirements could be frozen. It argued that requirements are dynamic and emergent. Therefore methodologies based on the erroneous assumption of frozen requirements are inherently flawed. The last chapter proposed an alternative paradigm to the software engineering metaphor; that of SSD as an interpersonal and inter-group communications problem. The model presented the SSD challenge as being one of how to coalesce disparate stakeholder and developers' visions of what is required into a coherent and, ultimately singular view of the required system. Whilst the Agile community recognised this problem, their approach has largely been solutions based, rather than theory based. Agile practitioners have generally adopted a collection of ad hoc methods to solve the problem they face without reference to solid theory to guide their choices. Without a coherent theoretical framework upon which to base decisions, it is hard to generalise, so what works in one place burns and crashes in another. The previous chapters argued that many SSD projects fail because the software engineering paradigm fails to provide a functional theoretical framework.

Overturning a paradigm that has stood for fifty years demands an alternative that is more convincing and leads to more effective ways of working. Providing such an alternative is a multifaceted challenge. First the alternative needs to have a coherent and sustainable theoretical foundation. Secondly it must resonate with workers in the field. Finally, it must lead to more successful, and preferably lower cost solutions.

The previous chapter instigated the process of providing an alternative model. The communications model of the process however is observational rather than predictive. It illustrates the problem but does not indicate a solution. Although it cannot be claimed that this chapter provides a solution[1] it does contribute further insight into

---

[1] Chapter 7 does make some suggestions.

© Springer Nature Switzerland AG 2020
C. Rosen, *Guide to Software Systems Development*,
https://doi.org/10.1007/978-3-030-39730-2_3

the problem. Open Systems Theory and the thinking that accompanies it, provides a different filter through which to consider SSD. Open systems theory is used in a wide variety of disciplines where the problem being addressed is complex and largely unstructured. By acknowledging that this is the nature of the SSD challenge, open systems theory promises to provide some insight into the problem. Some would argue that open systems theory lacks the precision and rigour of an engineering approach. The close alignment of SSD with mathematics and the historical association of computer hardware with electrical engineering has predisposed the discipline to an engineering mind-set. So, whilst methodologies based on open systems theory have been proposed for software systems development in the past, it is an approach that has not received wide spread acceptance. This chapter makes the case for considering SSD as being amenable to an open systems analysis and proffers some practical implications of open systems thinking.

The chapter begins by describing what an open system is and why open systems theory is relevant to SSD. Open systems theory leads to "open systems thinking" (OST). When applied to SSD, open systems thinking provides some insights into the SSD decision making process which could reduce the number of ill-fated projects being undertaken. It also raises some questions about the development process itself. As mentioned above, derivatives of open systems thinking, in particular Soft Systems Methodology (SSM) [2, 7, 21] have been around for some years without gaining a great deal of traction. SSM, as its name suggests, is a methodological approach rather than a theoretical concept. As such it can provide an implementation framework, but not a conceptual model. It can be argued that one reason for the poor uptake of SSM is the lack of theoretical foundation. There are certainly other reasons. There is always inertia about switching from one methodology to another. There has to be a very good reason for adopting what is quite a complex methodology requiring investment in training and tools. Software engineering is replete with methodologies and tools and seems to offer simpler answers. More evidence is required before a commercial organisation will change direction.

The argument presented here is intended to provide theoretical support for an open systems approach. It may not be sufficient on its own to overcome the inertia mentioned above, but it does suggest that open systems thinking provides a better analysis of the software systems development process than software engineering and provides a platform for further study.

This chapter recognises two distinct, but interrelated applications of open systems thinking to software systems development. The first, is in using open systems thinking as a means of analysing the requirements of a software systems development. This is how SSM, for example, has applied open systems thinking. The second application of OST is to view the software systems development process itself as a process in an open system.

3.2   What Is an Open System?

To understand open systems theory, it is necessary to provide a definition of a "system". At its simplest a system is a process chain where a process is defined as a means of transforming one or more inputs into one or more outputs. The output of one process forming the input to a subsequent process (Fig. 3.1).

As the system is composed of processes that can have multiple inputs and outputs, systems can become complicated quite quickly (Fig. 3.2).

However, processes are composed of sub-systems. The definition of a sub-system being that it is itself a system (i.e. a process chain). This recursive definition of a

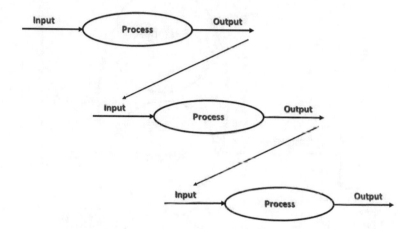

Fig. 3.1   A simple system

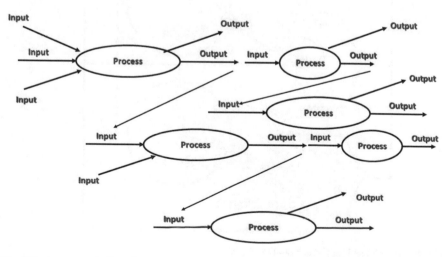

Fig. 3.2   A more complicated system

subsystem was elegantly drawn by Beer [4] when describing his "Viable Systems Model" (VSM) (Fig. 3.3).

Beer's model illustrates a process chain, Systems A, B, C and D. Progression between the systems is not necessarily linear as is shown by System B feeding back into System A. The output from any system can provide input for any other system. Beer also includes the concept that all systems contain subsystems. In the diagram this is only shown in Systems C and D, but all systems do incorporate subsystems. System C can be described as the Subsystems C's parent system. It can also be seen that Subsystem Cs and D are exact replicas of the parent model, illustrating that they

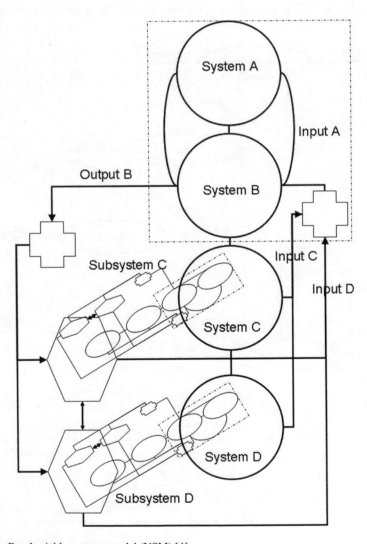

Fig. 3.3 Beer's viable systems model (VSM) [4]

are process chains where every process in the chain has one or more subsystems. Subsystems can connect with other subsystems as Subsystem C and Subsystem D do. They also provide feedback into their parent system. This feedback is attenuated meaning that it is sort of filtered and fuzzy as is the input from the parent system to the subsystem. This input and feedback is often difficult to describe and can be subject to change.

All systems exists within an external environment on which it is, to some extent, dependent. At the same time, subsystems have an effect on its parent environment. A system also consists of subsystems that are both dependent and affective.

For example, a car exists in its external environment, such as a city. The car relies on the city to provide its fuel, roads and the processes by which it was manufactured. The car has various subsystems such as a braking system, a fuel combustion system and a heating system. The car returns transportation as well as exhaust emissions and noise to the external environment. The car is only viable because of the parent environment and the parent environment both benefits and suffers as a result of the car.

Systems can be "open" or "closed". In theory, a closed system is one that is hermetically sealed from its external environment, that is, it receives no inputs from it and returns no feedback to it. In reality, very few, if any, systems exist in this state. Beer would consider any that do to be "non-viable". Electronic, embedded systems come the closest to this state, but still receive some input from the system in which they are embedded and also cause changes in their external environment. In practice, a closed system may be considered to be one that has very few inputs from the external environment. So for example an engine management system could be considered to be a closed system.

An open system is one in which there are innumerable inputs from its external environment, and often innumerable outputs that affect the environment. Social systems such as the education systems and biological systems are open systems. Socio-technical systems, by dint of the fact that they involve people are also open systems. Inputs are extremely diverse and might include thoughts, attitudes, emotions, economic factors, cultural factors, power relationships and many more. This results in making it extremely difficult to predict outcomes when one makes changes to the inputs into a social or socio-technical system.

3.3 An Open Systems Perspective of SSD

Open systems are relevant to software systems in two dimensions. Firstly software systems aim to model open systems when developing new products. It is this dimension of open systems that SSM and DSDM have attempted to encapsulate.

Secondly, the software system development process is itself an open system because the people involved in the development process are participants in systems.

These two dimensions interact with each other.

The function of a new software system[2] is to take an existing system and model it using program logic (sequence, data, iteration and selection) so that some portion of the original system can be replicated in a computer enabling (some of it) to be automated. To do this, the system's processes must be mapped. A process diagram (such as Fig. 3.2) has to be drawn (many different forms of Fig. 3.2 exist). The role of the system's designer is to map these processes. Open systems theory provides an model of the key decisions a designer has to make and a way of thinking about those decisions. This is viable because software systems conform to the open systems model in three respects:-

1. People interact with the system.
2. Software systems exist, operate and interact within an external socio-technical environment.
3. Developers also interact with their personal socio-technical environment.[3]

Software systems are far from unique in this respect. This presents the prospect that it might be possible to adapt some theoretical ideas from open systems theory to help to better understand the SSD processes. As ever, caution is required. As has been shown with regards to importing an engineering perspective into SSD without noting the significant differences between other engineered products and software systems, one needs to be cognisant of the differences between software systems and other socio-technical artefacts. In particular, the determinant nature of software systems imposes a discipline on SSD that is absent in other disciplines. Exploring both the similarities and differences holds the prospect of understanding the SSD process better.

Perhaps the greatest benefit of open systems theory is that it offers a different way of thinking about systems. In particular, systems become more complex than they appear from an engineering perspective because open systems theory registers the interconnectivity between a system and its environment. This interconnectivity cannot be taken for granted. The social and socio-technical factors are considered to have significance rather than being a nuisance the system must accommodated. SSM calls for sufficient emphasis to be given to understanding the potential influence of non-technical factors. SSM applies open systems thinking to systems development as a means of ensuring environmental factors are considered as part of the development process. In this book, open systems theory is used to help to understand the development process in principle and in practice as it applies to both the development methodology (dimension 1) and the development process (dimension 2).

---

[2]Games perform a different function although they can still be explained in open systems terms.

[3]The first 2 points represent the first dimension of how open systems are relevant to SSD and the third point to the second dimension.

3.3.1 The Interface Between People and Software Systems

Dimension 1 of open systems thinking refers to how the system under development is affected by its parent environment. One of the obvious points at which this is relevant is the human/computer interface (HCI).

Allied to HCI are the related disciplines of user experience (UX) research and research into technology acceptance (the Technology Acceptance Model (TAM)) which has considered the effect on people's attitudes towards the system of the effectiveness of the system [12]. Both approaches (TAM and UX) recognise that how people respond to the system is contextually dependent. Hornbæk and Hertzum in their review of UX and Tam identify 12 construct categories (ibid. p. 33:11) relating to the user that affect the user's attitudes towards the system. However there is little agreement regarding the weighting of affective factors which seem to depend on the wider context. In other words, how people feel about a system, and therefore how they interact with the system depends on the what, where, why and when of their interaction and can be influenced as much by the other people around them as any particular feature of the system. This fits in with an open systems approach in which people are part of a more global environment and must be understood within this environment. Checkland sees this as the "Weltanschauung" or world view [7] of stakeholders. The conclusion to be drawn from this discussion is that if developers are to deliver software systems that people are comfortable using, they need to get to know the people and the environment in which they work. Unfortunately, this is often not possible. In 1988 Curtis wrote

> Remoteness involved the number of nodes in the formal communications channel that infor-
> mation had to pass through in order to link two sources. The more nodes that information
> had to traverse before communication was established, the less likely communication was to
> occur... [Communication] were often preconditioned to filter some messages ... and to alter
> the interpretation of others (e.g. messages about the actual needs of users). [10, p. 1269]

This situation is unlikely to have improved since Curtis' original research.

This is a real problem for SSD and highlights the importance of the requirements analyst. The lack of significance afforded to this role, and in particular to the "weltan-schauung" (world view) of stakeholders can account for a large proportion of failed projects.

3.3.2 The Consequences of the Interaction Between Software Systems and Its External Environment

Beer's viable systems model provides insight into the interaction between an open system and its external environment. Every open system encompasses a subsystem. In software development, a recursive algorithm should always contain a binary conditional test that will either return the system sequence to the calling level of iteration or call another level of recursion. In an open system, no such test exists. A subsystem both returns feedback to its external environment and invokes a lower level subsystem. This accounts for the complexity of real life and consequently makes life difficult for IT systems designers. They must make conscious decisions about the systems boundaries. There is no lowest level. There will always be another subsystem which could affect the viability of the whole system. The deeper into the subsystem levels one descends, the more granular the detail of the operation. The more levels one chooses to include in the IT system, the more complex the system becomes, and the harder it is for developers to comprehend the whole system. When to stop accounting for lower level subsystems is a design decision of considerable importance; one that is rarely given the scrutiny it deserves. Often the base level is considered to be common sense, but unless the feedback from substrata are at least considered, the consequences can be severe. The possibility of failing to handle an interaction between processes in the process chain can bring the system down.[4]

A subsystem may be informal, that is there are few specific rules for how the process chain operates. This is particularly true for human to human processes. It may be possible to regularise some of these processes by introducing rules of engagement, but it is not always possible to predict what processes or even subsystems might be compromised. Any subsystem could generate unexpected feedback that has not been taken account of and could result in an unexpected response. In safety critical or mission critical systems this could be disastrous. One example of this was when the UK 1901 census records were first made available on line. Interest in the web site was underestimated by a factor of 100 causing the site to crash. This could be interpreted as the failure of requirements engineers to appreciate the weltanschauung of the British public and their desire to know about their past. Developers did not realise that changes in life expectancy and a greater sense of connectedness to 1901 differentiated attitudes to the 1901 census and the 1891 census which had been placed on line a few years earlier. Accessing the 1891 and the 1901 censuses was identical from a technical point of view. There was no reason to believe that any system parameters should need to change. The non-functional requirements also appeared similar. However, the parent environment of the system was a social system populated by people of a certain age, a much greater number of whom had grandparents they had known, and about whom they were interested to find out more. An apparently insignificant factor in the parent system resulted in a great change in the input to the 1901 census system which caused the system to crash.

At some point designers must make a decision to exclude a subsystem from the IT system. Take for example an intelligent stock purchasing system. Such a system could operate quite happily managing stock levels, purchasing from the cheapest suppliers, recording arrival and delivery times. The system could even make adjustments such as switching suppliers at different times of the year when shorter delivery times are more advantageous than lower price. If however a particular supplier phones up to say they have a new product available that is technically superior, but more expensive,

---

[4]The Boeing 737 Max aircraft disasters can be considered an example of failing to think far enough through the subsystem substrata.

human intervention is likely to be required. Purchasing the product may well depend on the relationship between customer and supplier. Decision support systems might analyse available data and offer recommendations, but they cannot assess trust and instinct.

Process chains that can be specified, can be computerised, but ones that rely on informal processes must have a structure imposed on them first. This can result in some of the richness of the interaction being lost along with the data conveyed in the interaction. It is often these informal processes that are overlooked or oversimplified during requirements elicitation. The consequences are unpredictable, but can result in usability problems or even incorrect assumptions being made. Appreciating this aspect of open systems can help to avoid some of these omissions and misunderstandings. When a conscious decision is made, it can be documented. Open systems thinking provides a cognitive model for recognising the importance of such decisions. Traditional technology based approaches have a tendency to oversimplify which causes difficulties later in the development. Sometimes the fault may not be discovered until the system is installed.

At the topmost level of socio-technical systems, there are multiple potential inputs to the IT system from the external environment. The IT systems designer must decide which of these the IT system will manage, and which will be excluded from the IT system. Take for example the IT system postulated in Chap. 2, that of an IT system to manage cross border trade across an international boundary. It would be possible to establish for example a network of sensors to detect when something crossed the border. Depending on cost, this could be a very comprehensive network, but what should the sensors detect? Should it just be goods vehicles, or should it include private cars? What about bicycles, or even people? After all, it is possible for them to smuggle goods. What about drones? How can data transfers or capital transfers be detected? The systems designers must decide which of these will be part of this system, and also how any of these features might need to inter-operate with other systems. Missing one potential input may undermine the whole system. Including too many different inputs, may overcomplicate the whole system increasing cost, time and complexity. Once again, the cognitive model provided by VSM helps to uncover these decisions and make them explicit. Designers and stakeholders can make more rational decisions with greater knowledge and awareness that a decision has actually been made. Open systems thinking emphasises the importance of boundary decisions and predisposes designers to give them due consideration.

Decisions at the topmost systems boundary and at the most granular level introduce risk into the project. At the lowest level, a process may return an event that has repercussions throughout the higher levels. At the upper level boundary of the systems model, there may be an expectation that the system manages a process that turns out to have been excluded from the system design. When this occurs it usually results in a failure to meet the expectations of one or more of the stakeholders, possibly the commissioning stakeholder. Making decisions regarding the systems boundary is one of the key negotiations that requirements engineers need to conduct with stakeholders.

3.3.3 People in the Software Systems Development Process

The second dimension in which open systems play a role is that people develop software systems and people belong to a parent social system.

In some ways, the role of people in the software systems development process has been addressed extensively [6, 9, 25] and many others. Often the approach has been from a managerial perspective. That is to say how do we manage people more effectively? Brooks for example proposed that development teams should be modelled on surgical teams with the chief surgeon directing the work of the other team members. Curtis' emphasis was on individual programmer's differences in programming capability and performance. He suggested therefore that team selection should aim to choose only the most capable programmers.[5] Weinberg's view was that programmers' attitudes were important. He suggested that programmers needed to be open to criticism; an attitude he described as "egoless" programming. This was latterly embodied in the design and code inspections culture [11] and pair programming [3, 8], a favoured method in Agile development. Agile methods also promote the idea of self-organising teams [18] guided rather than managed by a "scrum master". This contrasts with Brooks' surgical team organisation. The Scrum Master concept has attracted considerable attention within the Agile community.[6] However, the management and organisation of teams is a controversial issue that has kept theorists excited at least since Mayo's experiments in the Hawthorne Factory in the 1930s [13].

This chapter is concerned with systems thinking and from this perspective people are more than assets in the process or agents of production, they are the process. As such, personal, interpersonal and intra-group processes are subsystems in the development process that require as much consideration as any other process. The open systems model portrays all systems as multi-layered, and this applies as much to the people developing the system as it does to the system being developed. Within and amongst the development team, the model of the system being developed must be construed as a coherent vision from the highest level, to the most detailed. This vision must be simultaneously holistic and granular. If a person takes a strategic overview of the product however, it is difficult to appreciate some of the detail. Too much detail can obscure the bigger picture. In large systems, it is difficult for one person to master both the top level overview and all the detail. Without an overview, it is difficult to maintain a strategic vision for the product. The larger the system being developed, the less likely it is that one person can hold a complete vision of the system. This means that team members need the ability to communicate their detailed but partial vision between each other. A highly productive code writer who lacks the ability to communicate her/his conceptual understanding of the system may be less valuable than someone who is a slower coder but a good communicator.

At any point during the development, there may be a need for a particular new function or an adjustment to an existing function which had not been envisioned.

---

[5]It does however appear to be difficult for every software team to only be comprised of the most capable programmers.

[6]For a criticism of self-organising teams see Moe et al. [15].

Feedback from the most granular level might cause a ripple effect up the process levels requiring management at the higher level. Code encapsulation will minimise the risk of this happening, but if something cannot be predicted, it is difficult to manage.

Consider the example of the border control and management system introduced in Chap. 1. Before worldwide GPS, the concept of transporting goods using semi-autonomous aerial drones would have seemed pure science fiction. A systems designer at that time would not have given the idea a moment's thought. Today, serious research is going into how such systems can be made commercially available and are quite likely to succeed in the next few years. This change in technology changes little of the high level concept of managing goods traded across the border, but it could, for example, require additional sensors, the data from which would need to be integrated into the existing system. Developers need to transition their thinking between low level concepts such as the data formats, and high level concepts such as how the new technology affects the integrity of total system. Is there, for example, the potential for this new technology to compromise the security of the whole system? Designers might even be tempted to look further into the future to consider what other new technologies might affect the system. Being able to consider the detail whilst, at the same time, maintaining a clarity of vision of the total system is a high level skill. Being able to share this thinking with others is perhaps even more valuable. The open systems paradigm however, points to the requirement for at least some in the development team to have such capabilities.

All members of the team must be able to adjust their own conceptual model of the system as new requirements emerge. Such flexibility of thinking is required to be able to integrate new functions into the existing system. Additionally, developers need to be able to project onto the system the implications for the wider system of the modifications being considered. Less experienced programmers, used to being told what to do, may not, in some organisations, realise that this is expected of them. Developers need the capacity to conceptualise the system being developed as an open system. This points to the type of supportive learning culture required by an organisation to achieve its full potential.

This analysis uncovers some of the capabilities required by development staff beyond their ability to program or produce an entity relationship diagram. They must be able to think flexibly and respond creatively to changing conditions. Environments that are subject to rapidly changing requirements are inherently stressful. All software systems developments will be subject to some change, so for software systems developers, it is not a case of whether or not the working environment is stressful, but of how stressful it is.

A condition which will add to the level of stress is the overall volatility of the vision. If either key people in the development team are unable to develop a coherent vision, hold fundamentally different conceptual models of the product or are unable to articulate/communicate their vision to the remainder of the team, anxiety levels will be increased. Much research has shown that lack of senior management involvement [24], weak leadership [17, 24], and volatile requirements [14], are indicators of potential problems for the project, but fails to suggest why these failings result in problems. Without this understanding, it is hard to know what actions can be taken. Recognising that developers must create their own abstract conceptual model of the system and be able to share it with other team members provides the explanation as to how management and leadership affect the process. Vision creation and dissemination is one of the key roles of senior staff. When the vision lacks cohesion, it is likely to prove problematic.

Recognising the importance of the system vision offers the opportunity for a health check of the project to be conducted at an early stage. If vision holders are unable to articulate a coherent vision that can be understood by the rest of the team, the project will suffer. Further action should be taken to resolve the inconsistencies from wherever they arise. The vision need not be complete. Indeed as a conceptual model of the system under development it will be, by definition, incomplete, but it needs to possess sufficient clarity for progress to be made. Initially, this may be only a small number of steps, but it does have to be enough to indicate a clear sense of direction and to hold together as a coherent whole. Committing resources to a project when the overall vision is unclear, subject to change or cannot be clearly articulated would seem unwise.

Most often the vision is spread informally across a team with very little formal effort made to ensure consistency. Developers are expected to create their vision from the design documentation such as requirements specifications, use cases and so on. This documentation is not intended for this purpose and allows too much latitude for differences, even conflicts in interpretation. Achieving a common vision cannot rely on formal documentation. It requires interpersonal, face to face communication. Providing opportunities for this to happen would be a valuable addition to any development process.

The difficulty of the task of communicating the vision of the system to all members of the development team should not be underestimated. Bearing in mind that the vision as an abstract concept, the intangibility of software and the emergent property of system requirements, communication of software systems constructs is significantly more difficult than for other product developments. The tools available to software systems developers are much more limited. Data flow diagrams, entity relation diagrams, use cases, object relationships are all abstract descriptions of the system relying on expertise to understand and interpret. They rely on implicit assumptions regarding the user environment, and do not account well for non-functional requirements. "Quality Attribute Scenarios" [1] do provide a tool for establishing quality requirements, but as Van Landuyt and Joosen point out they are dependent upon assumptions made by requirements engineers [22]. In any case, quality attribute scenarios are themselves abstract models. How to improve the quality of communication of the vision seems to be one area ripe for further research.

Functional decomposition seems to provide part of the solution by breaking the problem down into comprehensible components. It also creates problems because it focuses developers' attention on the detail and this can be at the expense of the overall vision of the total system. This is particularly true for system wide non-functional requirements. It is less cognitively demanding to concentrate on the functional aspects of the system at the expense of the NFRs. A classic example of this is returning 'meaningless' error messages to the user from the operating system. Unless the user can interpret the message and translate it into taking some corrective action, the message only serves to confuse. To avoid this type of occurrence the developer needs to have some empathy with the user(s). As developers will rarely have direct contact with users, those developers that do must be able to communicate a good sense of the user as a person, not only the definition of the user interface with the system. Viewpoint analysis [20] can offer some help in this regard, but cannot easily capture the essence of the user in her/his environment.

3.4   Why Not Open Systems?

Methodologies based on open systems such as SSM have been promoted for many years. Whilst they are popular in university information systems departments, they have not gained great traction in industry. Methodologies based on the software engineering paradigm have overwhelming appeal in the commercial sector. The fallibility of waterfall methodologies has largely been replaced by the flexibility agile methods offer. But agile methods lack the coherence of a methodology per se. There is little evidence that organisations undertake the exercise Cockburn proposes of defining a customised methodology for the organisation. Adding one more text to the heroic failure of previous open systems avocations without understanding why open systems approaches have not appealed, would seem to invoke the unlikely prospect of hope triumphing over experience.

There are two reasons for attempting this exercise. Firstly, a more appropriate model of the software development process provides a better opportunity to understand that process. This is perhaps more of a long term endeavour requiring further research and theory generation. Secondly, the open systems model offers insight into the process that requires little detailed knowledge, understanding or investment in the approach. Previous attempts to promote open systems thinking have proposed a big picture vision of the development process involving radical change to ways of thinking about the development process within the development team and heavy investment in training. The open systems approach as described by Wilson and Haperen [26] is a radically different way of thinking about systems development. Such change has demanded too great a leap of faith on behalf of project managers.

The "scientific", method and the methodical certainty software engineering offers contrast with the subjective, imprecise, impressionistic methods attributed to open systems thinking in general and Soft Systems Methodology in particular. Furthermore, open systems seems to demand skills of empathic listening that are uncommon in the industry, skills that in some ways are alien to it. Open systems thinking places a greater emphasis on the people involved, thereby imposing greater psychological pressure on them. People become the focus, above the process. Judgement has more of a role than measurement. Managing uncertainty is required more than professional discipline. At least this is the perception of open systems methodologies, perhaps with some justification. That is not to say that process, measurement and discipline are not important in the open systems approach. They are, but people must use their judgment as to how process and measurement are used. It could be argued that much of this is also true of the Agile approach. The difference is that the Scrum Master can be seen as a proxy manager rather than a facilitator. Nevertheless, as Moe et al. [15] have pointed out, the Agile methodology still requires management support. SSM however requires a culture change within the organisation as a whole; one in which management cedes control over the development process to developers. This is often a step too far for senior managers who feel the need to be in control over the process. This need for culture change is one of the factors that has hamstrung the progress of SSM. Another is that adopting a new methodology requires commitment of time and resources. Taking on a few new methods is less of a risk. So, for example, running a staff development day on open systems thinking might be an easy first step for a manager to take that might benefit any development process.

The apparent lack of methodology in SSM appears to leave too great an opportunity for developers to spend too much time contemplating their own understanding of the system rather than make real progress. Managements often feel the need to be seen to be in control of the process. This line of reasoning however ignores the track record of over-promising and under-delivery of the engineering approach, but it still resonates with project management.

In some ways this argument parallels that of the wider questions society faces regarding the acceptance of human and interpersonal needs for wellbeing versus economic and rational progress [16]. For some in the 1960s and '70s technology seemed to offer all the answers to society's problems', but the philosophy that accompanies socio-technical thinking asserts that healthy societies need to engage the people affected directly. This requires addressing their emotional needs as well as their physical ones. In the same way technological change seems to create new problems as it solves older ones. Software engineering is ill-equipped to handle the subtlety, complexity and dynamism of user requirements. The larger and more novel the system required, the more complex and socially dependent the relationships will be with the external environment, so the less likely a purely software engineering approach is to succeed. Whilst this may be the case, as they say in the north of England, it butters no parsnips. The objective is to get the job done, not to pontificate over the sensitivities or inadequacies of the doers. A more prosaic, utilitarian argument is required. Open systems thinking about the development process provides some indicators as to how SSD can become more effective by avoiding some of the more damaging pitfalls.

Some observations that derive from open systems thinking are that the risk to a project will increase where:-

1. There is high volatility within the environment in which the system will operate.
2. The rate of technical change affecting the system is high.
3. The novelty of the solution in terms of similarity with existing systems is great.
4. There is a lack of availability of existing solutions.
5. The socio-technical complexity of the problem domain is great.
6. The scale/scope of the problem domain is high.

7. The level of integration and or inter-operability with other systems is demand-
    ing.
8. There is limited availability of existing and usable systems infrastructure to
    build upon.
9. There is a particular requirement for system longevity and/or sustainability.
10. Great diversity and complex socio-political relationships exists between stake-
    holders.
11. There are high numbers, range and complexity of inputs into the system.
12. There is a lack of detailed systems knowledge held by stakeholders.
13. The socio-technical impact of the system is high. (The system's feedback from
    the introduction of the system to its external environment.)
14. The greater the cognitive separation between stakeholders and developers.
15. The more pressing the cost and time constraints that are placed on the project.

These generic project risk factors are not necessarily independent of each other.
Interaction between risk factors may either compound the risk or possibly mitigate
it. This list of potential risks should be considered tentative. For any given project,
there may be more specific issues such as funding or management capability. The
risks identified above derive from systems thinking and apply to a greater or lesser
extent to all projects. This list offers the opportunity to assess the probability of the
project being completed on time, to budget and with acceptable quality.

The systems thinking perspective suggests that this risk evaluation is best conducted as part of a feasibility study. This differs from traditional understanding of
feasibility. Sommerville for example suggests that feasibility is

> a short, focussed study that should…answer three key questions: a) does the system contribute
> to the overall objectives of the organisation? b) can the system be implemented within the
> schedule and budget using current technology? c) can the system be integrated with other
> systems that are used? [19, p. 100]

This list suggests that feasibility should be a much more sophisticated and lengthier
activity focussed on the risks that are being undertaken. This list also differs from
previous, similar list of risk factors in that their purpose is to identify risk and mitigate it. Here the objective is to evaluate project feasibility. It is tempting to suggest
that these differences arise from the assumptions inherent in the software engineering approach that software can always provide the solution. Traditional SSD has a
tendency to focus on the solution before fully understanding the problem. The open
systems approach is more cautious because open systems theory implies that any
intervention in a system has consequences, and it is important to understand (as best
as possible) what those consequences might be. Pressure from the commercial imper-
atives of the industry seem to press for action and visible progress rather than greater
philosophical understanding. This risk inventory is one way of assessing an appropriate level of caution before over-committing resources to a project that potentially
has hidden depths.

One factor that does not appear in the list above is the size of the project. Clearly
this is important whether one takes an engineering perspective or an open systems

perspective. Size increases complexity and the number and diversity of the stake-holder population. Brooks [5] identified problems software has with the scalability of software systems, and any large project should bear in mind the increase in risk to a project as its scope grows. Open systems thinking suggests that the number of inputs to the system and particularly the potential for unanticipated inputs would be of greater concern as project size increases rather than size per se. Predicting the number of unanticipated inputs however may be multi factorial incorporating system's knowledge, volatility and the number of stakeholders, as well as scope.

In spite of the discussion above however, two questions remain regarding the open systems approach:-

1. How does open systems thinking actually help software systems development in a practical sense?
2. How can an open systems approach overcome resistance to its adoption?

The answer to the first question is perhaps easier than the second.

Whilst the open systems approach is a more permissive approach than say PMBOK or PRINCE II, it still provides frameworks for working and, more importantly, a framework for decision making. Furthermore, it drives that decision making earlier in the development process. For example, early assumptions regarding the system need to be made [23], but these are often unconscious and largely undocumented. The open systems model recognises the importance and value of these assumptions, but also the influence they have on systems design. Making them explicit and transparent enables them to be scrutinised. The open systems approach prompts a number of questions such as:-

1. What is the scope of the project? What is being excluded?
2. How well is the external (to the system under development) operating environment understood?
3. How resilient will the system be to excluded processes?
4. How well articulated is the project vision?
5. How stable is the project vision?
6. Are the communications protocols between the application and development domains appropriate to the project?

Once open systems thinking is applied to a project proposal, many more questions regarding the system and its environment may emerge. These help ensure that the project is actually feasible and that the product being developed can meet its stakeholders' needs.

However, there is a time and a cost involved in this process. It appears that during this time little actual progress is being made on the product. The lack of reliable cost/benefit evidence for conducting significant "pre-production" activity as advocated by Checkland [7], Stowell and Welch [21] and others [26] makes it difficult for project managers to justify in cost/benefit terms. Open systems thinking can be thought to be an expensive prologue to the actual hard engineering work required to develop the system. Although open systems are grounded in a solid theoretical framework, it is one that is largely alien to the engineering community, and so not particularly appropriate or applicable.

3.5 Conclusion

Open systems thinking has, in the past, appeared to be a radical departure from the software engineering approach. When applied as a total change in methodology, this argument has some validity. Practitioners must be trained, and there seem to be a lot of new processes and procedures to adopt.

When open systems thinking is applied to the development process itself, rather than being seen as a different methodology, the picture changes. It is possible to introduce some new ways of working without upending the whole applecart. Using an open systems approach, the risk to a project can be evaluated prior to overcommitting resources to it. Greater emphasis can be given to understanding the impact and cost of non-functional requirements. More time can be spent articulating the project vision. These are small steps and easily implemented.

They are also a Trojan Horse. They introduce new ways of thinking that eventually lead to cultural change within the development organisation and then on to structural change to provide improved opportunities for intra-team communications.

Open systems thinking is radical, but it is not challenging for systems' developers who are well versed in thinking about process in terms of sequence, iteration and recursion. The difficult part is opening up oneself to think about how a software system affects other people and how the development process affects oneself. That is the real challenge.

3.6 Discussion Questions

1. Why haven't open systems methodologies received more attention from the software development industries?
2. How can a common vision of the product be created given the intangible nature of software and how would we know it had been?
3. Are communication skills more important than technical skills?
4. How different is the open systems approach from the software engineering approach in reality?
5. What are the differences and commonalities between open systems thinking applied to the product being developed and the development methodology?
6. How can system boundary conditions be handled by software systems design?
7. Does their really need to be a radical change in management culture to accommodate open systems approaches to software systems development?
8. What would the outcome be of applying the list of 15 generic risks to a project to the example of a new international customs boarder discussed in Chap. 2?

References

1. Bass L et al (2003) Software architecture in practice, 2nd edn. Addison-Wesley, Boston, USA
2. Baxter G, Sommerville I (2011) Socio-technical systems: from design to systems engineering. Interact Comput 23(1):4–17
3. Beck K (2000) Extreme programming explained. Addison-Wesley, Boston
4. Beer S (1985) Diagnosing the system for organizations. Wiley, Chichester
5. Brooks FJ (1987) No silver bullet: essence and accidents of software engineering. Computer
6. Brooks F Jr (1995) The surgical team. In: Brooks F Jr (ed) The mythical man month. Addison Wesley, Reading, pp 29–37
7. Checkland P (1999) Systems thinking, systems practice. Wiley, Chichester
8. Cockburn A (2002) Agile software development. Addison-Wesley, Boston, Massachusetts
9. Curtis B (1994) Human factors in software development. In: Marciniak JJ (ed) Encyclopedia of software engineering, vol 1. Wiley, New York, pp 545–558
10. Curtis B et al (1988) A field study the software design process for large systems. Commun ACM 31(11):1268–1287
11. Fagan ME (1976) Design and code inspections to reduce errors in program development. IBM Syst J 15(3):182–211
12. Hornbæk K, Hertzum M (2017) Technology acceptance and user experience: a review of the experiential component in HCI. ACM Trans Comput Hum Interac 24(5):33:31–33:30
13. Mayo E (1946) The human problems of an industrial civilization. Cambridge, Massachusetts
14. Menezes J Jr et al (2019) Risk factors in software development projects: a systematic literature review. Softw Q J 27(3):1149–1174
15. Moe NB et al (2008) Understanding self-organizing teams in Agile software development. In: 19th Australian conference on software engineering, IEEE computer society, pp 76–85
16. Mumford E (2006) The story of socio-technical design: reflections on its successes, failures and potential. J Inf Syst 16(4):317–342
17. Sardjono W, Retnowardhani A (2019) Analysis of failure factors in information systems project for software implementation at the organization. In: International conference on information management and technology (ICIMTech). IEEE, Jakarta & Bali, Indonesia, pp 141–145
18. Schwaber K, Beedle M (2001) Agile software development with scrum. Prentice Hall, Upper Saddle River
19. Sommerville I (2011) Software engineering, 9th edn. Pearson/Addision Wesley, Boston, Massachusetts
20. Sommerville I, Sawyer P (1997) Requirements engineering. John Wiley, Chichester
21. Stowell F, Welch C (2012) The manager's guide to systems practice. Wiley, Chichester UK
22. Van Landuyt D, Joosen W (2015) On the role of early architectural assumptions in quality attribute scenarios a qualitative and quantitative study. In: 2015 IEEE/ACM 5th international workshop on the twin peaks of requirements and architecture. IEEE, Florence, Italy
23. Van Landuyt D et al (2012) Documenting early architectural assumptions in scenario-based requirements. In: Joint working conference on software architecture & 6th European conference on software architecture. IEEE, Helsinki, Finland, pp 9–75
24. Verner J et al (2008) What factors lead to software project failure? In: Second international conference on research challenges in information science. IEEE, Marrakech, Morocco
25. Weinberg GM (1971) The psychology of computer programming. Van Nostrand Reinhold, New York
26. Wilson B, Haperen KV (2015) Soft systems thinking, methodology and the management of change. Palgrave, London

Chapter 4
Team Management

4.1 Introduction

There is a basic assumption throughout this text that individual members of development teams possess positive attitudes towards the projects they are working on and are willing to contribute their expertise to achieve successful outcomes.

This subject has been extensively researched. Hall et al.'s review of the literature [8] identified 92 separate papers, and this review has since been cited over 60 times. Within software engineering much of the debate has centred on whether software engineers in general can be typified as possessing common characteristics that motivate them. Beecham et al. [1] found some support for this hypothesis. From over 2000 references to motivation in software engineering they provided a meta-analysis of 43 studies. They observed that 9 papers (21%) were concerned with what motivated software engineers. The most common finding was that software engineers were mostly motivated by the challenge of learning new skills. 7 of the papers (16%) found that software engineers required little social interaction and 7 studies reported software engineers prefer to be allowed to work autonomously. These findings suggests the majority of software engineers are, in Belbin's terms [2], "implementers" ("company workers").

The observation that software developers are more motivated by the intrinsic challenge of the task provides circumstantial evidence for the assumption above that software engineers are, by and large, committed to their work. This is a convenient working assumption as it allows further discussion of developer motivation to be taken off line.[1] Although motivation of software systems developers covers some intriguing ground, the theory supporting that discussion is not particularly distinct from general management theory, and can therefore be refferred to if the reader is interested.

---

[1]Interested readers can refer to the references identified at the end of the chapter.

© Springer Nature Switzerland AG 2020
C. Rosen, *Guide to Software Systems Development*,
https://doi.org/10.1007/978-3-030-39730-2_4

However, motivation theory itself does provide some pointers towards the management of software development teams that influences the debate on the software development process which is the central theme of this book.

Motivation theory can be traced back to the perennial debate between the Scientific School of Management and the Humanistic School of Management. Douglas McGregor's seminal paper "The Human Side of Enterprise" [18] exemplified this discussion.[2] McGregor labels the two schools of thought as "Theory X" and "Theory Y". Theory X characterises the Taylorist, scientific school and Theory Y, the humanistic school. These two theories might better be described as philosophical rather than scientific as they are based on beliefs about human nature. Whilst it would be unnecessarily distracting to revisit this discussion in detail, a brief overview of motivation theory will set the background for the discussion that follows.

4.2   Theory X Versus Theory Y

The philosophical differences between the Scientific School of Management (Theory X) and the Humanistic School (Theory Y) rests essentially in beliefs about human nature. The scientific school believes that human beings are basically indolent and need to be cajoled into doing anything beyond that required to meet their basic needs. They need to be motivated and managed with rewards and punishments. It cites Pavlovian stimulus/response conditioned behaviour [20] and later Skinnarian operant behavioural psychology [23]. This way of thinking leads to the belief that people at work need to be told what to do, managed on a day to day basis, rewarded for good behaviour and punished for not doing what they should.

The Humanistic School believe that human beings are more complicated and are motivated by things other than reward and punishment such as self-actualisation and the need for recognition. People perform better if they are encouraged to express themselves, show initiative and take responsibility. McGregor (ibid.) drawing on Maslow's "Hierarchy of Needs" [17] suggested that the reasons managers reject the Theory Y proposition is from fear that they will lose control over the production process. Thus managers adhere to the Theory X approach even if they would prefer to believe in Theory Y. Unfortunately, whichever position one starts from, one tends to find evidence supporting that perspective. McGregor has attracted a good deal of both support and opprobrium over the years, but as a categorisation of the two views, it has stood the test of time.

These two positions appear to be irreconcilable, and the shadows of them can be seen to influence debate today. One person who tried to reconcile the two was Charles Perrow using "Contingency Theory".

---

[2]These two conflicting theories of management were referenced in the discussion regarding Agile methods.

4.3   Contingency Theory

Contingency Theory Perrow [21] argues that the correct managerial approach is contingent on the type of work being carried out. Perrow identified two axes divided into four quadrants. On one axis was whether the work being undertaken is characterised by many or few exceptions. An exception or anomaly is any problem that might arise during the production process. On the other axis is whether the exceptions are difficult, complex and/or hard to solve, or simple and relatively easy to sort out (Fig. 4.1).

Perrow labelled each of the four segments created by the axes. The top left segment represents an industry that has a high proportion of complex problems, but few of them. When a problem does arise, it is often difficult to fix. This segment is characteristic of craft industries such as hand blown glass. The essential nature of the activity is such that it cannot be mechanised. The problems and intricacies associated with the product mean that each unit of production must be treated on its own merit.

Quadrant two is characterised as having a large number of exceptions each of which is complex and/or difficult to solve. He labelled this quadrant "Non-Routine" production. The exemplar Perrow used for this segment was the aero-space industry and elite psychiatric agencies.

If it became possible to increase ones understanding of the problems associated with this style of production, it would be possible to move the organisation towards cell three; non-routine, but well understood processes. Perrow called this class of organisation "engineering." Finally, if it then became possible to mechanise the system, the organisation would develop towards quadrant four; well understood, "routine" operation such as manufacturing processes.

The distinction between "non-routine" and the "engineering" is interesting in the context of SSD. If the problems that occur during software systems development were relatively straightforward to resolve, it would support the case for software to be categorised as an engineering technology. Generally however, the problems

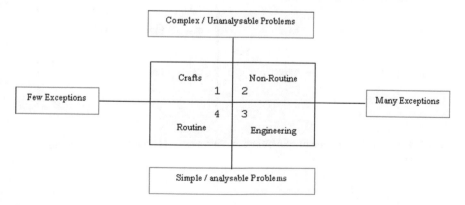

Fig. 4.1 Perrow's contingency theory

that arise during SSD require a level of expertise to resolve and should therefore be classed as complex.[3] It would be hard to argue that SSD is anything other than non-routine using this analysis. Production problems are common, and often complex and difficult to resolve, placing the activity in the non-routine quadrant rather than the engineering quadrant. This is more than a semantic point. According to Perrow, many of the processes and procedures adopted in each quadrant differ according to which quadrant they are in. Misclassifying SSD as engineering has consequences.

Perrow argued that the appropriate management structure and style was contingent on the quadrant within which the industry was operating. He deconstructed management into three functions: planning, technical control, and production supervision. (It is not necessary to consider further the planning function in this analysis.) The task requirements were disaggregated into four components:

- The discretion an individual possesses
- The power they have to influence goals and strategies
- Whether co-ordination of tasks could be achieved through planning, or was better achieved from feedback
- Whether there was a high or low level of interdependency between tasks.

These characteristics were mapped onto the previous grid in the manner shown in Fig. 4.2. For quadrant 2, the quadrant characterising non-routine organisations such as SSD, both technical and administrative supervisors would have high degrees of

	Discretion	Power	Co-ordination	Feedback	Discretion	Power	Co-ordination	Feedback
Technical	Low	Low	Plan		High	High	Feedback	
				Low				High
Supervisory	High	High	Feedback	**1**	High	High	Feedback	**2**
				4	**3**			
Technical	Low	High	Plan		High	High	Feedback	
				Low				Low
Supervisory	Low	Low	Plan		Low	Low	Plan	

Fig. 4.2 Perrow's classification of appropriate management style according to technology

[3]Interestingly, whilst engineering implementation might be categorised as engineering, by this definition, engineering design would be also be classed as non-routine.

discretion over day to day decisions, and influence over goals and strategies. Co-ordination would necessarily be through feedback,[4] and there would be a high level of interdependency between production groups. In other words a Theory Y approach would be most appropriate to SSD. Theoretically then development team members should be given a high degree of discretion, considerable power to make decisions, and be expected to coordinate their work through collaboration with their colleagues.

This analysis places further emphasis on the ability of team members to com-municate with each other. Not only must team members share a common vision of what needs to be achieved and an empathy with the users who will eventually own the system, but they must be able communicate with colleagues. Given that much research has shown how lacking in communication skills IT workers appear to be [24, 26], it should be a matter of concern that IT curricula place such little emphasis on developing communication skills. It might be argued that developing these skills is difficult and also hard to assess, but other professions such as teaching, social work and nursing require their graduates to demonstrate their ability in this area. The dominant software engineering paradigm has resulted in these soft skills receiving less attention than they require.

4.4 Communication Skills

Whilst most software engineering texts recognise the importance of interpersonal communications in the software systems development process (SSDP), few have much to say beyond this. What is meant by "good communications?" How are "good communications" fostered? What are the implications for software development staff and staffing? Engineering science has little to contribute towards answering these questions. Instead it is necessary to turn towards the "softer" sciences where ideas or theories are less determinant, but can provide insight into complex problems.

When it comes to dealing with people, as individuals, in groups or between groups, there are few rules and often impressions, and even intuition can be as valuable as theory. Theories can nevertheless offer a basis or precursor for judgement and provide structure to the thinking process. However, this is not the same process of observa-tion and analysis as exists in the "harder" sciences. It involves greater subjectivity and is less reliable. Perhaps this is why software engineering texts are reluctant to stray into this area. Having placed such emphasis on interpersonal communications, avoidance of this topic is not an option here. There is much more scope for argument and disagreement in social science discourse. However, there are theories that can be considered relevant to the situations in which software systems managers and developers find themselves.

The starting point is to consider what is meant by "communication skills". The focus in this book will be on interpersonal, interactional communications rather than asymmetrical skills such as report writing and presentation skills. Whilst these skills

---

[4]Feedback in this context refers to seeking expert knowledge.

are undoubtedly important, they have far less impact, and certainly far less immediate impact on relationships between people (or at least most people) than face to face communications. They therefore have less impact on the development process.

There are four levels or situations in which interpersonal communications occur within SSDP

- the internal psychological level
- the individual person to person level
- at the intra-group level
- at the inter-team level.

The first of these, the developer herself/himself, is both relevant and important. Much has been written on the subject, but here the discussion is restricted to how individual feelings, emotions and reactions affect the process rather than individual capability and the relationship between the person and the program as these topics have been discussed at length elsewhere.[5]

4.4.1 The Person to Person Communication Level

It is often assumed that person to person communication is easy, and not worthy of in depth analysis because everyone does it all the time and therefore everyone is expert at it. This assumption is invalid. Most of the time, all that is needed for people to be able to acquire the information they need to manage their lives, and even to form quite meaningful relationships, is a relatively superficial level of communication. People who need to develop deeper relationships with others, people such as counsellors, social workers and, to some extent, teachers, recognise the need for a more empathic level of communication. In particular, in everyday communication, people do not need to pay a great deal of attention to what other people say, and even less to how they say it. They do not need to listen intently. Deep concentration and awareness of what others are saying is rarely needed and so most people are not particularly good at it. This form of intensive, observant, "active" or "empathic" listening takes a great deal of practice to develop.

4.4.2 Active Listening

In recent years it has become fashionable to talk about body language, particularly when observing sports players and politicians. But body language is just one element of everyday non-verbal communication that people subconsciously express. Hand gestures, voice tone and volume and eye movements make up some of the other

---

[5]The Psychology of Programming Interest Group (PPIG) is a very good resource in this respect. See http://www.ppig.org/.

elements of nonverbal communication. Experts estimate that a good majority of all human communication, possibly up to 70% is nonverbal (although this is extremely hard to measure). The important point however is that everyone uses nonverbal behaviour to communicate extensively in everyday life and we are all affected and influenced by it. Most people pay little conscious attention to non-verbal signals because this requires a good deal of concentration and energy; too much energy for most purposes compared to the benefit gained. These non-verbal signals are referred to as "leakage" because most of the time, most people are unaware that they are using them. Active listening includes attending to a person's nonverbal leakage. The non-verbals offer insight into a speaker's inner world; what they are actually thinking and feeling as well as what they are saying.

In addition, there are three other elements to active listening. The first is paying much more careful attention than is usual to how the words are being used, such as the choice of words, pauses between words and the intonation. Perhaps most importantly, active listening includes checking understanding of what is being said. All interpersonal communication is interpreted by both parties within and into their own frame of reference. Misunderstanding occurs when this translation process goes wrong. Active listening requires the listener to check that their understanding matches the speaker's meaning. Finally, active listening places the speaker in control of the conversation. An active listener should allow the speaker to pace the conversation and say what they want without interruption. This is a rare commodity in everyday life. In normal conversation, most people are framing their response whilst the other person is still speaking. Indeed, it would be a very stilted conversation if each person had to wait until the other person had thought about their response before replying. Because active listening is rare, it can also be somewhat embarrassing for the speaker and frustrating for the listener; particularly when all that is required is a simple exchange of information. Active listening should therefore only be used when appropriate.

Software systems developers are not counsellors or social workers who use active listening skills in their work. Software systems developers do not need the same level of active listening skill. This means that developers need to be more sensitive to when active listening is or is not appropriate and take greater care to establish a suitable environment to exercise active listening. This requires self-awareness and situational sensitivity, something that is not normally associated with software systems developers. Social awareness and active listening are not part of the software systems developer curriculum. They are not skills high on the agenda when selecting developers. Perhaps it is not surprising therefore that miscommunication occurs in the SSDP and costly mistakes are made. Indeed research using the Myers Briggs inventory suggests that software systems developers are predominately ISTJ (Introverted, Sensing, Thinking, Judgemental) [5]. Although these findings should be treated with caution[6] as Cruz, Silva et al. point out, anecdotal reports have resulted in the stereotypical nerdish characterisation of software systems developers; not qualities often

---

[6]As should the Myers-Briggs inventory itself.

associated with active listening skills. The underrepresentation of Extrovert, Intuitive, Feeling, Perceiving (EIFP) staff would point towards potential problems with interpersonal communications.

4.4.3   Interpreting Information

If eliciting information from clients and fellow developers is more complex than it appears, then interpreting that information in an accurate way is equally complex. The difficulty arises from what soft systems methodologists call "Weltanschauung" or world view. The problem is that each person's world view is a unique construction born out of a lifetime of previous experience. Construct Theory [13] suggests that the process by which a world view is formed is an inexorable, recursive process of comparing and contrasting previously formed constructs as new events are experienced. A "construct" is an individual's way of making sense of the world. It consists of both the experience (which can be of a person) and the emotions connected to it. So for example, as a child we might have a construct of a bicycle as a two wheeled toy, but associated with that construct might be fun days in the park with our parents, or alternatively, frustration at not being able to stop and crashing into a tree. The construct might be framed by our existing feelings with regard to our parents as soothing and supportive or angry and critical. In one world view, the bicycle construct is associated with fun, freedom and caring, in another with failure, pain, and unworthiness. Bicycles might then be contrasted with say a construct of a car which has been construed in a similar process. The car construct might represent freedom to travel and a sense of speed and exhilaration. Alternatively it could be of interminable journeys locked up with our winging, whining sister. So one person might have a world view of car good, bike bad, another person the exact opposite. These types of simplification help us make sense of a highly complex world and lead to us making assumptions about it. So, for example, when we see a cyclist riding on the pavement, we might, as a result of previously formed constructs, catch ourselves thinking that all cyclists are lawless, arrogant egomaniacs who have no concern for other road users. On the other hand, the thought might cross our minds what a fun loving, eco-friendly, companionate person. "I wish I was on my bike right now". According to construct theory such thoughts come to mind unbidden and often unnoticed, but they influence how we interpret new events. For a software systems developer, this might be a client or colleague passing on information about the system. Depending on the developer's world view, she/he might pay more or less attention according to their construct of that person, introducing a subjective bias regarding the value of the information. ("I wish I was on my bike right now.") This can easily lead to different understandings of the system and different decisions being made about it. Minimising these subjective biases requires developers to be sufficiently self-aware to be able to pay attention to their own inner dialogue and analyse how it is influencing their thought processes.

Furthermore, some people hold a more rigid a world view than others. A person's world view formed from the individual constructs connected in a multi-dimensional, multi-layered matrix of relationships between one construct and another; bikes connected with parents, holidays by the sea, boring Sunday afternoons, Auntie Abigale. There is a certain amount of psychological pain associated with changing one's world view. After all, we have spent a lifetime constructing it, it has worked well enough so far, why change it? If one were to modify one construct in the light of new evidence, what is to say that the whole edifice might not change? ("Okay, so he does ride a bike. He's still a nice chap.") The more central a construct is to a person's sense of identity, the more difficult it becomes to change. A passionate cyclist might find it difficult to believe there are some malevolent bike riders. On the other hand, because of their world view, someone else might actually enjoy changing their world view. They might find the psychological pain stimulating, recognising new possibilities in the changed perspective. Software systems developers probably need to be closer to the later personality than the former. With reference to Myers Briggs Type Indicator (MTBI), Intuitive, Feeling, Perceiving people might be more likely to hold flexible world views than Sensing, Thinking, Judging people. If a developer lacks the self-awareness to challenge their own preconceptions, assumptions regarding the system or its users might bias the delivered system, in favour of those the system's designer approve of.

It would be stretching the point to suggest that construct theory can be used to explain the high incidence of software system failures, but communications failings have often been cited as a major issue [9, 10].

Construct Theory is itself a construct intended to help to make sense of a complex world. However, it does highlight the principles that (a) preconceptions regarding systems need to be identified and challenged and (b) it is not always evident that assumptions have actually been made as they can be deeply engrained in developers' world views and therefore not available to inspection. An example of this from the medical world is that drugs are often only tested on young people because young people volunteer for drugs tests. The assumption is made that the drugs will work in the same way for elderly people. Clearly this may not be the case, but the assumption has remained unchallenged for many years.

The principle here is that a purely engineering view of SSDP cannot provide a comprehensive solution if the human perspectives is not given sufficient attention.

4.4.4 Intra-group Communication

There are a plethora of theories relating to team dynamics.

As can be seen from Fig. 4.3, this is a complex, well established field, and it is not possible to explore all these theories here, so the most commonly used approaches and those most appropriate to SSDP have been selected.

Figure 4.3 identifies four general areas of group theory.

1. "Socio-technical approaches" whose main concern is organisational and adopts a primarily objective approach.

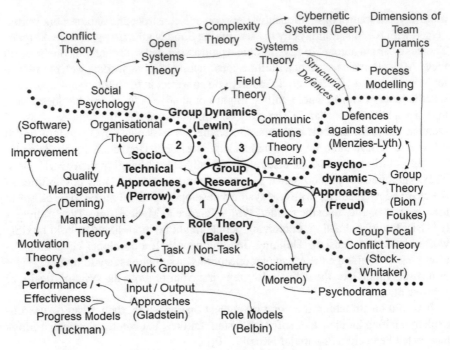

Fig. 4.3 Group dynamics theories

2. The "role theory" approach that explores what positions people adopt within a group.
3. The "psychodynamic approach" that explores the unconscious motivations of group members.
4. The "group dynamics approach" that considers how people interact with each other within groups.

Each area provides a way of exploring groups. Traditionally, software engineering has favoured a socio-technical approach with a bias towards process control and process improvement. Process control and improvement are a means of constraining the factors affecting an open system (as discussed in the Chap. 3) and regard the interpersonal/intra-team communications elements of SSDP as noise in the process.

Role theory is represented in the discussion below in the sections on Tuckman and Belbin. Psychodynamic approaches are in sections on Bion and Menzies-Lyth. Group dynamics is considered in the sections on Lewin and DOTG,

Whilst each is discussed in its own section, interconnections abound, and Fig. 4.3 should be seen as an epistemology, not an ontology. As such the boundaries and interconnections between concepts are fluid. Figure 4.3 should be taken as illustrative rather than definitive. Readers may readily construct their own mapping which would be equally valid.

4.4.4.1 Team Dynamics Tuckman [25]

Perhaps the best known model of team development is Tuckman's team progression model consisting of "forming", "storming", "norming", "performing" (and "adjourning") stages [25]. Tuckman developed this as a result of observation of small groups in the US Navy and from extensive literature reviews. This popular model, states that all groups have to progress through three unproductive stages before they achieve a working state, the "performing" state. Later Tuckman added a fifth state the "adjourning" state. Whilst clearly influential, Tuckman's model has been heavily criticised [4]. It has been challenged on the grounds that many groups fail to follow this progression. There are few suggestions as to what influences the rate of progression. Whether different parts of the group can be in different states simultaneously and whether a group necessarily ever achieves the performing state is questioned. For the purposes of better understanding the SSD process, the main problem with Tuckman's model is that it addresses what happens when team members communicate, but not how team members communicate with each other. Nevertheless, the idea that a group might be in a collective state at a given time may help a team manager understand what is happening within her/his team.

4.4.4.2 Field Theory Lewin [15]

Kurt Lewin who first coined the term "group dynamics" was one of the most influential thinkers on group theory of the 20th Century. His "Field Theory" (ibid.) has resonances throughout management, organisational and group theory. His idea was that every person has a unique psychological field around them that is composed of their thoughts, feelings, aspirations and expectations. This field, which is analogous to a magnetic field influences other people's response to them. In a group, one member might wish to move in a certain direction from A to B, and expect one of the other members to move in some other way (from C to D). As a result of their interaction, Person A may end up at point E and Person B at point F. This dance will be performed between each member of the team. The outcome will depend on the sum of all the forces and whatever external forces are affecting the team as a whole. This provides a visualisation of how individuals in the team and the team as a whole might respond to any stimulus or intervention.

> Field theory implies both the concept of dynamic equilibrium and also reciprocality of movement. Regarding equilibrium it implies that as long as there is no change in the psychological field, there will be no change in the person's behaviour…However, there may well be tensions. The driving forces and the restraining forces may be equal, but they may well be forces of considerable strength. [6, 7, p. 53]

This metaphor provides a means of observing people's behaviour in groups by seeing how they interact with each other and react to each other. Such interactions may, or may not be logical in that they may not be in either person's best interests. Instead they may be serving an internal, unconscious psychological need. By accepting without judging[7] how members of a team behave within the group, it is possible to read the group dynamics. This takes skill, but can help to better understand group outcomes.

Lewin is also credited with the maxim "there is nothing quite so practical as a good theory". This can be interpreted along the lines that although all theories are flawed in some respects and should not be taken as factually correct, they can still be valuable as approximations or guidelines. In other words, as constructs they can provide a useful description of real world situations, but should be applied flexibly rather than dogmatically. It is worth keeping this in mind when considering all the theoretical constructs discussed here.

4.4.4.3   Belbin's Self Perception Inventory [2]

The Belbin Team Roles Self Perception Inventory (ibid.) derives from research initially done in the 1970s that discovered that teams, even those made up of the brightest people often failed to achieve what might have been expected of them. Belbin's research identified that the most successful teams consisted of a balance of people who felt comfortable fulfilling particular roles. Each role provided a valuable contribution to the team effort, and no one role was any more important than any other. Belbin's thesis was that teams consisting of high performing individuals did not necessarily perform well as a team because they failed to mesh together. Having a balance of roles was more important than having large numbers of high performing individuals.

The Self Perception Inventory is not a personality test although quite a lot of research has been done comparing it to personality profiles. People are expected to change their role depending upon the context, environment, other people in the team and broader interests, etc. (unlike personality tests).

Belbin's self-perception inventory has been very popular. It is relatively easy to understand and to administer. Although intended to be used in effect as a recruitment tool to create well balanced teams, this is rarely possible in practical SSD, as it would require a pool of underemployed developers with known profiles to be available for new projects as they arise. However, there are three ways in which Belbin can still be useful.

1.   Firstly teams can analyse themselves to see which roles are covered within the team, which are over-represented and which are lacking. The team can then decide how they might compensate for the problem areas. In this way the inventory provides a tool to support team decision making and communication.
2.   A second use of Belbin is by the team manager. She/he can use their knowledge of the profiles to identify weaknesses within the team and misalignment of functions among the members. So, for example, an implementer in a requirements elicitation role might not be the best fit. If a manager can reallocate work to

---

[7]Being non-judgmental is important because judgmentalism infers that the observer's own feelings and emotions interfere with the observational process. This is unhelpful because it introduces a bias into the interpretations being made.

reflect the team members' preferences, this could lead to better performance. This would require the team manager to be well versed in Belbin and a good observer of her/his fellow workers.

3. The third application of Belbin would be by the team member themselves. Once the person knows their profile, and recognises themselves in their preferred roles, they would be better informed about the type of work that appeals and can make better career choices.

4.4.4.4 Basic Assumption Theory Bion [3]

Bion's Basic Assumption Theory is a state model that is very different from Tuckman's group development model. It is perhaps the most difficult of the models to understand or use. It derives from Freudian psychology. For Bion, groups can be in one of three "basic assumption states"; "dependency" (B*ad*), "flight or fight" (B*af*) or "pairing" (B*ap*). These states exist to protect the group from anxiety and are characterised by a commonly held group belief. States have no priority or order and can change very quickly. The first state (B*ad*) is characterised by the belief that the group leader will protect them. The group has become dependent on an authority figure in the team, usually the team leader, expecting that person to make all decisions for the group. When the authority figure is not the team leader, conflict can be high and a decision making paralysis can result. If the authority figure fails to lead the group to the satisfaction of the group, she/he becomes the subject of negative, even hostile feelings.

In the second state (B*af*) the group believe that it is prepared to fight for its survival and/or to abandon a member if necessary to his/her fate. In B*af* team members waste energy challenging the authority of the leader (fight) or in finding ways to avoid (emotional) contact with each other (flight).

The third state (B*ap*) is characterised by the belief that a pair within the group will produce a messianic saviour to rescue the team. Thus they will hang around waiting for this mythical rescuer to arrive. Even if, on the rare occasions a saviour does emerge (possibly a new manager is appointed or a bright new person joins the team), it is unlikely that she/he will be able to solve the group's problems because they are born out of anxiety, not reality.

All these states are borne out of anxiety within the group and impact the team's ability to work together. One ever present source of anxiety is whether or not the team is doing what it should be. i.e. has it got the right requirements and the requirements right?

It is only when these basic assumptions are challenged that the group can work effectively on the task. However, even for a trained Freudian group psychotherapist these states are difficult to recognise.

Practical application by a project manager seems unrealistic on a day to day basis for managing a team. Nevertheless, two practical ideas emerge from Bion's thinking.

1. That either an unconscious individual angst, or a collective group anxiety might affect the performance of the team. Being aware of the potential anxieties enables a team leader/project manager to mitigate the anxiety.
2. Project managers may be irrationally criticised by the team for perceived failures that result from team members' own anxieties rather than anything the manager has, or has not done. Project managers who are aware that this can happen are more likely to be in a position to identify the true source of the anxiety rather than feeling personally attacked.

4.4.4.5   Dimensions of Team Dynamics Rosen [22]

Belbin's Self Perception Inventory provides a snapshot of a team's role structure. Rosen proposes a more dynamic approach. The purpose of Dimensions of Team Dynamics (DOTD)[8] is to encourage open dialogue between team members by exploring assumptions team members make about each other. It is not intended to create a team profile, although this is one way that the team could enhance their own understanding of the team. It provides a framework to explore similarities and differences between team members' ways of working and their perceptions of each other. The assumption behind DOTD is that any relationship can be defined by what cannot be discussed, the taboo subjects, rather than what is openly spoken about. This relates back to Bion's Basic Assumption States. Enabling team members to talk more openly about each other using a relatively unthreatening language and structure improves group communications. This promotes team cohesion and better equips the team to access all its resources.

Similar to Belbin's self-perception inventory, the effective use of DOTD depends upon the team manager being able to facilitate a discussion between team members, and having the opportunity to do so. As a manager, it is often difficult to work out why a perfectly capable team of people is not achieving the expect results. A team might be performing reasonably. No one person is letting the side down, but team members are not gelling together. DOTD is an observational tool that provides a language and a model that encourages intra-group dialogue.

Derived from theories of group dynamics such as Bion (op. cit.) and Menzies-Lyth [19] that suggest unconscious interpersonal processes affect task achievement, DOTD supports the raising of awareness of the team's dynamics. DOTD provides a schema for examining how the socio-dynamic relationships within the team affect the group process. The hidden, intrinsic strengths and weaknesses of the team can be identified, appropriate action can be agreed and the outcomes monitored in a safe and unthreatening way.

DOTD has 6 "dimensions":

1. Leadership and initiative taking
2. Structure and flexibility

---

[8] See Appendix A.

3. Group or self-motivation
4. Task or social orientation
5. Acceptance of responsibility
6. High/low self-belief.

In addition, it challenges the assumption of a common and stable vision (identified as "Valence of Vision" in the framework).

These dimensions emerged from empirical observations of teams in both commercial and educational settings. The DOTD instrument provides a medium for managers and group members to exchange ideas and promote a group's discussion about itself.[9]

DOTD is describes as an "epistemological", "non-orthogonal" and "non-judgemental" framework. "Epistemological" in this context denotes that each team member has their own interpretation for the meaning of each dimension. Discussing how team members have understood the dimensions is one of the ways in which differences in members' perceptions can be explored.

"Non-orthogonal" refers to the fact that the dimensions interact and affect each other and cannot be totally disassociated from each other. These two attributes provide a mechanism for encouraging dialogue. Users of the framework will construe their own understanding of the model and apply it accordingly.

DOTD, perhaps more than Belbin, requires a facilitator who can explore and challenge differences in perceptions between team members in a non-confrontational manner. For example team member "A" may see themselves as innovative, but this might not be the view of other team members. This might be because when "A" makes a suggestion it is not heard by other members of the team, but when B makes the same suggestion it is acknowledged. This would be an indicator of status differences within the team between A and B. The consequences could be that A stops making suggestions and the overall potential of the team is reduced. A responsive team manager might pay greater attention to A's ideas and ensure that they are heard in team meetings. Another example might be that team member C is seen by the team as being individualistic, not letting other team members know what she/he is doing. In C's case, the team manager might work to find a way of helping C become a more integrated member of the team. DOTG does not aim to provide answers, just more data for both team members and the team manager. Its effectiveness relies on a supportive, collaborative, constructive culture being generated, and team management is particularly influential in this regard.

4.4.4.6 Defence Against Anxiety Menzies-Lyth [19]

One of the theories to emerge from observation of the nursing practice that appears to have relevance to SSD is Isabel Menzies-Lyth "Defences Against Anxiety" (ibid.). Menzies-Lyth observed that nurses on wards rarely spoke to patients as if they were human beings, referring to them as, for example, 'the leg in bed 4'. Another example

---

[9]Further description of the dimensions can be found in Appendix 1.

of defence against anxiety was the imposition of a highly structured regime on the working day such as wake patients up at 6:00 am, serve breakfast at 6:30, start ward round at 8:15. Menzies-Lyth concluded that these structures were little to do with patient welfare and much more to do with managing the distress and anxiety of the nurses themselves caused by the emotionally and physically difficult environment they were working in.

This phenomenon has been widely observed in many other work environments [6, 7]. It is not hard to draw parallels with SSD. Anxiety caused by tight deadlines, uncertainty regarding requirements and whether the system will ever work correctly, results in the defensive implementation of procedures. Such procedures offer little in the way of quality assurance and lead to longer development times. These defence mechanisms are particularly evident when using traditional development methodologies. With Agile approaches, they are less obvious, but still present. Recognising when a process or procedure has become a hindrance to the development process is difficult. Disposing of it is even trickier. Awareness of the psychological role the procedure fulfils can help to reduce their negative impact.

4.4.4.7 Groupthink Janis [11]

Groupthink is another example of a defensive mechanism and fits well with both Menzies-Lyth and Bion. It results from both a perceived external threat to the group and over-identification with the group. The groupthink phenomenon manifests itself as a failure to challenge authority within the group even when a team member, or even a group of team members believe that something might be going wrong. Many factors might contribute to groupthink occurring; a (perceived) external threat to the existence of the group, unequal power relationships within the group, an overbearing sense of group identification and/or a lack of diverse and divergent thinking within the group. Groupthink can, and often does lead to incorrect decisions going unchallenged resulting in the requirement for rework later in the process. In the case of the Challenger space shuttle, groupthink is considered to have contributed to the catastrophe. Groupthink can be mitigated by introducing greater cultural diversity amongst team members and the positive encouragement of divergent thinking, but as has been suggested above, this can be a challenge in its own right.

4.5 Inter Team Dynamics

In 1971, Weinberg [27] called for developers to become "egoless programmers". His idea was that programmers should be sufficiently detached from the code they write to be able to submit their code to the scrutiny of fellow workers in code reviews. However, it is difficult to disassociate this conception of egolessness from the sense that most programmers have of personal identification with the code they write.

Getting a co-programmer to check ones code is one thing, having someone from outside the team testing ones code before it is ready, is a totally different prospect.

The role of the testing team is to find faults in a program. Good testers have a knack of finding bugs. Sometimes, at least from the programmer's point of view, they are too good judging from the anecdotal evidence of arguments between coders and testers. The number of reposts along the lines "that's not a bug. That's a feature!" or "of course the program gave an error. Did you read the spec?" are legend. The rights and wrongs of the particular discussion are less important than the vehemence with which they are conducted and the vitriol that emerges from the confrontation. The point they illustrate is that programmers and testers, although they work for the same organisation and ostensibly have the same objectives, do in fact have very different personal motivations and allegiances. Programmers want to develop clever systems. Good testers want to find faults in programs. So if a "half baked" tester criticises a programmer's program, the tester is criticising the programmer. Egolessness goes out the window.

This example of conflict between individuals often represents a conflict between groups; the programmer identifying as a member of the programmers' group and the tester a member of the testers' group. The other group is seen as defensive, aggressive and divisive. This is known in organisational psychology as "splitting" [14], a Freudian concept that seeks to project any negative feelings experienced by a person onto someone else attributing the cause of those feeling to the other person. The same process was first applied to groups by Jaques [12], DeBoard [6, 7] since when it has emerged as a field of research, social defence theory, in its own right [16]. Programmers and testers are just one example within SSD. Stereotypes of various groups can emerge such as "All systems architects have their head in the clouds", "all marketeers are interested in is protecting their own bonuses." These examples are symptomatic of splitting. Because SSD occurs in an environment of uncertainty, software development project teams can readily revert to defensive postures that can undermine inter-group cooperation and result in production delays.

4.6 The Role of the Project Manager[10]

Too often the role of the project manager can be reduced to one of managing resources and meeting deadlines. This is a very limited view of the role and fails to address the issues arising from the discussion above. Of course, most commentators on management recognise the importance of leadership, people management and motivating staff played by project managers. The problem however is that few appreciate the complex social issues managers need to deal with, and therefore provided little training for the role. This is particularly true for SSD project managers who, more often

---

[10]Team leader can be substituted for Project Manager is this section. a team leader is taken to be the person leading a single team whereas a Project Manager may be responsible for several teams.

than not are promoted to management positions as a result of their technical capability rather than their social skills.

The argument above provides a theoretical landscape in which a software development team operates. There are few rules as to how a manager might intervene to enhance the success of the team or teams involved in the project. This is left to the skill of the project manager. The project manager needs to become consciously aware of, and sensitive to, the unconscious currents that flow between team members and between teams. This is a role for which they are often unprepared, and ill-equipped.

Being from the development community as they often are, project managers will often exhibit the same personality profiles (using MTBI inventory) as team members; that is a bias towards thinking, judging and sensing when the skills called for are more associated with feeling, sensing and perceiving. For a person who is uncomfortable dealing with other people's emotions it is difficult to find the right sort of response to an expression of feeling, or even recognising that a situation is emotion filled. A sensing/thinking person might deal well with the logic and the logistics, but less well with any underlying anxiety. Strong emotions such as anger and aggression might be particularly challenging. Such a person might miss the signals that suggest more substantial problems with the project.

4.7   Manager's Power and Authority in the Team

There is one further factor that has not so far been discussed in relation to the project manager's role that emerges from a social psychology perspective; that of the manager's perceived power and authority. Much has been written regarding leadership and power in teams, but the focus taken here is on the power relationship between the project manager and team members. This is an intricate theory developed by Klein [14] using a concept known as "Transference" first observed by Freud. Without expanding on the complexities, the theory suggests that a manager will elicit two simultaneous, conflicting emotions from a team member; dependence on the manager to lead and make decisions and hostility to the manager for their imposition of authority. If a manager fails to lead and make decisions they will be vilified as weak and ineffectual. If they make decisions that a team member or members consider wrong, they will be criticised for being over-authoritarian. These positions are rarely expressed openly to the manager as they hook into deep and usually inaccessible parts of a person's psyche. Nevertheless, they can impair communications between staff and managers without either party really understanding why. Managers wishing to improve communications in a team or between teams therefore face an additional challenge of how to manage the transference. To do this, a manager needs to be aware of the possibility (some would say the inevitability) of transference in the manager/team member relationship, and to be sensitive to it. The Tavistock Institute has made addressing transference a core element of its management training programmes and its research for many years, but few other management and training organisations recognise it as significant.

Whilst transference is a central and integral concept in social-psychology literature, it is rarely, if ever, mentioned in the SSD field yet it is likely to play a central role when dealing with uncertainty and constant change.

4.8 Conclusion

This chapter has introduced various theoretical ideas and a several tools managers could use to improve their understanding of the team process. A number of these ideas will be considered implausible, unscientific mumbo jumbo by hard scientists concerned with verifiable proof and facts. Software engineers in particular would most likely prefer to put their faith in processes, procedures and standards to achieve their required outcomes. Yet time and time again, projects fail to deliver to order and when they are delivered they fail to deliver the expected returns. It is evident that process alone is insufficient.

The concepts discussed here require a different mind-set. They are not proven laws of nature, but simplified metaphors for complex phenomena. They do not aspire to truth, but to insight. They will be intrinsically unappealing to many and regarded sceptically by others, questioning their authenticity and usefulness. Lewin's maxim quoted above that "there is nothing quite so practical as a good theory" has to be appreciated to understand the value of these theories and this approach. The theories provide a way of making sense of the world and predicting what might happen. It is not possible to predict what will happen, but it is better than having nothing to go by, which is the alternative. One might expect that a "shaper" from Belbin's model might not make a great job of meticulous research. If someone of low status in a team isn't credited with their ideas, they will probably stop putting new ideas forward. This may seem obvious, but it is only obvious if one is looking for it, and most of the time, most people are too preoccupied to notice. The theories above are intended to draw attention to these phenomena so that they can be examined. The concept of the unconscious is generally accepted as useful these days, but the implications for human behaviour are poorly understood and less widely accepted. One of these implications is that interpersonal, intra-group and inter-group communications are much more complicated than they initially appear to be. In everyday communications this is not a particular problem. Most people learn to read the signals other people give off and adjust their own behaviour accordingly. We have many years of practice before we're expected to become good at it. This sees us through most situations more or less successfully.

The argument throughout this book is that SSD is not a normal situation. It is not one that people learn to cope with during their upbringing. That is not to say that developers do not learn to cope. Generally they do. The question is whether coping is sufficient. Is SSD significantly different from other environments to require special attention to be paid to the communications processes? Some would argue that paying more attention to communications and personal emotions is important anyway. The wellbeing movement is founded on this principle. This book argues that the fundamental nature of SSD is unique. It therefore require specific intellectual and practical inquiry into the consequences of that uniqueness.

SSD is a communications process. It requires people to share intangible concepts with a precision required of engineering activities. This is not required in the production processes of other intangible products. This uniqueness has consequences. One is the rapidly changing and unpredictable nature of the SSD work environment. It creates a work environment that is ill defined, ambiguous and pressured. These are just the conditions likely to generate anxieties, and, if one is prepared to accept some of the theory above, lead to unconscious defence reactions. Defensiveness leads to barriers being created to communication; just the opposite reaction to that needed for effective development. Thus paying greater attention to potentially detrimental unconscious communications processes is central to establishing a constructive working environment. The management role is crucial in this process, so managers need to equipped and skilled in social behaviour, beyond normal people skills. This level of skill requires specific training. Process control can only ever provide a partial answer to the SSD conundrum. Understanding the human aspects of the process offers the insight that is lacking from the social perspective of this socio-technical activity.

4.9   Discussion Questions

1. When might it not be appropriate for a software systems designer to use active listening skills?
2. How might communication skills be included in a software systems development curriculum?
3. What role should self-awareness play in the role of a software systems project manager?
4. How might counter transference affect software systems project manager?
5. Is performance anxiety a significant influence is software systems development?
6. Is SSD sufficiently different from other forms of development to warrant paying much more attention to interpersonal communications?

References

1. Beecham S et al (2008) Motivation in software engineering: a systematic literature review. Inf Softw Technol 50:860–878
2. Belbin RM (1981) Management teams: why they succeed or fail. Heinemann, London
3. Bion WR (1961) Experiences in groups. Routledge, London
4. Bonebright DA (2010) 40 years of storming: a historical review of Tuckman's model of small group development. Human Res Develop Int 13(1):111–120
5. Cruz S et al (2015) Forty years of research on personality in software engineering: a mapping study. Comput Human Beh 46(94–113)

6. DeBoard R (1978) The psychoanalysis of organisations. Routlegde, London
7. DeBoard R (1978) The psychoanalysis of organizations. Tavistock Publications, London
8. Hall T et al (2008) What do we know about developer motivation? IEEE Softw 25(4):92–94
9. Hall T et al (2007) Communication: the neglected technical skill? In: SIGMIS CPR '07 proceedings of the 2007 ACM SIGMIS CPR conference on computer personnel research: the global information technology workforce. ACM, St. Louis, Missouri, pp 196–202
10. Hayes JH (2003) Do you like Pina Coladas? How improved communication can improve software quality. IEEE Softw 20(1):90–92
11. Janis I (1971) Groupthink. Psychol Today 43–76
12. Jaques E, Klein M, Heimann P, Money-Kyrle RE (1955) Socialsystems as a defence against persecutory and depressive anxiet. In: New directions in psychoanalysi. Tavistock Publications, London, pp 478–498
13. Kelly GA (1991) The psychology of personal constructs. Routledge, London
14. Klein M (1952) The origins of transference. In: Mitchell J (ed) The selected works of Melanie Klein. Penguin, London, pp 201–210
15. Lewin K (1951) Field theory in social science. Harpers & Row, New York
16. Long S (2006) Organizational defenses against anxiety: what has happened since the 1955 Jaques paper? Int J Appl Psychoanal Stud 3(4):279–295
17. Maslow AH (1970) Motivation and personality. Harper & Row, New York
18. McGregor D (1960) The human side of enterprise. McGraw-Hill, London
19. Menzies-Lyth I (1959) The functioning of social systems as a defence against anxiety. In: Menzies-Lyth I (ed) Containing anxiety in institutions. Free Association Press, London, pp 43–85
20. Pavlov IP (1927) Conditioned reflexes; an investigation of the physiological activity of the cerebral cortex. Dover Publications, New York
21. Perrow C (1967) A framework for comparative analysis of organizations. Am Sociol Rev 32(2):194–208
22. Rosen C (2008) The influence of intra-team relationships on the software development process. Comput Sci (Keele Staffordshire, Keele, PhD)
23. Skinner BF (1948) 'Superstition' in the pigeon. J Exp Psychol 38(2):168–172
24. Teague J (1998) Personality type, career preference and implications for computer science recruitment and teaching. In: 3rd Australasian conference on computer science education (ACSE '98). ACM, Brisbane, pp 155–163
25. Tuckman BW (1965) Developmental sequence in small groups. Psychol Bull 63(6):384–399
26. Varona D et al (2012) Evolution of software engineers' personality profile. ACM Sigsoft Softw Eng Notes 37(1):1–5
27. Weinberg GM (1971) The psychology of computer programming. Van Nostrand Reinhold, New York

Chapter 5
Project Management Decision Making

5.1 Introduction

As a guide to software systems development, this book places considerable emphasis on understanding stakeholders and the stakeholder environment. The theoretical
foundation used is open systems theory. Open systems theory is used in two distinct,
but interrelated contexts as noted in Chap. 3. The first explains the complexity of and
the problems associated with software systems development. The second views the
software systems development as an open system. This chapter explores the second
of these two propositions in more detail. In particular how SSD relates to its parent
system.

Beer's Viable Systems Model (VSM) [2] argues that a viable system

(a) Is always contained within a parent system.
(b) Receives inputs from that parent system.
(c) Provides feedback to the parent system.

A systems approach to the project management of SSD therefore needs to start
with a consideration of the context set by the parent system. What is this parent
system with regards to the management of the project, what are the inputs from the
parent system and what is the feedback to it?

Clearly there are many different contexts in which SSD takes place; embedded
systems, control systems, end user systems and so on. It is difficult to develop specific guidelines for each of these contexts. This chapter will focus on large business
oriented systems as this type of development touches on many of the problems other
development contexts face to a greater or lesser extent. As the chapter title suggests,
it will also focus on the decision making aspects of project management rather than
project planning, work and cost breakdown structures or task allocation. These latter
concepts are extensively covered in the literature [20] and there are tools available
such as Prince II, Microsoft Project and spreadsheets to help with the process. These
lower level activities however are predicated on decisions that must be taken regarding which projects to undertake in the first place, how the projects will be carried out

C. Rosen, *Guide to Software Systems Development*,
https://doi.org/10.1007/978-3-030-39730-2_5

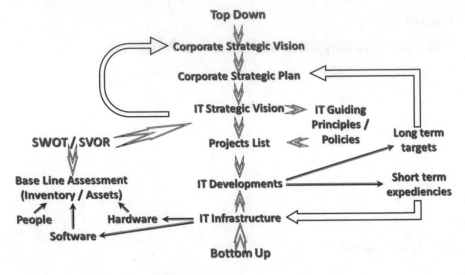

Fig. 5.1 Project selection decision making process

and who will be doing the work. It is these decisions that are the considered here. Figure 5.1 illustrates the process.

5.2 Top Down Decision Making

For business orientated systems, the parent system within which software systems exist is the business organisation. Most, if not all, medium to large businesses are guided by a vision for the future and a strategic plan to achieve that vision. This corporate business strategy may be more or less formal and more or less long or short term. This strategy forms the future vision for the organisation. Smaller organisations may operate on a more opportunistic basis, but as they grow, the pressure to develop a more disciplined approach becomes greater as the range of opportunities grows and priorities have to be set.[1]

This corporate strategy[2] should be the starting point for a systems development strategy. The principle behind a systems development strategy should be 'how can the IT strategy best support the corporate strategic plan?'. In other words, the IT strategy should align with the corporate strategy. The IT strategy should incorporate

---

[1] Developing a corporate strategy is covered extensively in the business literature. An introduction can be found in Grünig and Kühn [11].

[2] Whilst the following argument is couched in terms of a business milieu, the argument applies equally to not for profit organisations which hope to be able to offer their services to a broader clientele.

an IT strategic vision that provides a general direction in which the IT system(s) need to develop.

The resultant systems development strategy provides the context within which decisions on potential systems development projects should be prioritised.

Alongside the IT strategic vision, a set of guiding principles and policies is required. This consists of the following sections as a minimum:

- The criteria to be applied to potential projects for a given level of resourcing.
- How well the project needs to fit with the IT strategy.
- Who should be consulted.
- What level of risk assessment needs to be undertaken.

These principles should be considered guidelines rather than strict criteria. Few projects will satisfy precise criteria and there is always that project opportunity that is just too good to miss.

Applying these principles should lead to a project development list (sometimes called the project backlog) that prioritises potential projects and allocates resources. Decisions on which projects are actually funded can be taken on the basis of the estimated return on investment (ROI) although this is not an exact science. On large projects both cost estimation and evaluation of benefit are difficult to assess as will be discussed later. The significant point is that decisions are made in the context of an IT strategy that supports the corporate strategic plan. The IT strategy is integral to the corporate strategy, not independent of it.

One of the attributes of software systems developments is that they tend to provide unforeseen further development opportunities. The classic example of this was the Tesco loyalty card scheme [9]. In 1994 the supermarket chain Tesco decided to introduce a loyalty card scheme to encourage existing shoppers to return to shop with Tesco rather than visit competitors and spread their spend. Tesco required a software system to administer the scheme. A pilot program was duly developed. The system required, large quantities of data about customers to be collected.

The data analysis company, DunnHumby who developed the pilot system, presented an analysis of the data they had collected to the Tesco board. This led to the commissioning of the full system which not only boosted the company's market share, but provided a great deal of information regarding the behaviour of Tesco's customers. This led to changes in Tesco's marketing approach and had a profound effect on the retailer's growth strategy. It could be argued that ultimately it was one of the major initiating events of the data analytics revolution. This relatively unambitious software systems development project resulted in major changes to Tesco's corporate strategy and demonstrates the general principle that software systems developments can significantly affect the broader operating environment. It is an example of Beer's (ibid.) VSM in operation; subsystem feedback to its parent system.[3] Organisations that have mechanisms in place to monitor the influences systems developments are having on their business can derive considerable benefit as a result.

---

[3]The changes made by Tesco affected its parent environment, the retail sectors as competitors had to respond with similar schemes. This in turn influenced the business world as a whole and contributed to the instigation of the data analytics revolution.

In some organisations, decisions on IT developments seem to be taken completely divorced from the corporate strategy. Whilst opportunistic IT developments can provide efficiency gains, a lack of strategic alignment between IT and the rest of the organisation can result in lost opportunities to make corporate gains.

5.3 Bottom Up Decision Making

The top down decision making process described above is often confused by, and sometimes with, bottom up decision making.

Any organisation will already own legacy systems. (In some organisations these may even be manual, paper-based systems, although these days this is rare and becoming rarer.) These systems require maintenance and upgrading. The more sophisticated the system, the more likely they are to require continual reinvestment. (An IT system is for life, not just for Christmas!) The demands on resources from legacy systems cannot be ignored and usually compete with new systems developments. The lower half of Fig. 5.1 illustrates this tension.

Thus a list of potential development projects consisting of both new developments and legacy maintenance projects emerges. Some projects will be long term, strategic projects usually designed to deliver some form of competitive advantage. Other projects will be short term expediencies needed to manage existing infrastructure. Each type of project will need to be assessed and prioritised according to criteria for that category of development. A balance needs to be struck between the two types of project. If short term expediency projects are not funded, the infrastructure of the organisation can be compromised. If strategic projects are not resourced, the long- term competitiveness of the organisation can be at risk. One thing that can be guaranteed (along with death and taxes) is that there will be more potential projects than resources allow. For this reason, having clear criteria for assessing the relative worthiness of projects is necessary. The principles and policies support the selection process. The more clarity there is in the corporate strategy and the better defined the IT strategic vision, the easier it is to assess the potential benefits of the proposed projects. Of course, there may be a case for skunkworks type projects; speculative projects that do not conform to any of the criteria. If these are low cost, cause minimal disruption to workflow and promise good returns, they may be worth the risk. This decision can only be taken in the knowledge that such a project would be speculative and provided the risk of failure is appreciated.

5.4 SWOT and SVOR

Organisations often make use of SWOT (Strengths, Weaknesses, Opportunities and Threats) or SVOR (Strengths, Vulnerabilities, Opportunities and Risks) to inform their corporate plans. It is probably less commonly used to inform the IT strategic plan. Evidence to inform the SWOT/SVOR process should come from an assessment of the currently available resources. This assessment includes not only an evaluation of the hardware and the software assets, but also the skills, knowledge and capabilities of the people within the organisation. The assessment of resources forms a baseline for conducting the SWOT/SVOR.[4]

5.5 Selecting from Potential Projects

5.5.1 Strategic Versus Tactical Projects

As mentioned above, when selecting potential projects, the first consideration is to decide whether the potential project is intended to support the strategic plan or whether it is an expedient, tactical development designed to maintain or enhance the organisational infrastructure. Benyon-Davis [3] suggests dividing tactical developments down further into tactical and operational management as this provides a pyramidal structure in terms of the number of projects undertake. Most projects are likely to be operational, with fewer tactical projects. There will be even fewer strategic projects. (See Fig. 5.2.)

This stratification reflects some common correlations relating size to resource consumption, duration, and therefore, quality of knowledge available for making the decision and the associated risk. The Pareto rule is a useful guideline here. 80% of the projects will be relatively small, tactical and consume around 20% of the resources. The remaining 20% of projects will consume the remaining 80% of the resources.

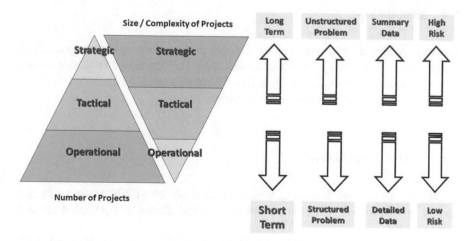

Fig. 5.2 Characteristics of systems developments (derived from [3])

---

[4]SWOT and SVOR are covered extensively in the literature.

Strategic projects are most likely to be bigger in terms of scope, complexity and duration. Strategic projects obviously take longer, but also have greater impact on the long term operation of the organisation. The understanding of the problems will be most structured, more clearly defined and most comprehensible for operational projects. The problem domain will be least structured, less well defined and less well understood for strategic projects. To compound the problematic nature of strategic projects, the quality of the data available in terms of the levels of precision and stability will be lower than for operational projects. Taken together this results in strategic projects inevitably presenting far greater risk than the operational projects. Depending on the complexity of tactical projects, they can be placed somewhere in the middle of each of these attributes.

The lack of detailed information available for strategic projects leads to a tendency for under assessing their complexity. It is easy to become seduced by the promise they offer and the allure of new technologies. Furthermore the negative effects of system changes are obscured and often only emerge some time after the new system has become operational. The greater the novelty of the new system, the fewer the analogous systems it can be compared to, so the more difficult it becomes to antic- ipate downsides. This might be an example of "Oversimplification Syndrome".[5] Non-domain, lay-people such as CEOs or politicians are particularly prone to this syndrome. Nevertheless, despite the uncertainties, decisions still need to be take.

Such risk must be measured against the potential gains. None of the risk factors identified in Chap. 3 are unique to SSD projects, but the determinant and intangible attributes of software systems contribute more to oversimplification syndrome and this needs to be factored in.

5.6 Feasibility

Having determined whether a potential project's primary purpose is strategic, tactical or operational, a feasibility study can be conducted. This consists of a risk assessment, capability assessment and a cost estimation. These are normal business practices, but the nature of SSD adds additional complication.

5.6.1 Risk Assessment

In addition to the risk factors identified in Chap. 3, two further sources of risk should be considered. These are potential external threats and potential internal disagreement.

External threats are likely to have been considered during the development of the corporate strategic plan or during a SWOT analysis, but SSD has attracted additional

---

[5]See Chap. 2.

threats such as to data security, systems resilience to malicious attack, and the potential for technological change to undermine potential benefits. The more ambitious the project, the more prone it will be to these risks. High profile projects such as government initiatives are perhaps even more vulnerable than commercial projects. Oversimplification syndrome is a particular threat for governmental projects as additional political factors can influence decision making, and the fact that non-domain experts hold the decision making prerogative. Outside government, the decision maker will probably hold some expertise in the operation of the organisation if not in the technology being proposed. Within government, it is quite possible that the decision maker possesses little expertise in either.

Internal conflict can be related to lack of a common vision as discussed in Chap. 2, or, potentially as a result of differing organisational perspectives. SSD organisations may be no more prone to internal dispute than any other type of organisation, but the complexity and lack of definitional precision provide greater scope for disagreement. Adding to this difficult decision making environment is another of the attributes of software that Brooks identified [4]; that of the "essential" malleability of software. Because software can be moulded to whatever shape is required, it can offer all things to all people. However, trying to please all the people has cost implications. Drawing the line will inevitably disappoint some people. It can be easier to avoid conflict by employing constructive ambiguity in the specification. This defers the decision making to later in the process, but adds to the risk that the system fails to satisfy anyone. The increased possibility of this scenario places considerable emphasis on the authoritativeness of decision making. Much research suggests that a large proportion of SSD project failure is a consequence of "management failure". Charette [5] identified 12 causes of software failure of which all could be considered management's responsibility.

There is no lack of advice either on what project managers should do. Khan and Malik [15] identify 33 separate standards to which project managers can work. But these are all task oriented procedures. The standards do not address the reasons why project managers "fail" to do their job. The standards are analogous to self-help manuals. Everyone knows that they should go to the gym more often and eat more healthily, but there are probably good reasons why this doesn't happen. Similarly, project managers know they should be attentive to the standards in PmBok or SWBok, but without an awareness of the particular circumstances of a particular project manager, it is unhelpful to be saying you should be doing this or that. In reality, the volatile nature of the SSD environment is a rich breeding ground for individual anxiety and hence volatile interpersonal relationships within the development team and between teams [7, 18]. Managing in these circumstances places considerable emphasis on the authoritativeness of decision making and decision makers. Processes, procedures and standards are a second best.

5.6.2   Cost Estimation

Cost estimation in SSD is a controversial subject. There are several cost estimation approaches based on predicted lines of code, function point analysis and the number of use case scenarios. The reality is that:

(a)   There are too many variables affecting the cost of development on large projects to derive a usable cost estimation.
(b)   Cost estimation is dependent upon project size. Project size estimation is subject to oversimplification syndrome.
(c)   As the systems specification is volatile, the basis for calculating cost is unstable.

There are five approaches to address these deficiencies. The first is to keep it simple, but that is not always possible. The second is to attempt to break down the problem into the smallest possible functional units (top down functional decomposition) so that the cost of each unit can be calculated. The problems with this approach are that:

(a)   It is difficult to ensure that all functional units have been identified and accounted for.
(b)   The cost of integrating the functional units is often not considered or underestimated.
(c)   The cost of building in and testing non-functional attributes is difficult to assess and often unaccounted for.
(d)   Small underestimations of cost for each unit accumulate to a large discrepancy in the final cost estimation.

The third approach is to estimate based on similar projects undertaken by the organisation (cost estimation by analogy). The problem with this approach is that one never steps into the same river twice. This is particularly true of SSD. Many of the factors that influenced the cost of the previous system, will not pertain to the current development. This may lead to overestimation, but what seems to happen is that the estimate of the new system is over reduced because the value of the learning from the previous system is over estimated and the problems that arise during the new development are never the same.

A fourth approach is to not to try to calculate the cost. Under normal circumstances this is considered unacceptable, however, in effect this is what much Agile Development attempts to do by breaking the development down into small increments, but failing to predict how many increments there will be before the final system is delivered. This 'pay as you go' scheme is an effective way of hiding the true cost of a systems development. Whether this is a collusive obfuscation between the developer and the client is unclear, but clearly some client organisations are prepared to accept it. How much the organisation eventually pays for the system and whether this is larger or lower than if an alternative approach were to be taken is usually undetermined, and possibly indeterminate.

The final approach is estimation by intuition or guestimation. It might more accurately be described as finger in the air, but may be as accurate as any algorithmic cost estimator. The usual approach when adopted is to ask at least three experts to estimate the cost and to take an average of the three. It is probably better to take the highest estimate, and then, to account for oversimplification syndrome, multiply by between 1.5 and 10 depending on the predicted size and complexity of the project. (The list of potential risks identified in Chap. 3 can be used to assess this multiplication factor.) Finally add a further one third to account for integration costs. Cost data from previous projects may help to inform the original guestimate, but should be handled with care for the reasons stated above.

This approach might appear to be flippant, and may lead to an over-estimation of costs. However when deciding on whether to proceed with a project, it may be better to overestimate than to be unreasonably optimistic. It is probably the most reliable approach given the currently available understanding of SSD cost.

Designing and building in the cost of non-functional requirements adds additional uncertainty to the project's cost. Some non-functional requirements may be relatively easy to calculate, such as the cost say of disaster recovery if required, but are often forgotten. A checklist approach to identify potential costs that might be overlooked might help in organisations where checklists are considered culturally acceptable. Other non-functional requirement costs may be multi-factorial and therefore difficult to assess. It is recommended that an independent costing exercise be conducted into non-functional requirements as this would ensure that greater emphasis is placed on the likely impact of the hidden costs associated with quality requirements.

5.7 Capability Assessment

Assessment of an organisation's capability is probably no more reliable than evaluating potential cost. Early studies [6] suggest that there is a factor of ten between the least capable and the most productive programmers. This however was not necessarily adjusted accurately for the quality of their work. Measuring both code productivity and quality is notoriously difficult. Number of lines of code produced is a poor measure of productivity. It is easy to produce large quantities of code when the problem is relatively simple, when code segments are closely related to each other or if code reuse is possible. In many respects this discussion parallels that regarding code complexity [8]. Both complexity and programmer productivity are complex concepts for which no single measure is appropriate. An individual programmer's productivity in practice is usually determined by subjective criteria which are hard to evaluate. De Aquino Junior and de Lemos Meira [14] suggest a meta-model approach based on stakeholder perceived value. That is, they offer a process model for identifying metrics stakeholders believe to be valuable, but these, in turn are largely subjective.

This difficulty applies equally to the organisation's capability. Programming per se can be considered one of the less demanding skills required of systems developers. Designing implementable solutions is a high level skill for which there are no metrics. The time taken will depend upon the complexity of the problem. The project's novelty, as well as familiarity with the problem domain are significant factors. Awareness of complexity increase with knowledge of the problem to the point, (and sometimes beyond), when the problem has been solved.

An organisation's best method of assessing its capability is therefore by considering what projects it has previously completed successfully along with the resources it has available, or is prepared to commit to the new project. If those projects were of similar size, complexity and in a related domain, it can be reasonably assured that it has the capacity and capability to manage the new project. The greater the gap between previous experience and required knowledge, the greater the risk the organisation is taking. As with all risk estimation, this is an inexact science, but better a poor estimation than no estimation. However, there may also be risks involved in not undertaking the project, or outsourcing the project to a third party which need to be considered.

5.8 In-house or Third Party Development

Many organisations adopt a corporate policy regarding SSD. They argue that they if they are not in the IT business, they should leave IT development to the experts that are in that business and so any SSD project should be contracted out to a third party. The economic theory of "comparative advantage" [12, 19] suggests that this should be the wise thing to do. A non-IT company's IT department should therefore be responsible only for maintaining their current systems.

The principles of comparative advantage may have currency for some products and services such as catering or even telecoms facilitation. However, there are a number of additional considerations in SSD, particularly SSD that is intended to support corporate strategy by delivering competitive advantage. Obviously, if the organisation does not have the capability the decision is straight forward, but at what point should the opportunity cost afforded by third party delivery fall short of the benefits to be gained by an in-house development?

Rather than this decision being a matter of corporate policy, organisations need to recognise that, as the company grows beyond a certain size, SSD becomes core to its continued growth rather than a cost to the business. The interdependence between IT strategy and corporate strategy has particular consequences for SSD when considering contracting out a development. These additional considerations are:

(a) Who will hold the intellectual property rights (IPR) to the software?
(b) How will detailed knowledge of the system be shared between client and vendor?
(c) How will the system be maintained in the future?
(d) Whether (parts of) the system can be reused for other organisations?
(e) What level of communication will pertain between client and vendor, how that communication will be effected and at what levels between the two organisations will it operate?
(f) What level of domain expertise does the vendor have?

(g) How wide is the communications gap between supplier and vendor?

These are more than academic questions. It is notoriously difficult to understand someone else's code. Understanding how an unfamiliar group of people have constructed a complete system is extremely difficult. It would require, as a minimum, accurate, detailed and current design documentation. Maintaining this level of documentation is costly in both resource and elapse time, which adds costs to the project. However, such documentation is essential as, if a system is "mission critical", it may be necessary for a different organisation to enhance and maintain the system if the original organisation is no longer willing or able to provide maintenance and/or enhancement services. A client organisation can find itself dependent on the developer organisation which would place the client in a very vulnerable position. Projects need not be very large or complex to become integral to the effective operation of an organisation, but they may still be intricate enough for a third person to find it difficult to maintain.

Software systems are particularly prone to the need for enhancement, both before the project has been completed (as has been previously stated) and after implementation in response to changes in its operating environment. If mutually agreed arrangements for meeting these needs cannot be found, it can be a source of major disagreement between client and vendor. As has previously been discussed, specification changes which are common in SSD, can cause considerable disruption to the development process. Having arrangements in place that satisfy both client and vendor are essential to the successful completion of the project.

A consideration for an organisation embarking on a project intended to deliver competitive advantage is ownership of the system. If a third party developer owns the IPR, it may identify an opportunity to exploit part or all of the system with a third company, possibly even a competitor, thus undermining the accrued competitive advantage. Avoiding this happening should be subject to agreed contractual arrangements. A supplier may not wish to have its ability to reuse its code constrained, so finding agreement may require delicate negotiation.

On the other hand, the IP of the system may be of little value to the commissioning organisation as, without a detailed knowledge of the code structure, it is likely to be very difficult to make any changes to the system. Software systems consist of delicate and often obscure interconnections even in the most carefully, modular designed, object oriented systems (as the story of Ariane 5 graphically demonstrates [17]). Making changes to unfamiliar software systems should not be undertaken without very careful consideration.

It has already been shown how important communications are between developers and users. The cultural gap between a third party supplier and a client will inevitably be greater than the gap between in-house developers and users within their own organisation.[6] Working out the arrangements by which cognitive distance between user and developers can be reduced is another key to a successful development. Various methods can be used;

---

[6]This is not necessarily true however in large organisations where the IT department is remote, even in a different country from the users.

- prototyping,
- incremental development,
- incorporating user feedback,
- focus groups,
- embedding developers in the client organisation,
- embedding users in the development organisation.

There are however costs associated with adopting these methods which need to be considered in the overall evaluation of the project. It is possible that this is one of the hidden sources of underestimating project costs.

It is the commissioning organisation that carries the ultimate risk of an IT project failure, not the supplier. For this reason, the client organisation cannot abdicate its responsibility or delegate it to the provider.

This is more imperative than in other customer/supplier relationships as it is even more difficult to attribute fault in SSD contracts, especially when requirements have not been clearly (or possibly too precisely) defined. For this reason the commissioning organisation still needs to hold a high level of expertise regarding the system so as:

1. To facilitate the change management process during development.
2. To facilitate as problem free a handover of code and documentation as possible.
3. To ensure the successful implementation of the system and resolve any problems that may arise.

This project manager role within the client organisation is highly skilled, multi-faceted and carries a high level of responsibility. It constitutes yet another hidden cost of contracting out SSD.

These arguments do not make it inevitable that strategic software development is undertaken in house although they do bias the decision in that direction. The counter argument is that there is a considerable overhead in maintaining an in-house SSD capability. If a particular in-house development does not contribute a great deal to the corporate strategy, or is relatively disconnected from future developments, for example a web site upgrade, then carrying a permanent SSD capability may not be viable. There is an additional management overhead of maintaining a SSD department which might be beyond the management expertise of the organisation. An in-house SSD capability may not necessarily reduce the cognitive distance between developers and users if the department is allowed to become isolated from the rest of the organisation or fails to communicate effectively with users. This depends upon the attitudes, values and structures within the organisation in general and the SSD staff in particular. Having the right people is not only a matter of having the right technical capability as has been the argued throughout this book.

Adopting a corporate policy in favour or against maintaining an in-house capability and choosing one approach as a result of the policy is probably a mistake. Large organisations can accommodate the overhead, but may not always have the right expertise. On the other hand, the cognitive distance between developers and users is likely to be greater the larger the organisation. Medium sized organisations may face a dilemma with each project they undertake. Small organisations may not have any choice other than to buy in the expertise causing IT aware CEO's to suffer considerable angst knowing that an essential function of their organisation is in the hands of an external company over which they have little control.

5.9 Informatics

More recently the balance of whether to maintain an in-house SSD capability has shifted more in the direction in-house arrangements. This is due to the emergence of the potential of data analytics. The example of Tesco cited above may have been the start of the data revolution, but the power of data analytics has become generally acknowledged. Even small organisations have the capacity for improving their efficiency using data collected from within the organisation or from customers. This is not dependent on a loyalty card scheme. Indeed, arguably, almost all organisations are now information management businesses.

To benefit from data collection, data has to be transmogrified into information, and this depends on understanding the data in relation to the organisation. The better the data analysts understand the organisation and the business of the organisation itself, the better use they can make of the data. Turning data into information is not just a matter of number crunching. Real insight into the numbers only comes with insight into the business. This makes it more important that the organisation has full control over the data it collects and the data it is able to collect. This means it is more important that it has control over the software system that collects that data.

If, for example, a sandwich shop has an idea that men buy more chicken sandwiches and women buy more tuna sandwiches. If more women tend to come in on Monday after their palates class, and men on Fridays after a pre-weekend gym workout,[7] it would only be possible to confirm this insight if the data collection system collected data on which sandwiches were sold on what days to whom. An apparently small amendment to the database may incur a significant development cost if no customer data is currently collected, but would cost very little if all that is required is an additional gender field to an existing customer table. Knowledge of, and the ability to change the database enables development decisions to be taken quickly. Having to request changes from a third party slows down both the decision making and the implementation, and probably increases the cost. One insight often leads to another. One system change therefore often leads to another, so the change requirements accelerate. There are good reasons for maintaining control over the system and its rate of change as entropy can set in. There is a marginal increase in the difficulty of making a change to a system with each change that is made. Eventually, further change becomes unsustainable and the system must be replaced. Knowledge of the legacy system then becomes essential to keeping it running longer, designing the new system and smoothing the transition from the old to the new system. If that knowledge resides with a third party organisation, it may not be accessible to the

---

[7]Apologies for any gender stereotyping.

client organisation. This might well be another headache for the IT aware CEO of a small, growing business.

5.10   Systems Procurement Options

Once a decision has been made to proceed with a project, the next question is how to deliver it.

There are basically five options regarding the procurement of a system:

1. Building a new, bespoke system.
2. Integrating a number of existing systems.
3. Tailoring or customising an existing system or systems infrastructure to the operational requirements of the organisation.[8]
4. Purchasing an existing product off the shelf (sometimes known as a "shrink wrapped" or "components off the shelf" (COTS) products).
5. End user development (EUD).

5.10.1   Bespoke and Integration Projects

Bespoke refers to having the system designed and developed specifically for the organisation. In general, these are medium to large projects for which no existing product meets the organisation's requirements.

Major integration projects amalgamate a number of different systems or system units. They share many of the same characteristics of large, new development projects. In many ways, integrating different systems is often more complex than totally new developments due to the constraints caused by the existing products. Often, unforeseen complications emerge that require considerable ingenuity to resolve. New software is usually required to provide the communications link between different program units and this can result in performance difficulties or even security vulnerabilities. Anecdotally programmers will say that they would much prefer to work on a new, "green fields" project than mess with interconnecting legacy systems. Many would argue that the former option usually proves to be cheaper in the long run, although this is extremely hard to verify and may be subject to a "not invented here" bias. Integration projects can be considered in the same way as bespoke projects with regards to the analysis below.

Integration projects are likely to become more common as the "Internet of Things" becomes more prominent. This is because each "thing" has been built as an independent system and to its own standards. Common interfaces do not yet exist although IEEE have produced a draft standard [13]. However, even when this standard has

---

[8]Software as a Service (SaaS) usually takes this form.

been agreed, it is unlikely that all products will conform completely and there will still be many legacy systems in existence that do not comply. Communications interfaces will be required to link systems. Developing much of this software is likely to be challenging.

5.10.2 Tailored Projects

A tailored system is one that has a generic infrastructure upon which additional functionality is built to satisfy the specific needs of the system. This additional functionality may be offered from pre-existing library functions or be specially written functions, queries, reports and so on.

A tailored product is usually provided under a consultancy agreement and provided by the consultancy company. The consultancy company will contract to provide additional functionality to their generic product to meet the needs of the client organisation. This can be an attractive offer as the generic product provides the infrastructure and is therefore considerably cheaper than developing infrastructure from scratch. However, future changes can be costly. This arrangement also ties in the client organisation to the supplier as changing suppliers probably means abandoning the system and rewriting. It can also incur high data transfer costs.

5.10.3 Component Off the Shelf

Component Off The Shelf products (COTS), as described, are available, pre-existing products packages and apps such as word processors, spread sheets, accountancy packages, graphics packages and so on. COTS products provide generic solutions for common problems. They usually have some (limited) capacity for tailoring, and it is often these tailoring facilities that are used as the basis for end user development (see below). COTS products usually do what they say on the tin, but may be platform specific and sometimes incompatible with similar products from different stables. They are designed for the mass market and satisfy users' needs within the constraints of the package. The tailoring facilities may not meet the integrity requirements of the organisation, and, if available across a network, could provide a backdoor for malicious access. This is discussed below.

5.10.4 End User Developments

End user developments (EUD) usually start out as small projects intended to reduce an individual's or small group's workload. Often they are unsanctioned and undocumented. They have a tendency to expand to meet different user's needs without any preplanning and in an ad hoc manner. Each additional change or fix adds complexity of the overall product and makes future maintenance and enhancement progressively more difficult. Functionality is generally given higher priority than quality. It is not unknown for EUDs to grow into mission critical products without the organisation recognising the product's significance to the business, their size or the effort that has gone into its maintenance and enhancement. Having started life as a below the radar skunkworks, the organisation can end being dependent upon a hacked together macro containing a spaghetti of jumbled code that few people have any idea about the way it works. Having been developed without following the normal controls and procedures they are likely to lack quality attributes such as resilience, reliability, security and so on. This lack of documentation can leave an organisation highly vulnerable if the main developer leaves the organisation. Lack of quality concern during the development could, for example, lead to a data breach and malicious attack. Were a data breach to occur, the fact that an organisation had not sanctioned the development would provide no defence against the provisions of GDPR. So, whilst the benefits of EUD might be felt in the short run, companies need to have procedures in place to ensure that they can acquire control over these systems in the medium and long term.

End user developments should be regarded as assets of the organisation and treated in the same way as any other organisational asset.

These five options have been placed in cost order, options 1 and 2 being the most costly, at least before any hidden costs are taken into consideration. However, cost is not the only consideration. There are wider, commercial factors to be considered.

5.10.5   Procurement Option Conclusion

If the new system is of strategic importance, it is more likely to be required to deliver some competitive advantage to the organisation. In this case, there will be a requirement for at least some novel, unique functionality. The choice will be between a tailored product and a specially written bespoke product. The procurement decision will depending on how specialised the system needs to be. Two further factor might need to be considered:

1. Who holds the IPR.
2. How much of the development effort might effectively be wasted reinventing the wheel.

In tailored systems, IPR usually resides with the infrastructure provider who will usually provide the additional functionality and retain IPR for that. This can tie in the organisation to that particular provider for the life of the system. On the other hand if the required system has a lot of commonality with pre-existing systems, rewriting that code could be expensive and unjustifiable if the only grounds are owning the IPR. These can be finely balanced decisions.

A second dimension to the product procurement decision is the expected complexity of the new system. Again oversimplification syndrome is a factor here. It is in the interests of vendors to suggest that they have already solved a particular problem and that it is a relatively straightforward development for them to provide a particular specialised function. This helps to sell the overall product. The particular problem may have hidden complexity of which only domain experts are aware. In particular, the exceptions to the normal process can present additional problems. This is something to be aware of when considering the potential complexity of the proposed system.

Complexity and originality of function provide two dimensions of a matrix that can be used as a guideline for deciding on the procurement approach to be taken as illustrated in Fig. 5.3.

If the system is complex, but not particularly new or original (quadrant ①), then an off the shelf package is likely to be optimal. If the complexity is low as well as the originality (quadrant ②) it may be possible for an end user to provide a solution (end user development or EUD) or there may be a suitable off the shelf package available. Quadrant ③ represents a relatively simple, but specialised system. These programs tend to be quite specific to the business; repeated tasks that can be relatively simply automated. The lowest cost solution in these circumstances might well be an end user development. A well-constructed and properly documented development could be of high value to the organisation. However, it is in the nature of such developments for them to be poorly documented and lack robustness as discussed above. There are hidden costs to EUD development that often go unrecognised until it is too late.

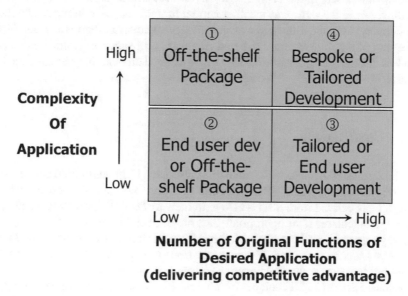

Fig. 5.3 Procurement decision making matrix

Alternatively there may well be a third party provider with a product that could be tailored to meet the organisation's needs.

Some commercial products that are designed to be tailored to meet specific customer needs are very sophisticated, modular component systems. The product being marketed may exceed the customer's requirements. The client organisation's strategic plan plays an important role in these circumstances as it helps determine the head room required for expectations of future growth and therefore how much of the product on offer that might be needed. An EUD may be appropriate for a single development, but not as part of a continuous growth strategy. Agreeing a flexible programme of developments with a trusted supplier may well be a better option for a growth plan.

The final quadrant (quadrant ④) is where the problem is both complex and original. Tailored solutions may be possible in these circumstances, but the more specialised the system, the more likely it is that a bespoke system is required. Quadrant ④ developments constitute major investment decisions and require as much consideration as any other investment decision the organisation might take. Indeed as software systems can impact the whole operation and the culture of an organisation, such developments can have a more profound impact on an organisation than many other investments. Managing such change is, potentially, another hidden cost to the organisation that is not always considered when making the investment decision. All the hidden costs of strategic SSD that have been identified in this chapter need to be accounted for when considering the cost/benefit of the development. In addition, there will most probably be recurrent costs such as maintenance and future enhancement as well as the initial capital cost. Investment decisions on software demand due diligence in the same way as other capital investments. According to Bannister and Remenyi [1], due diligence was not always apparent in their study conducted at the start of the millennium. Frisk and Bannister [10] suggest that the tendency to give less detailed consideration to SSD investments than other investment decisions persists.

5.11 Cost/Benefit

The difficulties associated with calculating cost have been considered above. Measuring the benefit or "value" (Bannister and Remenyi ibid.) of SSD, or even defining what value is derived from SSD is also extremely difficult. Efficiency gains per person can be calculated if the appropriate data has been collected, but if the real benefit from say a graphics package has been the ability to create a new character for a show, how would this be measured. If the system leads to unpredicted developments that cannot be foreseen, evaluating benefit in advance is impossible.

Balanced Score Card techniques or other positivist tools can be applied to support decision making,[9] but purely logical decision making is probably impossible. On the

---

[9]A more detailed discussion of positivist approaches is provided by Kramer [16].

other hand, intuitive decision making is inherently unreliable, and decision making regarding IT investment particularly so due to the paucity of data with which to make decisions. Nevertheless, having some notion of the cost, including the hidden costs, however inaccurate and some idea of the benefit expected to derive from the system, will help to inform the decision. It is likely that the judgement of benefit or value will be influenced by intuition or instinct (Bannister and Remenyi ibid) informed by knowledge and experience. A more detailed discussion on decision making has been presented by Frisk and Bannister [10] in which they conclude that investment decisions are more successful when made more collaboratively, but that this would require cultural change within many organisations.

5.12 Conclusion

IT strategic alignment with the organisation's corporate strategy is clearly a sensible policy for an organisation to adopt, but, as with all strategic decisions, the principle can easily be subverted by the day to day need to fight fires. Strategic investment decisions are made in a context which is less certain, lacks concrete, structured data and is more vulnerable to change. Strategic developments are also more expensive.

Strategic IT developments are no different in this respect than any other investment decisions. One historic difficulty however has been that IT has been seen as a cost overhead rather than an investment in the future. The consequence of this has been a lack of management board level interest in IT investment decisions and a disconnect between corporate strategy and IT strategy. Potential synergies between IT development and corporate development has been missed. An additional factor contributing to this scenario has been the limited comprehension of how to cost large IT development, how to assess the potential value of IT developments and how to decide whether to contract out the development. This has led to legitimate anxiety regarding any large IT development. A vicious circle exists.

> Evaluating both the cost and the return from IT investment is very difficult, but seems to be essential. Treat it as a cost of doing business so it is not necessary to try to evaluate cost/benefit as would be required for any other investment...
>
> Best leave IT investment decisions to the experts who know about these things...
>
> IT cost have often been a lot more expensive than expected and failed to deliver the expected returns because IT experts have failed to involve stakeholders and corporate decision makers in IT decision making ...
>
> Anxiety regarding IT development has increased as the result of IT failing to deliver...
>
> Better not get involved, leave it to the experts...

It is tempting to speculate that this has helped fuel the interest in Agile development approaches as a means of reducing the risk associated with IT. As has been shown, Agile is not necessarily the best approach and potentially results in additional cost. Bridging the gap between IT managers and corporate decision makers requires better understanding of the decision making process, better understanding of the costs (including the hidden costs) and benefits (including the feedback into corporate growth) and, above all, better communications between corporate decision makers and IT experts. This is, by no means, a recipe for success, but it may help to reduce the failure rate.

5.13   Discussion Questions

1. Does comparative advantage apply to software systems development?
2. Is informatics a game changer when it comes to software systems development?
3. How do you work out the cost benefit of a software systems development?
4. How would you decide whether or not to maintain an in-house software development team?
5. Critique Curtis' (1998) [6] paper on the differences between the best and the poorest systems developers.
6. Perform a SWOT/SVOR on a software development organisation with which you are familiar.
7. Research into software project failure seems to equate project failure with management failure. Is this valid? Is this justified?
8. How realistic is the CCCC role play exercise in the back of this book [Appendix C]?

References

1. Bannister F, Remenyi D (2000) Acts of faith: instinct, value and IT investment decisions. J Inf Technol 15(3):231–241
2. Beer S (1985) Diagnosing the system for organizations. Wiley, Chichester
3. Beynon-Davies P (2002) Information systems: an introduction to informatics in organisations. Palgrave, Basingstoke
4. Brooks FJ (1987) No Silver Bullet: essence and accidents of software engineering. Computer 10–19
5. Charette RN (2005) Why software fails. IEEE Spectr 42–49
6. Curtis B (1988) The impact of individual differences in programmers. In: Working with computers: theory versus outcome. Academic Press, London, pp 279–294
7. DeBoard R (1978) The psychoanalysis of organizations. Tavistock Publications, London
8. Fenton N, Bieman J (2015) Software metrics: a rigorous and practical approach. CRC Press, Boca Raton
9. Flemming M (2019) How tesco revolutionised loyalty with clubcard. https://www.marketingweek.com/tesco-clubcard-loyalty. Accessed 04 Oct 2019
10. Frisk JE, Bannister F (2017) Improving the use of analytics and big data by changing the decision-making culture. A design approach. Manag Decis 55(10):2074–2088
11. Grünig R, Kühn R (2018) The strategy planning process. In: Analyses, options, projects. Springer
12. Hunt SD, Morgan RM (1995) The comparative advantage theory of competition. J Mark 59(2):1–15

13. IEEE (2019) IEEE Approved draft standard for an architectural framework for the internet of things (IoT), IEEE
14. De Aquino Junior GS, de Lemos Meira SR (2009) Towards effective productivity measurement in software projects. In: Fourth international conference on software engineering advances. IEEE, Porto, Portugal
15. Khan HH, Malik MN (2017) Software standards and software failures: a review with the perspective of varying situational contexts. IEEE Access 5:17501–17513
16. Kramer J (2014) Defining value when managing it investments. In: Annual SRII global conference (SRII). IEEE, San Jose, CA
17. Lions JL (1996) ARIANE 5 Flight 501 Failure Paris, European Space Agency
18. Menzies-Lyth I (1959) The functioning of social systems as a defence against anxiety. Containing anxiety in institutions. Free Association Press, London, pp 43–85
19. Ricardo D (1817) On the principles of political economy and taxation. John Murray, London
20. The Project Management Institute (2017) A guide to the project management body of knowledge (PMBOK guide). Project Management Institute, Pennsylvania

Chapter 6
Software Systems Quality Assurance and Evaluation

6.1 Introduction

It would be remiss to write a book on software systems development without giving considerable thought to the quality of the systems being developed. This is because quality sits at the nexus between the technical, what the system does, and the social, how well it does it. The technical is embedded in algorithms, procedures and data. Technology encapsulates systems within well defined boundaries. Within those boundaries the system has a rigorous logic that predetermines what will happen in response to a limited range and type of stimuli.

For the system to be usable however, it must have at least one interface with a system, or systems outside of itself. In "embedded" systems, these interfaces are usually sensors that have tightly defined parameters.

For non-embedded IT the interface is far less constrained. The interface could be through sensors, with another system or with a user interface. Even when the interface is apparently quite constrained such as a sensor interface, the sensors are subject to the external environment. The sensor can fail or misinterpret conditions and pass misleading data across the interface as happened in the tragic case of the Boeing 737 Max [44].

When the system interfaces with its external environment is through a user interface, the internal world of the system is constrained by its operational parameters, but the external world is far less constrained and more unpredictable. Chaos theory appears to be applicable here. The number of potential affective factors result in indeterminacy creating severe difficulties for interface designers and input handlers. How well the technical system deals with the incongruence between its internal world and the external world can be described as its quality. The quality of the system therefore is dependent on the contingencies it provides for dealing with its external environment. Systems that appear to have low incongruence with their external environment will be perceived to be of high quality. Systems that clash with their external environment will be thought of as having low quality. The systems development process has to address this issue.

© Springer Nature Switzerland AG 2020
C. Rosen, *Guide to Software Systems Development*,
https://doi.org/10.1007/978-3-030-39730-2_6

6.2   Context

Recognising that software systems' quality is how well it interfaces with its external environment is all very well, but it is not particularly helpful other than in conceptual terms. "Well" is a catchall word that hides a world of meanings open to interpretation. It is necessary to deconstruct "well" before considering "how" a software system might be constructed to be considered to be of high or low quality. One thing is apparent from this analysis however: that the quality of a system cannot be divorced from the environment within which the system operates. The external environment determines the assessment of quality and therefore frames the discussion on quality. This is in contrast to classical approaches to quality that have attempted to define quality in reference to the internal attributes of the system.

6.3   Classical Approaches to Software Quality

The traditional debate on software quality has concentrated on three issues:-

- What is meant by quality; its definition and ontology.
- Software process improvement (SPI) intended to improve the quality of the developed systems.
- The metrics for measuring quality.

Two issues that have featured very little are

- How to design a quality system.
- How to balance the effort required to achieve a given standard of system whilst managing the overall cost and timescales of the project.

Before considering all these aspects of software systems' quality however, it is helpful to outline the theoretical background of the classical approach. Whilst logically it would be sensible to discuss the definitions of software quality before addressing software process improvement (SPI), it is very difficult to disassociate SPI from the historical background of software systems quality. This discussion of SPI appears therefore before definition of quality.

6.3.1   Theoretical Background to SSD Quality

Consistent with the software engineering approach to SSD, much thinking about software quality derives from analogy with other forms of product development, in particular manufacturing. The quality movement in the USA and subsequently in the UK and other Western countries was galvanised by the success Japanese companies had following the 2nd World War. Deming [12], who is widely credited for his part in the renaissance of Japanese industry drew heavily on Shewhart's ideas [34]. Shewhart proposed that faults and inefficiencies in the production process should be eradicated using statistical analysis to identify fault patterns [39]. This statistically based exercise has become known as the "Shewhart Cycle" and relies upon repetition of the process enabling patterns to emerge. Product quality is achieved through continuous refinement of the process [12, p. 88]. To achieve this two things were required; firstly that the process must be defined, and secondly that the workforce was involved in the optimisation process through such activities as quality circles and defect analysis.

Figure 6.1 illustrates the quality improvement cycle advocated by Shewhart and Deming. Observation of the process leads to a formal definition of that process and its documentation. Statistical monitoring enables benchmarks to be set for product quality. Once the product has been produced, it can be evaluated against the benchmark, faults and potential improvements can be identified and implemented. The whole process is then repeated; each time a little bit more efficiently. These principles can be applied to any or all subsystems of the process, so the whole production process will gradually improve over time.

Clearly compliance to the documented process is required. In some organisations, policing of compliance is felt to be needed which is effected through audit. Deming himself considered policing to be counter-productive. Nevertheless, it has become a common activity in quality management.

The last stage, refining the process has been the most controversial in practice. Deming felt that the experts in this field were the people closest to the process, usually those who were charged with operating the process. This led to the introduction of Quality Circles,[1] a cause championed within SSD by Peters, Waterman

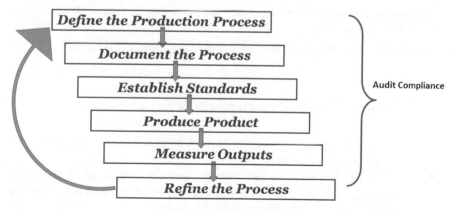

Fig. 6.1 The Shewhart Cycle [12]

---

[1]Quality circles are team meetings at which process improvements are identified and actions agreed that will improve the efficiency of the process. Defect Analysis (DA) meetings are conducted when a fault in the process has occurred and can be the subject of discussion for the quality circle. The DA meeting has the dual purpose of identifying the cause of a fault and how to eradicate it. Quality

and Austin [32, 33] and used extensively in Japanese industry. In practice, at least in the West, quality circles encountered some difficulties. The process improvements identified by these employee groups often lay outside the group's circle of influence and sometimes conflicted with other groups' interests [38]. Secondly, worker involvement bumped up against the manager's right to manage and was, in some organisations felt to undermine her/his authority. This was another example of the Theory X, Theory Y debate [27] being played out in the real world. Implementation therefore differed between (and sometimes within) organisations, but the main principles of the Shewhart cycle have been largely accepted within manufacturing industry.

The software industry was perceived to have a problem in both quality and productivity [41]. The main problem was perceived to be the amount of rework required. Faults in the software were found late in the development cycle, very often after the system had been handed over to the users. The "V Model" [37] suggests that faults found late in the process, were introduced into the system early in the development process. The earlier in the development process they are introduced, the more costly they tend to be to fix. The reputation of the software industry for quality was (perhaps still is) very poor. If faults could be eliminated at source, many of the problems software development had could be overcome. The mantra became "right first time, on time, every time" [7]. This was to be achieved through a regime of inspection and defect analysis, supported by statistics on the number and type of faults found and where the hot spots for introducing the faults were to be found [15]; a precise parallel to Shewhart.

It seemed that if these practices could be adapted to SSD, many of the problems software systems faced could be, if not solved, greatly reduced.

Deming's ideas, first adopted by Japanese software factories [11] became

the dominant approach for improving quality and productivity in software development organisations [30, p. 100]

This has become known as Software Process Improvement (SPI).

6.3.2 Software Process Improvement (SPI)

The hoped for gains from SPI have not materialised. Indeed, there is a strong argument that the SPI approach is in a mess.

Rodriguez et al. [36] describe the "current standards as a standard quagmire" (reproduced in Fig. 6.2). They identify well over 100 different tools in current use across the various stages of the development life cycle.

This diagram illustrates the complexity of quality assurance. The tendency towards the proliferation of artefacts when one attempts to fully document a process is predictable, even inevitable from a systems thinking perspective. Beer's [6] definition

---

circles are intended to encourage employees to accept responsibility for the quality process and quality improvement.

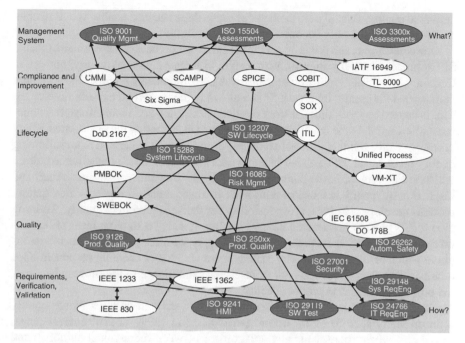

Fig. 6.2 The standards quagmire for the quality of the software process and product. (ibid. p. 14)

of a viable system is that a viable system consists of a chain of processes in which every process in the process chain contains a process chain. Attempts to define the process lead to ever more detailed definitions of the process as one descends further down the subsystems levels to less and less formal processes. Feedback from the lower levels back to higher levels disrupts the "normal" operation of the process. This results in striving to understand these lower level processes; chasing the rabbit further and further down the rabbit hole. Where it will end, nobody knows. It is, in a practical sense a blind alley.

SPI is a one way ticket to more and more quality process documentation. As this is infinitely recursive, the need for more and more documentation is never ending. Quality manuals that contain the process documentation expand to the point at which they are no longer navigable or comprehensible. It is a path that ensures that quality managers are never unemployed and forever vilified.

If documenting the process is ineffectual why is it so popular?

Documenting the process is the first step towards managing the process. Documentation in turn appears to provide some control over the process. However, if substantive elements of the lower level processes are not well understood, they cannot be accurately documented. This does not seem to prevent people and organisations producing process documents and seeking that measure of control.

The control is illusory. The lack of control will find a way of expressing itself. In the case of SSD it is through extended timescales, higher costs and/or poorer delivered quality. Usually it is the latter of these three because quality is less visible, harder to assess and only becomes apparent later in the process.

One could argue, and this is one of the cornerstones of the Agile movement, that the SPI approach to quality improvement results in poorer delivered quality, not better. Certainly, and this is another point made by Agile proponents, possibly the argument that has had the greater influence, SPI results in higher costs and extends timescales. This is caused by the additional work required to develop and maintain quality documentation, and the time delays and costs involved in executing the procedures. Many developers have felt that little actual quality improvement is derived from following quality procedures. This has led in some cases to a "tick box", compliance culture which in turn has led to the policing of compliance by quality managers. Audit and inspection by quality authorities reinforces extrinsic authoritarianism. True quality requires developers to accept responsibility for delivering product quality. Auditing the process places emphasis on process quality. It adds yet another level of bureaucracy in attempting to ensure developers comply with the process. This is vicious circle which results in the quality management authority becoming responsible for quality rather than the developers themselves. Compliance to the process becomes the objective rather than product quality.

Genuine adherence to quality is most likely to exist in cultures where quality is intrinsically seen to be important, particularly in safety critical environments. In cultures where there is already antagonism between hierarchical authority and developers, quality control procedures are likely to be perceived as further imposition of authoritarianism, resented and resisted. Organisations that are insensitive to these dangers can face major difficulties. Morale is affected, and productivity is reduced. Perhaps the most damaging side effect can be that good will is withdrawn and creativity stifled.

The Agile approach may appear to be the more practical approach. However organisations that pursue a laissez faire approach to quality may have other problems regarding quality. Inayata et al. [20] in their meta-analysis found that lack of development documentation can be problematic when modifications are required, and that non-functional requirements are often "neglected" (ibid. p. 925).

The documentation and compliance dilemmas identified above are applicable to quality assurance and quality control regimes in any occupation. "Good" management and sensible documentation procedures can often ameliorate potential problems. This is not the case for SSD. The application of Shewhart's quality cycle and Deming's quality programmes, require three conditions for the quality cycle to operate effectively. These three conditions are:-

1. Effective process definition.
2. Process repeatability.
3. A "stable system" [12, p. 313]; that is low numbers of exceptions in Perrow's [31] terminology.

These three conditions do not pertain for software systems development.

6.3.2.1 Process Definition

The classical approach to SPI attempts to define the process, but misses the target. SPI suffers from a fundamental confusion between the conceived process and process itself. The conceived process is based on SDLC. Even if SDLC were a more accurate model of the process than it is, it does not describe the process at the appropriate substrata for the purposes of process definition. SPI confuses outputs from the process such as documentation and code with the process itself.

In Chap. 2 a system was defined as a process chain where the output from one process provides the input to one or more following processes. A process was defined as

$$\text{Input(s)} \rightarrow \text{Transformation} \rightarrow \text{Output(s)}$$

The transformation is itself a process chain. In the SDLC model, the outputs from one state supply the inputs to the following state; that is SDLC is defined as a process chain. However, the transformation in each state consists of process chains which themselves have inputs and outputs.

In software systems design and programming the transformations from input to output are achieved as a result of creative activities and it is the creative process of people that constitutes the level at which process definition is required. Not only do no two people perform these activities in the same way, there are no convincing protocols of how to perform them. Furthermore, it is in the gift of the individual whether or not and to what extent they share their creative talent.

Inputs and outputs from design and programming activities are usually some type of document. The format and structure required of these documents can be documented, and this is what SPI process documentation does. But, for quality management purposes, it is the design and programming sub-process chains, the creative activities that actually need to be documented. Little is known about the creative process so it is difficult to document them. This missing link undermines the effectiveness of process documentation. Consequently there is little evidence of significant correlation between the quality of the documentation and the quality of the product itself because the process is being defined at too high a level of abstraction. This can be evidenced by the fact that "poorly written" code can perform well as far as a user is concerned (although the code may not be particularly maintainable) and "well written" code guarantees little in terms of delivered quality. (Obviously the same can be said for design documents.)

6.3.2.2 Process Repeatability

There are two reasons why, in SSD, the process is never repeated.

- Design and coding are problem solving activities, and are therefore dependent on the problem itself. Once the problem has been solved, there is no reason to solve it a second time.
- The people involved in a project are inevitably changed by their involvement in that project. Developers have gained experience, new skills and possibly, a little wisdom. The stakeholders, even if they are the same people, will similarly have been changed by their previous experience. It is also likely that the membership of both groups will have changed and so the relationship issues will also be different from first time round. This is a case of never being able to step into the same river twice.

It could be argued that these differences do not make any real difference to the process, but this relates back to the definition of the process. When the process is defined as the way that individuals in the process interact with each other and the task rather than as SDLC, then the changes in the process between one project and the next will be significant. Clearly the process will be similar for similar projects for the same client, or projects in the same series of developments, but it is questionable how much benefit SPI is to these types of project. A quick review identifying learning points might be sufficient.

6.3.2.3   Process Stability

The software systems production process must respond to constant change so in Perrow's terms [31] has many "exceptions". Many of the exceptions that arise raise problems that have to be worked through and potential solutions checked to ensure that any ripple effects can be accommodated. This requires expertise (and often complex scrutiny) that cannot be automated. In Perrow's taxonomy SSD therefore occupies the non-routine quadrant. For Deming this would constitute process instability, and therefore would by unamenable to the Shewhart cycle.

A fourth, more prosaic reason, has probably undermined the SPI movement more than any of these theoretical failings; SPI is expensive and leads down what is essentially a blind alley. Maintaining process documents is costly in terms of resources. It takes time and effort to maintain. The change management process to both process documentation and to development documentation adds further cost. When the innate volatility of the specification is accounted for, development documentation requires constant reworking so the cost and time required to ensure that it reflects the current state of the system is considerable. Many organisations believe these costs to be unsustainable. Adopting an Agile approach has been seen as a justifiable way of avoiding many of these costs.

In spite of these flaws in both the theoretical and practical foundations of SPI, process control, management and assurance have become a totem for the industry. One might ask why this is the case. One possible explanation is that the industry has grown up around the misconceptions. The momentum behind CMMI, TickIT, SWEBoK, and a wealth of IEEE and ISO standards is impressive, fuelled in part by the need to be seen to be doing something to address the quality gap. Quality stamps and kite marks afford insurance to businesses if something goes wrong. Government agencies want to be seen as doing things by the book. Kite marks are of considerable commercial value in seeking new business, particularly government business[2] as well as in defending against operational failures should they occurs. How tenable this veneer is may yet be tested, but it has survived 40 or so years to date. It has however diverted effort and attention from understanding what actually constitutes software systems quality and how it might be improved. The following sections aim to redress this balance.

6.4 Definition

The enigmatic quality of quality means that there is no unambiguous definition.

There have been numerous attempts to define software systems quality. The most commonly referenced is the ISO/IEC standard 25010 [21]

> [The] degree to which a software product satisfies stated and implied needs when used under specified conditions (ibid.)

and variations of this.

Leaving aside the phrase "specified conditions" that allows the specification of quality to be changed as required, the term "stated or implied needs" allows any functional or non-functional aspiration of any stakeholder to be considered to be a legitimate quality attribute. Such a definition therefore is inoperable as it fails to limit what can and what cannot be considered to be a quality criterion.

The vagueness and ambiguity of this definition, reflected in similar efforts to define quality, demonstrates how ephemeral quality is and leads to attempts to clarify the concept by further decomposition into lower level concepts. Wagner [42] identifies three approaches:

> hierarchical models, meta-model-based models and implicit quality models [42, p. 29][3]

6.4.1 Hierarchical Models

Hierarchical approaches decompose quality into sub-terms. ISO/IEC 25010 and its predecessor ISO/IEC 9126 are typical examples of this. Hierarchical models are the

---

[2]The cost of achieving a particular kite mark is relatively high so can be off putting for smaller organisations. Government agencies that insist on these kite marks therefore exclude smaller firms from competing for contracts. Thus there is some vested interest in maintaining the status of kite marks by larger, established companies for whom the proportional cost of a kite mark is lower.

[3]Wagner's treatment of software quality is much more detailed than can be covered here.

most traditional approach and typified by Boehm et al. [9], McCall et al. [26] and
Grady and Caswell [19]. These models offer a taxonomy of quality concepts which
are decomposed into lower level constructs known as attributes. The objective is to
end up with a set of measurable constructs that can be used to assess the quality of
the software. Usually the constructs are applicable at the systems level rather than
for individual modules, procedures or objects within the system. This approach has
been criticised on the grounds that the terminology used is too vague and ambiguous
to be measurable [42, p. 30].[4]

ISO/IEC 25010 has identified two types of quality attribute. The first "Quality
in use" is the quality of the product the user sees Fig. 6.3, the second is "Product
quality" that relates to the internal quality of the software system Fig. 6.4. Estdale
and Georgiadou [14] provide a critique of the model. Biscoglio and Marchetti [8]
observe that the standard

> only provide[s] a conceptual framework, and not a ready-to-use solutions usable in every
> context (ibid, p. 65)

The definitions provided for the terms used are ambiguous and open to wide
interpretation. There is, what might be termed a semantic hiatus between the upper
level terms and their sub-components. In other words, there is no clear derivation or
link between the upper level concept and the lower level concepts. There is an implied
one to one relationship between them in the standard, when clearly it is possible for
one concept to interact and interfere with other concepts either at the same level, or
between levels. Some sub-concepts could clearly belong to more than one top level
concept depending on its interpretation.

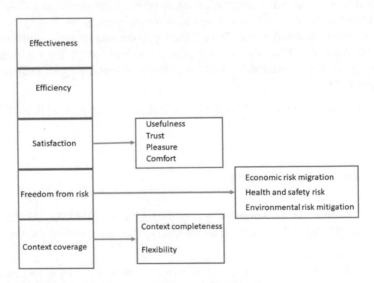

Fig. 6.3 ISO/IEC 25010 "Quality in Use" Standard Model [21]

---

[4]Wagner outlines FURPS Grady and Caswell [19] as an example of a hierarchical model of quality.

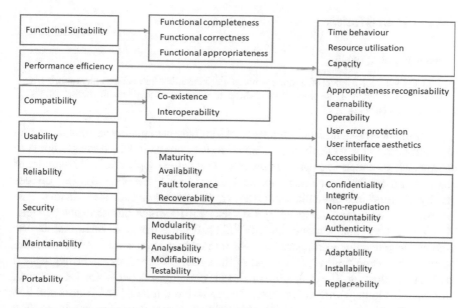

Fig. 6.4 ISO/IEC 25010 "Product Quality" Standard Model

The distinction between "quality in use" and "product quality" is also open to question. Is security (or the lack of) for example not a risk to the product in use. Finally there are some concepts that do not seem to have been identified at all, such as "sustainability". Mohagheghi and Aparicio [29] point out that the standard fails to incorporate constraints such as legal constraints and political considerations.

The definitions provided do not satisfy Doran's requirements for S.M.A.R.T objectives [13]:

Specific – target a specific area for improvement

Measurable – quantify or at least suggest an indicator of progress

Assignable – specify who will do it

Realistic – state what results can realistically be achieved given available resources

Time related – specify when the result(s) can be achieved (ibid., p. 36)

Mohagheghi and Aparicio [29] found that, in practice they had to add a third level. Their experience seems to suggest that the model may provide a starting point, but a great deal more work to tailor the model to a given context and adapting it to meet the specific needs of stakeholders is required. Given that, in the systems they were connected with implementing, they identified over 1000 quality scenarios, this is no small task, for which the effort required should not be underestimated.

6.4.2 Meta-Models

A meta-model of quality

> A meta-model...is a model of the quality model, i.e. it describes how valid quality models are structured. In addition, the proposals also differ to what extent they include measurements and evaluations [42].

Meta-models recognise the complexity of the concept of quality and that the model of quality used in practice must be adapted to the context in which the system is to operate. Meta-models attempt to define rules that can be applied to build a model of quality for a particular situation. One such example is Quamoco [43]. This divides quality "factors" into those that affect the whole system and code level factors. This is similar to the distinction made by ISO/IEC 25010 which differentiates between "Quality in Use" and "Product Quality" [21]. Factors have measures that can be assigned to it and an "instrument" or instruments to calculate value of the measure when applied to an "entity", an artefact of the system. The values can be aggregated to give an evaluation. The evaluation process is complicated, but Wagner, Goeb et al. provide tools to help with the process. Quamoco has a total of 284 factors and 544 instruments, which demonstrates, if nothing else, how complicated measuring quality is when done systematically.

Wagner [42] discusses meta-models in much greater detail than can be covered here, but, as he observes, they have failed to coalesce into a coherent overall approach even given his and his colleagues efforts in the interim.

There is an obvious danger with the meta-model approach of trying to multiply apples by oranges and ending up with cabbages. The resulting metrics require calibrating and benchmarking against previous products before they can be interpreted in the context of the current project. The questions that meta-models have not answered, and perhaps cannot answer, are whether such an exercise provides a cost/benefit to an organisation and whether the additional effort required to develop a quality system affords a cost/benefit. (This latter question is discussed below.)

It is conceivable that using a meta-model approach over a long period of time and analysing the results may help to identify hot spots responsible for generating system faults and so can be targeted for fault reduction activities, but this is far from certain. This uncertainty is likely to be a major disincentive to commercial application.

6.4.3 Statistical Models

Implicit models are statistical attempts to predict faults through, for example, complexity indices or maintainability indices. This approach is analogous to cost modelling. Due to the potential number of factors affecting the outcome, statistical models need to be calibrated for a given organisation. However, past performance is no guarantee of future success. Mathematical models may demonstrate correlation between a factor and a fault prediction, but not causation. Nor can the model preclude new factors becoming significant or existing factors becoming more or less significant over time. Unforeseen changes between one development and the next could render the previous statistical model invalid. So if there are environmental changes, the reliability of the model becomes questionable. It may be that, given sufficient data, data analytics could reduce the number of factors required to make a reasonable prediction within a given level of confidence. It may also be possible, with sufficient data, to calculate the probability of the success of the forecasts. The proviso of sufficient data however is a limiting factor for this particular line of research.

6.4.4 Non-functional Requirements (NFR)

The term "quality requirement" is further confused by the use of the term "non-functional requirement". NFR is, by and large, seen and used as synonymous with "quality requirement". NFR however is no less ambiguous than quality requirement as Glinz [17] has identified.

Semantically, the distinction between a functional requirement (FR) and an NFR is that a functional requirement is a binary function; it is either present or absent from a system. An NFR is analogue. It represents a potential range of values from high to low or good to bad. Glinz (ibid.) argues that the difference between an NFR and an FR can be (is?) representational in that at least some NRFs can redefined as FRs. His example using security access being redefined from a probability of unauthorised access (an NFR) to access not being permitted without a username and password (an FR) illustrates this point. But whether all NFRs can be redefined in this way is unclear. It may be that it is the missing knowledge that turns an FR into an NFR. Using Glinz' example, the functional form of the requirement does not include other means of access, or that user name and password may not be sufficient to allow all access. For example disallowing access by an authorised person from an unauthorised IP address. The NFR form is vague enough to cover many different circumstances and potentially some unknown circumstances. It is precisely the vagueness of the NFR that affords them their power, and consequently creates the headache for the system's developer.

6.5 Quality Metrics, Measurement and Evaluation

The often quoted Lord Kelvin is an apt place to begin this section

> when you can measure what you are speaking about, and express it in numbers, you know something about it; but when you cannot measure it, when you cannot express it in numbers, your knowledge is of a meagre and unsatisfactory kind" (William Thomson (Lord Kelvin) 1824–1907)

Thompson's aspirations may have been judged to be unrealistic in the post-modernist age, but the idea that a concept that is not measurable, is open to wide range of interpretation can be validly applied to the metrics being offered to measure software quality. One should also bear in mind Fenton and Bieman's admonition to ensure that the metrics being used are actually measuring what was intended [16].

Basili advocates the "Goal, Question, Metric" (GQM) paradigm [5]. In this approach the developer should identify what the objective is (the goal), how it will be known whether the objective has been achieved or not (the question) and therefore what measure (the metric) will be used to assess whether or not the objective has been achieved. Sommerville [40, pp. 712–714] suggests that GQM is particularly appropriate for process improvement.

Doran's S.M.A.R.T criteria [13] were originally intended to inform management objectives and have been used extensively in that field, but could also provide a basis for quality metrics. If the quality objective cannot be ascribed a metric it probably means that the problem is not understood well enough. This assertion is not intended to imply that it is always possible to understand the problem "well enough". Not being able to ascribe a testable criterion however would point to an area of risk for the system for which a risk assessment, mitigation or avoidance could be considered. It would not be possible to eliminate all risk (it never is) or possibly even reduce the risk involved, but an activity of this sort could assist in making an assessment of the overall risk involved and support the decision making as to the scope of the project. It might also be possible to determine incremental steps to help define the problem more clearly over a period of time.

GQM and SMART metrics could be applied to quality scenarios [22] and "Exception Scenarios". Exception Scenarios are generated by asking stakeholders questions such as "what goes wrong in your work?", "what causes you problems?", "is there anything that happens, possibly rarely, that the current system doesn't cater for and you have to do something different or special?". ATAM (ibid.) uses the term "external stimuli" and provides a list of questions to explore the stimuli in detail.[5] ISO/IEC 25010 could also be provide a checklist to help to identify some of these scenarios. The better non-standard, informal process and non-functional scenarios are understood, and the more priority they are given the less like it is that important aspects of the system as a whole are overlooked during the development process. Metrics could play a part, but perhaps a more productive idea comes from evaluation. Evaluation is a more subjective assessment than a metric, and fits better with the idea of "good enough software [4]. Ultimately stakeholders will be the arbiters of what is good enough, but the more aware developers are of what might constitute good enough, the more likely there are to be able to deliver it.

A principle here should be that at least as much time should be spent on identifying exceptions from the normal process and NFRs as is spent on defining the functional

---

[5] ATAM does not propose a particular architecture, but suggests an "architectural style" that supports the NFRs identified by the analysis of scenarios. In the early stages of a development, the architecture itself can be highly fluid, which, to some extent undermines the early evaluation of architectural artefacts.

requirements. The more mission critical, or safety critical the project is, the greater the effort required to identify and evaluate the non-functional requirements.

6.6 Development Realities

6.6.1 The Programmer's Dilemma

The nub of the developer's dilemma is how much effort she/he must put in to satisfy a quality requirement if it is imprecise. The analogue nature of NFRs allows for a range of values, but not necessarily precise boundaries to those values. A specification document might put a number to an NFR, but almost certainly this number fails to represent the stakeholder's actual requirement. The precise figure is likely to be fuzzy at best, or even merely an aspiration. For example, a metric for usability might be say a maximum 10 h training to learn to use the system. Why 10 h? Would say 10 h and 30 min be a problem or even 15 h? Is this a problem at all or a proxy measure for comprehensibility?

Two further problems exist for the programmer. Firstly, if it is unclear how precise a target has been set, when a Pareto function of marginal gain over effort is applied to the work needed to meet the target, is it valuable time spent trying to reduce the learning time from 10 h 30 min to 10 h?

Secondly how will the developers know what they need to do to meet the target and how will they know if they have actually met this target? Testing of the target cannot begin until much of the system has been completed, and this is probably way too late to do much about it? A user may complain about how complicated the system is to use, but the commissioners of the system are not likely to be prepared to delay installation for this problem to be fixed, even if it were possible to do so. A mock up, or a prototype might help to assess the learnability in this case, but that may well add to the development elapse time, and may not represent the actual complexity of the finally delivered system. In this type of scenario, pragmatics are often more persuasive than principle. Project managers will mostly take the view that it is better to deliver something even if it is less than ideal, rather than have nothing to hand over. One can have an argument about how good something is. If nothing is delivered, there is no argument.

On the other hand, developers who understand the real needs of stakeholders and who have some concern for them, are more likely to try to satisfy the stakeholders. Having a personal connection with someone helps to engender empathy with and a sense of responsibility towards them. A developer with such a connection is more likely to want to do their best by the stakeholder and to feel uncomfortable when they know something is not quite right. Project managers have the responsibility to decide what and when compromises need to be made in order to deliver a "good enough" product. This may cause a rift between developers and managers if the developer's idea of good enough conflicts with that of the manager. Another of the responsibilities of the manager is to manage that relationship. The manager of a SSD project, amongst many other skills needs to be a skilled diplomat.

6.6.2 The System's Developer Dilemma

The system's developer faces more problems. Take for example the concept of "maintainability" from the FURPS hierarchical taxonomy [18, 19]. Providing a measurable metric for this concept is challenging in the first place, but whatever metric is agreed, how could a systems developer predict what maintenance might be required in the future? Certainly it might be possible to include some tracing functions or ensure code is adequately commented, structured and so on, but would these measures satisfy the requirement?

Budgen [10] for example discusses attributes of a good design including "simplicity" "modularity" "cohesion" and "information hiding", but does not argue that these techniques necessarily lead to a "good design". Neither does he clarify what a "good design" might be other than to say what a good design should not contain. With regards to considering how one ensures that a software system meets a particular quality standard Budgen concludes that

> no degree of quality can actually ensure some particular degree of quality in the product (ibid. p. 82)

but that design quality has an important influence.

To make life more difficult for the designer, many quality requirements are defined at the global level of the system and are therefore an aggregate measure of the total system. This means that any component could contribute towards the final system. An example of this is performance. There are several valid measures of performance, and these can usually be assessed, but performance is dependent on where it is measured and all the components of the system between the transactional element of the systems and the point at which the measurement is conducted. A slow Ethernet bridge or congestion in the system could result in poor performance. These things may not be in the control of the designer.

The global nature of many quality requirements results in no one person, and often no one group being responsible for the system's quality. A quality failure might result in an unfortunate and unforeseeable combination of two different perspectives. For example providing an interface to enable the interconnectivity of two incompatible systems could potentially lead to a security vulnerability from the accumulation of encryption data. This component of quality contravenes Doran's (op. cit.) 3rd S.M.A.R.T attribute; that of accountability.

Sometimes a failure might result in a direct conflict between two quality requirements A conscious decision to prioritise one quality requirement over another could well have been taken. The now largely forgotten Y2K bug was an example of this. The need to minimise process time and memory use led to the adoption of 2 bytes of data to store a date. This seemed entirely reasonable in the 1970s and 1980s when computer processing units were much slower and costly than at present. It was also assumed that the programs that were written at that time would no longer still be in use 20 or 30 years later. 2 bytes should be sufficient. In the 1990s when those systems were still being widely used the original decision proved to be very costly to fix. This particular problem is very unlikely to reoccur, but it is in a class of problems that almost certainly will happen again. Reading the future is a difficult business.

There are no rules regarding the managing of global quality. Design guidelines may help in certain circumstances, but precise rules would be ineffective. Perhaps this is why Ameller et al. [2] were able to report an almost casual attitude to NFRs apart from in safety critical systems. Architects they interviewed tended to create their own NFRs with little consultation with stakeholders, hold an almost dismissive attitude to documenting NFRs, and sometimes took the view that NFRs would have to be fixed at the subsequent version of the software.[6] It appears that in a practical sense, unless it is essential, architects have, in effect given up on quality requirements. It is hardly surprising therefore that software systems have a poor reputation for quality.

If Ameller et al. findings are representative of the industry, the best that can be hoped for is that, architects, designers and developers are subconsciously adjusting for quality requirements in their decision making. Better understanding of developers' attitudes in this regard may help to raise their conscious awareness of users' perspectives of quality and increase their effort to satisfy those expectations where possible. It is possible that developers' attitudes towards the Capability Maturity Model at least partially results from a hiatus between process improvement and actual product quality. Ply et al. [35] report that employee cynicism towards their organisations increases as those organisations ascend the CMMI levels, though this tentative finding could be organisation specific (only 2 organisations in their study were at level 4 or 5) or may be affected by other factors.

6.6.3 Design Patterns

Some argue that the use of design patterns with known behaviours minimise the unpredictability and improve the quality of software systems designed using patterns. Khomh and Guéhéneuc [23] found this not to be the case. In fact they found

> Some patterns are reported to decrease some quality attributes and to not necessarily promote reusability, expandability, and understandability. (ibid. p. 278)

In their 2018 retrospective Khomh and Guéhéneuc (ibid.) identify numerous ways in which design patterns might support the design process. They found one study (Ali and Elish [1] that reported design patterns had a negative impact on "maintainability [and] evolution and change-proneness" and could not draw conclusions for other quality attributes. This suggests that, at best, with regards to design patterns improving quality, the jury is still out.

---

[6]No first time, on time, every time here!.

6.6.4   Model Driven Development (MDD)

Model driven development [28] is, at its simplest a means of using abstract modelling tools to models the system. These modelling tools may or may not provide automated generation of a lower level of model abstract, down to the code level. Ameller et al. [3] identify 3 levels of abstraction above code; Computational Independent Model (CIM), the Platform Independent Model (PIM), and the Platform Specific Model (PSM). In their systematic literature review they identify 15 approaches to using MDD as a means of incorporating NFR coverage into architectural design. Of these most addressed security, and/or reliability. Some incorporated "quality of service" which was interpreted as service availability or response time. However, none of the approaches at the time of the study had provided evidence of this approach working in an industrial setting. Clearly this is a work in progress.

6.6.5   Test Driven Development (TDD)

Test driven, or test first systems development has been around a long time. According to Larman and Basili [25] test driven development (test first) was first used in the early 1960s on N.A.S.A's Mercury project. The idea is that being able to design the test of a unit of code demonstrates that it is sufficiently understood to write the code. This understanding is tested further by being able to automate the test. The automated test can then be included in a regression test suite so that with every increment of the software, the test is rerun to ensure incremental compatibility.

The concept did not achieve a great deal of popularity until it was promoted by Beck as part of the promotion of Extreme Programming. Having an ever expanding regression test suite becomes much more important when more, and more frequent changes are being made to the system, as they are in XP.

TDD is an effective way of verifying that the functional code does what it is specified to do, but it is more questionable how effective it is for non-functional requirements. It can ensure validity of code, that is that the specification is correct. The difference between code verification and system validity is important and refers back to the question of whether the requirements have been correctly interpreted and applied. TDD, as it is applied at the unit level, has little influence at the global level. The system's level can only be finally verified when the system is tested in its working environment. The cumulative effect on systems quality of a large number of small changes can be dramatic. This is why Agile methods require continuous installation of small increments as they are produced; an approach that is better suited to products where discrete enhancement is possible rather than closely integrated mission critical or safety critical systems.

Most of the problems of quality assurance have been known for a generation [24], but unless the circle of precisely defining imprecise concepts can be squared, they will remain. The uncomfortable conclusion is that the solution can only be found in managing the imprecision at the social level, not continuing to search for an elusive technical solution.

6.7 Quality at the Interface

This chapter was introduced with the concept that quality is determined at the interface between the software system under construction and its external environment. This highlights the difference between verification (does the system behave as specified?) and validation (does the system behave as it should?). Understanding the "should" means

1. understanding the system outside the software system beyond the interface
2. understanding the nature and variety of the inputs to the interface
3. how the output is used
4. the effects of feedback through the parent system environment back into the software system.

This more holistic view of the system needs to be applied as much to testing the system as it does to specifying the system bearing in mind what has changed in the interval between specification and implementation. Boundaries may well have shifted, but rather than attempt to offload responsibility for the system no longer synchronising with the external environment, a more constructive approach is to understand the changes and how they have affected the system. There is little value in railing against this entirely predictable occurrence. A more realistic approach is to have a process in place to manage the necessary changes when the inevitable occurs. Construing the post installation phase as a recognised phase in the development process would constitute a radical change in systems developers' attitudes along with it being part of the developers' role to understand the external environment. Agile methodologies probably require this change more than traditional methodologies, but encouraging development staff to become more outward looking would be a first step.[7]

6.8 Culture Not Compliance

A recap

1. SPI is a one way ticket to ever increasing documentation, additional process complexity, higher costs and longer timescales.

---

[7]The post installation phase does appear in the SDLC as maintenance and enhancement, but in reality this phase is not considered to be part of the development activity. It may be part of a service contract, deemed to be a new development contract, or support for the client organisation. Rarely is it considered to be the developer's responsibility as it occurs after acceptance and handover. "Job done; let's move on to the next job.".

2.   The Shewhart cycle is inapplicable as there is no repetition. Continuous improvement is not possible. Quality has to be reinvented every time.
3.   "Laissez Faire Agile" tends to neglect quality criteria which leads to unmaintainable software.
4.   Quality is an ephemeral concept that is hard to define and difficult to measure.
5.   Quality is a key element of the acceptability and longevity of software systems.
6.   Quality is not the responsibility of one person or one group, but is the result of collective collaboration.
7.   Tools are only ever going to provide part of the answer.
8.   A post-installation change management phase is inevitable and should be considered as an integral part of the development process.
9.   Understanding the systems outside the systems boundary is a distinct advantage, if not a necessity for quality assurance.
10. Quality is a matter of organisational culture and not of procedures and processes; a conclusion that Deming (op. cit.) would have agreed with.

Whilst some of these assertions may be uncomfortable, they flow inexorably from the analysis of the problem from an open systems perspective. Stating a problem however is only the first step toward a solution. The next step is accepting that there is a problem, and rather than clinging to a surrogate for comfort, addressing the real problem.

The analogy is with an alcoholic whose first step to recovery is to accept "I am an alcoholic". In the case of SSD, the intoxicating substance is SPI for some and Laissez Faire Agile for others. It would be unrealistic to propose total abstinence for either patient, but some attitudinal and cultural changes might be helpful in the first instance.

Systems developers at every level in the development process need to be much more familiar with the systems outside the systems boundary. Rather than focussed on the problem solving aspect of systems development, they need to be focussed on understanding the problem they are trying to solve. If a developer does not understand why something is a problem from the stakeholders' point of view, they cannot know that they are solving the right problem. Problem solving is important, but problem solvers should not be perceived as occupying the highest status in a systems development team. That accolade should go to those team members that understand the problems in the greatest depth and from the broadest viewpoints.

In order to facilitate this change, developers at all levels need to be more closely aligned to stakeholders and the environment in which stakeholders work. Development silos need to be broken down. Hierarchies of power, status or decision making need to be deconstructed so that, as near as possible, equal status is afforded to all members of the team. Quality needs to be felt more than measured, and the most junior member of a team may have as much capability in this respect as the most senior. Furthermore, quality assurance cannot be a matter of compliance. It has to be a matter of commitment. This can only be assured if all members of the team identify equally with the objectives of the team.

SPI can be seen as occupying one end of the spectrum, "Laissez Faire Agile" (LFA) the other. SPI is addicted to documentation, LFA to production. There is a role for documentation, but process documentation can be considered to be a failure of culture. If people need to be directed in what they have to do, they are less likely to be committed to it. Responsibility comes with autonomy and process documentation inhibits autonomy.

A distinction needs to be made however between process documentation and development documentation. The purpose of development documentation is to aid the development process and support subsequent maintenance. Therefore sufficiency of development documentation should be the objective. Unfortunately there is a tendency in LFA towards an insufficiency of documentation. Achieving sufficiency is a matter of establishing cultural norms and enculturation rather than autocratic rule making.

If this sounds like "Theory Y", it is, but it is not anarchy. Developers need to understand, and respect the culture of the organisation that they are working in as much as they understand and respect the culture of the organisation that they are working for (i.e. the stakeholder organisation.) Facilitating this enculturation is one of the roles of project managers, possibly one of the more difficult roles.

6.9 Discussion Questions

1. How practical are PMBok and SWeBok?
2. Is CMMI cost effective?
3. In practice, how different are Agile systems development projects from traditional methodologies?
4. How can a software developer know whether their code is "good enough"?
5. How do you know when you have the right level of process definition?
6. What should be the role of a quality manager?

References

1. Ali M, Elish MO (2013) A comparative literature survey of design patterns impact on software quality. In: International conference on information science and applications (ICISA). IEEE, Pattaya, Thailand
2. Ameller D et al (2013) Non-functional requirements in architectural decision making. IEEE Softw 30(2):61–67
3. Ameller D et al (2018) Non-functional requirements in model-driven development of service-oriented architectures. Sci Comput Program 168:18–37
4. Bach J (1997) Good enough quality: beyond the buzzword. Computer 8:96–98
5. Basili VR (1992) Software modeling and measurement: the Goal/Question/Metric paradigm. College Park College Park Maryland, University of Maryland
6. Beer S (1985) Diagnosing the system for organizations. Wiley, Chichester

7. Birchinall W (1990) Prevention in ICL. TQM Mag 2(2):113–116
8. Biscoglio I, Marchetti E (2015) Definition of software quality evaluation and measurement plans: a reported experience inside the audio-visual preservation contex. In: Holzinger A, Cardoso J, Cordeiro J et al (eds) International conference on software technologies (ICSOFT 2014). Springer, Vienna Austria
9. Boehm BW et al (1978) Characteristics of software quality. Amsterdam North-Holland
10. Budgen D (2003) Software design. Pearson Addison Wesley, Harlow
11. Cusumano MA (1992) Shifting economies: from craft production to flexible systems and software factories. Res Policy 21:453–480
12. Deming WE (2000) Out of the crisis. MIT Press, Cambridge Mass
13. Doran GT (1981) There's a S.M.A.R.T way to write management's goals and objectives. Manag Rev 70(11):35–36
14. Estdale J, Georgiadou E (2018) Applying the ISO/IEC 25010 quality models to software product. In: X L, I S, R OC, MR On-Line (eds) Systems, software and services process improvement EuroSPI 2018, vol 896. Springer, pp 492–503
15. Fagan ME (1976) Design and code inspections to reduce errors in program development. IBM Syst J 15(3):182–211
16. Fenton N, Bieman J (2015) Software metrics. CRC Press, On-Line
17. Glinz M (2007) On non-functional requirements. In: 15th IEEE international requirements engineering conference (RE 2007). India Habitat Centre, New Delhi IEEE Computer Soc, pp 21–26
18. Grady RB (1992) Practical software metrics for project management and process improvements. Prentice-Hall, Englewood Cliffs NJ
19. Grady RB, Caswell DL (1987) Software metrics: establishing a company-wide program. Englewood Cliffs Prentice Hall
20. Inayata I et al (2015) A systematic literature review on agile requirements engineering practices and challenges. Comput Hum Behav 51:915–929
21. ISO, IEC (2011) ISO/IEC 25010:2011: systems and software engineering—systems and software quality requirements and evaluation (SQuaRE)—system and software quality models 34
22. Kazman R et al (2000) ATAM: method for architecture evaluation. Carnegie-Mellon University Pittsburgh, Defense Technical Information Center, p 81
23. Khomh F, Guéhéneuc YG (2008) Do design patterns impact software quality positively? In: 12th European conference on software maintenance and reengineering. Greece IEEE, Athens, pp 274–275
24. Kitchenham B, Pfleeger SL (1996) Software quality: the elusive target. IEEE Softw 13(1):12–21
25. Larman C, Basili VR (2003) Iterative and incremental development: a brief history. Computer 36(6):47–56
26. McCall JA et al (1977) Factors in software quality. Springfied The National Technical Information Service
27. McGregor D (1960) The human side of enterprise. McGraw-Hill, London
28. Mellor SJ et al (2003) Model-driven development. IEEE Softw 20(2):14–18
29. Mohagheghi P, Aparicio ME (2017) An industry experience report on managing product quality requirements in a large organization. Inf Softw Technol 88:96–109
30. Ngwenyama O, Nielsen PA (2003) Competing values in software process improvement: an assumption analysis of CMM from an organizational culture perspective. IEEE Trans Eng Manage 50(1):100–112
31. Perrow C (1967) A framework for comparative analysis of organizations. Am Sociol Rev 32(2):194–208
32. Peters T, Austin N (1986) A passion for excellence: the leadership difference. Fontana/Collins, London
33. Peters T, Waterman RH Jr (1982) In search of excellence: Lessons from America's best-run companies. Harper-Collons, London

34. Petersen PB (1987) The contribution of W. Edwards deming to Japanese management theory and practice. In: Academy of management best papers proceedings, vol 1987(1), pp 133–137
35. Ply JK et al (2012) IS employee attitudes and perceptions at varying levels of software process maturity. MIS Q 36(2):601–624
36. Rodriguez M et al (2019) Software verification and validation technologies and tools. IEEE Softw 36(2):13–24
37. Rook P (1986) Controlling software products. Softw Eng J 1(1):7–16
38. Rosenfeld RH, Wilson DC (1999) Managing organisations. McGraw-Hill, London
39. Shewhart WA (1931) Economic control of quality of manufactured product. D. Van NOstrand, New York
40. Sommerville I (2011) Software engineering, 9th edn. Boston Mass, Pearson/Addision Wesley
41. Standish Group (1995) Unfinished Voyages. Standish Group research. 2005, from http://standishgroup.com/sample_research/unfinished_voyages_1.php
42. Wagner S (2013) Quality models. Software product quality control. On-Line, Springer, pp 29–89
43. Wagner S et al (2015) Operationalised product quality models and assessment: the Quamoco approach. Inf Softw Technol 62:101–123
44. Woodrow Bellamy III (2019) Lion air 737 MAX final accident report cites AOA sensor, MCAS among multitude of contributing factors. Retrieved 30/10/19, 2019, from https://www.aviationtoday.com/2019/10/28/lion-air-737-max-final-accident-report-cites-aoa-sensor-mcas-as-contributing-factors/

Chapter 7
So What?

7.1 Introduction

The intention of this book has been to present a more practical theoretical framework to provide better support for the software systems development process than the software engineering paradigm offers. The contention here has been that software engineering has not, and cannot, deliver the required mechanism because:

1. The SDLC model at the heart of software engineering has been misconstrued as a stage model rather than a state model, and therefore has little to offer in terms of describing the process.
2. SDLC cannot discriminate between appropriate and inappropriate methodologies and methods because it is a description of all software development. That is, all software projects pass through all states. The difference between software projects is in the level of formality applied to the process, not in the process per se.
3. The engineering metaphor does not incorporate the sociological aspects of a sociotechnical problem.
4. By claiming to provide a model of the process, the software engineering paradigm has

    a. inhibited alternative model making
    b. overly prioritised tools development ahead of theory development.

The alternative model that has been proposed is a communications model based on the observations by Brooks and Dijkstra of the intangible and determinant attributes of software. This model is supported by theories derived from other domains, namely communications theory, group dynamics theory, open systems theory and management and organisational theories. All of this is all well and good, but, as they say in the north of England, it butters no parsnips.

SSD is a practical occupation and essential to everyday life. It must deliver new systems. The pertinent question is "so what?" What difference does a different paradigm make to how software systems are produced? This chapter addresses that

© Springer Nature Switzerland AG 2020
C. Rosen, *Guide to Software Systems Development*,
https://doi.org/10.1007/978-3-030-39730-2_7

question at three levels. The theoretical level, the practical level and the relationship between theory and practice.

The proposed new paradigm has implications for the higher education curriculum, research and the profession of software systems development. This chapter will address each of these in turn.

7.2   Implications of the Theory and for Theory

This book has proposed a different way of understanding the problems of SSD from a communications perspective. The Abstract Conceptual Model (ACM) arises from the intangibility of software. This model illustrates the need for the inhabitants of the development domain to communicate with the application domain. It requires system requirements, particularly non-functional requirements to be communicated across the application domain (AD)/development domain (DD) interface from stakeholders to developers. It requires developers to create a shared vision for the system in the absence of physical models. It requires developers to communicate with project managers so that resource management can be done effectively. The communications model illustrates the problem. It does not provide a solution. Clearly tools will be requires to facilitate this communication. Some tools already exist, but before further tools are developed, the problems need to be better understood and more detailed contextualised models developed. The model raises a number of questions including the following:

(a)   What factors facilitate mutual understanding across the AD/DD divide?
(b)   Are these factors context dependant and if so what affects context?
(c)   How do cultural factors affect mutual understanding and what are the relevant cultural factors?
(d)   How can non-functional requirements be identified, understood and verified to the point of mutual understanding?
(e)   What factors affect environmental volatility with regards to SSD?

Some of these questions have been addressed by, for example, cognitive psychology, but not in the context of SSD.

Similarly, the identification of SSD as an open systems problem creates a number of questions regarding defining boundaries, handling infinite recursion of subprocesses, accounting for feedback from subsystem to parent system. Soft Systems Methodology has offered some insight into these problems [31], but offers practical solutions rather than theoretical understanding. Could, for example, a model be developed for determining the level in the subsystem at which an "acceptable" percentage of exceptions was achieved?

Perceiving SSD as a sociotechnical process raises other theoretical questions such as how are the sociological factors identified, tracked, incorporated into design? Does the sociotechnical nature of the SSD process actually affect the development process, and if so how?

One theory identified that seems to be pertinent is that of defences against anxiety [24]. This is the idea that when people are anxious they tend towards defensive behaviour such as applying overly rigid procedures and offloading blame for failure onto others. There is a clear case that due to the uncertainties inherent in SSD, developers are likely to be under stress, but how relevant is this, and, if relevant, what are the inferences? Can this phenomenon be modelled? Could this modelling potentially lead to a better understanding of decision making under uncertainty in SSD, or produce better risk or cost models?

There are two further implications of the analysis in this book pertaining to theory.

The first is of immediate and direct benefit to developers. It is that SSD is intrinsically hard. It is (both actually and metaphorically) rocket science. The challenge of SSD is to hit the bull's eye on an out of focus, continuously moving dart board, that has no defined shape and for which everyone will allocate a different value for hitting the target [29]. It is not generally appreciated how difficult SSD is as an enterprise. The general impression is that because a 14 year old whiz kid is capable of writing a multi-million pound application in their bedroom, writing software is easy. The truth is that writing software is not difficult. Developing a reliable, resilient, fully working industrial strength software system is an entirely different proposition. The whiz kid app has almost certainly required many hours of further development and refinement before becoming a commercial product. Being able to make this distinction enables the case to be made for appropriate resources to be allocated to SSD projects. Many programmers find programming easy. Possibly because of this they tend to remain in the closeted world of writing programs and solving abstract logical problems. Once the sociotechnical factors of the outside world intervene, the problems become infinitely more difficult. Making commissioning bodies aware of this distinction is the first step to narrowing the gap between application domain inhabitants and development domain inhabitants. Software systems developers will probably always be up against the layperson's perceptions, but the analysis here provides some of the ammunition needed to change these perceptions.

The second outcome of the analysis here with regards to theory is that less time and effort by researchers and academics should be spent developing tools and more energy should be devoted to developing and testing theory. The wealth and range of disputed theories in management science and psychology has not hampered the growth of public business schools, private consultancies and academic psychology departments. Theoretical models provide the foundation stone upon which discussion and debate can occur. The consequences of the lack of theory for computing and professionalisation are discussed below. The lack of theory also holds back the development of the discipline in other ways. Without theoretical models, methodologies, methods and tools cannot be evaluated. This leaves the industry open to fads and fashions in a search for a holy grail that does not exist. It is time for SSD to emerge from this self-imposed cocoon.

7.3   Practical Application of the Theory

Progress in the theoretical sphere requires a community of practice to emerge. This can, and often does take a long time. It is one of the reasons why new paradigms in any academic domain struggle to become established. One challenge to existing paradigms arises from a mismatch with current practice, and whilst practice is often led by theory, it is not necessarily so. Changes in practice occur because they make sense to the practitioners. Throughout this book there have been suggestions made to do some things in a different way as a result of the different way of thinking about the process. These proposals relate directly to practice and, if they make sense to organisations, could simply become the way of doing things. This section looks at some of these ideas.

7.3.1   Greater Priority Given to Requirements Elicitation

(a)   Recognition of the skills required by requirements elicitors.
Open systems theory identifies some fundamental difficulties with requirements elicitation.

   i.   All systems are sub-systems of a parent system. They receive input from the parent system and return feedback to it. This means that a software system is intricately connected with its parent system. Requirements elicitors must become very knowledgeable about the environment in which the software system will operate, and how the environment interacts with the software system. The operational environment is not just physical, it includes the people concerned with the parent system and the part they play in the system's operation. Often people are the critical element. They are most often there for those processes that cannot be automated. The requirements elicitation process must understand how and why people make their decisions. Acquiring this understanding requires high level communication skills and an empathic connection. The elicitors understanding must then be passed onto other members of the development team. The language and culture of the development team are very different from those of the application domain environment. The requirements elicitor must therefore be a skilled translator. These are critical activities in the SSD process and require highly skilled personnel to achieve them successfully.

   ii.   The infinitely recurrent attribute of an open system makes defining the scope of the software system very difficult. There will always be a level of functionality that could potentially be incorporated into the system. The requirements elicitation function must recognise this potential, but must also decide what will and what will not be included in the project.

   iii.   The most difficult features of a system to incorporate in a software system are the informal processes. Informal processes are those processes that do not conform to the normal procedures and for which there are no clearly defined actions. The requirements elicitation process must decide how the software system manages these situations.

iv.   The non-functional quality requirements determine the ultimate acceptance of the software system. Defining and describing them in an implementable mode is very challenging, but essential for the project.

v.   Systems are often highly efficient when they work within their specified parameters. Problems arise when, for whatever reason, they are required to handle exceptions to normal operation. The requirements elicitation process must identify as many of these exceptions as possible and find ways to handle them. Systems fail most catastrophically when an exception occurs that is not handled safely.

(b) Higher status for requirements elicitation (RE)

It follows from point "a" above that requirements elicitation is a difficult and complex activity, yet too often project managers curtail the activity prematurely because it appears that no visible progress is being made. This reflects the status of requirements elicitation in the development process as a necessary evil. "Let's get on with the real work developing the system!" Open systems theory points to the complexity of requirements elicitation and suggests that more effort should be expended on it rather than less.

There are probably a number of reasons why RE is not a particularly revered activity. The elicitation process seems to go round in circles with no obvious end, so arbitrary decisions are taken to end it. The elicitation process is seen as being unreliable. Requirements continuously emerge during the development process and thus undermine the outcome from the activity. Understanding the volatility of the environment in which the software system will operate is one of the activities that should be included within RE. It might not be possible to predict what changes might occur, but it may well be possible to estimate how likely they are to occur. Whatever the case, the failure to respect the RE process will undermine the overall project. Understanding the complexity of the activity will help promote its importance in the development process.

(c) Priority given to understanding non-functional requirements

A great deal has already been written on the importance and difficulty of non-functional requirements. Quality is recognised as important in the industry. However, possibly due to the fact that NFRs are difficult, much more attention is paid to delivering the functional requirements than the NFRs. Various suggestions have been made over time for managing NFRs, but this area is still problematic. Kazman et al. [19] proposed developing "scenarios" for NFRs. Their proposal identifies three different types of scenario; "use cases", "growth" and "exploratory". They suggest that these scenarios could be processed into measurable targets. This has proved more difficult than suggested. Nevertheless, quality scenarios could be used to raise the profile of quality requirements during the development process. Knowing what is important to stakeholders is more important than being able to measure it precisely. Having an idea of what needs to be taken into consideration is better than writing it off because what is needed is ambiguous. Quality scenarios have the advantage of providing a description of what concerns stakeholders and can be given to developers to aid their understanding. Developers however do need to take heed of them.

(d) Exception scenarios

Alongside quality scenarios, exception scenarios can support developers' understanding of the application domain. The exception scenario catalogues what happens when the normal process goes "wrong", that is when the unexpected happens. Human actors have a way of adapting and take such events in their stride. Often a human actor will draw on her/his tacit knowledge. This knowledge is, by definition, hard for a requirements elicitor to access. One scenario can easily snowball into several variants as the informant remembers similar, but different situations. Each scenario may result in a different action being taken. Sometimes the cause of the difference is obvious. Other times, not so obvious. As with capturing informal processes, exceptions can spiral into infinitely recursive sub-processes, and the developer will have to decide what level of granularity the software system should handle. With exceptions, a failsafe mechanism or exception handler will be needed to terminate the recursion appropriately. Understanding how human actors handle exceptions provides insight into the true operation of the system rather than an idealised version of the system. Exception scenarios can sit alongside quality scenarios as supporting reference material. Both quality scenarios and exception scenarios make the task of requirements elicitation more challenging, but ultimately more complete.

7.3.2 Project Management

(a) Project risk evaluation

In Chap. 3, a list of 15 conditions that pose potential generic risks to a project was proposed. This list should be considered as an initial starter pack. The purpose of this list is to scope the size of the challenge being set. It can feed into an initial costing exercise (see below). If big ticks are placed against a number of these risks, a big sign "PROCEED WITH CAUTION" should be placed against a project. The list is not definitive however and does not necessarily lend itself to mitigation as is normally the intention of risk evaluation exercises.

Research into project failure, however that is defined, has identified many contributory causes of failure such as time constraints, incomplete functional requirement specifications or staff turnover. These are often referred to as "risk factors". Verner et al. [32] identify 57 potential risk factors contributing to project failure, the most common of which were unrealistic completion date, underestimated cost, failure to manage risks, failure to reward staff, and failure to evaluate requirements correctly. However these are not risks, but symptoms.

The 73% of projects that failed where lack of risk management contributed to the failure (ibid.) suggests that insufficient attention was paid to risk management. Why was this the case? It could be that managers in those projects just had a blind spot with regards to the risks they were running, or that they had no way of mitigating the risk anyway. If there is not much you can do about it, there's not much point wasting energy trying to control the uncontrollable. The 93% of projects where timescales and the 81% where cost was a factor in failure (ibid.) suggest that the generic risk factors identified in Chap. 3 were given lower priority than winning the business in the first place, or some other such consideration. Project managers are not to blame for this situation. They are required to play the hand they are dealt. Some managers may be better finessing the jokers[1] than others, but the point is that

- Unless the reasons for the "management failures" are known, it is not possible to offer any guidance on how to avoid them.
- If no overall evaluation of risk to the project is conducted along the lines of those identified in Chap. 3, it is not possible to estimate the life chances of a project in the first place. It is quite conceivable that none of these projects (or any other failed project) ever had much chance of succeeding.

How aware project managers are of hitting the jackpot or picking up the wooden spoon may vary, as does their potential room to manoeuvre, but equating project failure to management failure in the absence of understanding the constraints, constitutes a rough justice from which nobody benefits, and does nothing to advance understanding of the problem domain.

(b) IT strategic alignment with corporate strategy

Chapter 6 observed that IT strategy and corporate strategy were not always closely aligned. Divergence can result from the competition for resources between strategic systems developments and the need to maintain and enhance legacy systems. Meeting short term expediencies will most often win out over long term targets because of the immediacy of the problem and because short term problems are a lot easier to resolve. IT systems have a tendency to promise more than they deliver, but they can also create opportunities that were never envisaged before the system existed. Close collaboration between corporate planners and IT experts suffers from the same malaise as that existing between other stakeholders and software systems developers; the language, communications and culture gap. There is no simple solution to bridging this gap as there is no simple solution to bridging the gap between the application domain and the development domain. It relies on the skills of people. At least, if there is an aspiration to align IT and corporate strategy, mutual understanding can be worked on and enhanced.

---

[1] Apologies for the mixed metaphor.

(c)   Pair designing

Software systems design is often considered to be a solitary activity. This is in contrast to say architecture where design is often a team collaboration involving many people. Al-Kilidar et al. [2] experimented with pair design with final year students, but had mixed results. Canfora et al. [9] had slightly more positive results (also working with students). But whilst pair programming has attracted a great deal of attention, pair design is largely overlooked. It may be that the intangible nature of software makes it difficult to share design ideas. This is precisely the reason pair design is proposed here. If an idea can be articulated well enough to share, it suggests that that idea is concrete enough for it to be recorded. If it is not, more work is required and working through the problem with another person could help to resolve the ambiguities. Research is required in this area. This book has identified the communication of abstract concepts as the central problem for software systems development. Pair design may offer one way of reducing the difficulty.

(d)   Independent cost estimation of NFRs

It not often recognised that there is a cost involved in satisfying NFRs. Non-functional scenarios suggested above are a way of helping to understand how NFRs affect the system, but they are of little value unless they are explicitly referenced during the development process. NFR scenarios can provide a vehicle for facilitating ongoing communication between developers and stakeholders as called for by Baxter and Sommerville [3]. They can also provide a mechanism for identifying cost drivers that are often unaccounted for. It may be that, as Glinz observes [16], a number of the NFRs can be reframed as sets of functional requirements. The problem with this idea is that it may result in many more functional requirements being needed as requirements analysts try to identify all the potential conditions that could occur. NFR scenarios help to improve the calculation of the cost in two ways.

1st.   By improving general understanding of these requirements even if they do not eliminating all the ambiguity

2nd.   By recognising that there is a cost to satisfying NFRs.

Cost estimates are notoriously imprecise. NFR scenarios will help to highlight the need for the cost of satisfying quality requirements to be taken into account and thereby reduce the inaccuracy of SSD costing.

(e)   More conservative approach to cost estimation

Text book methods of cost estimation identify various techniques. In software engineering many of these are based on mathematical algorithms such as COCOMO [5] or its derivatives. The problem with these approaches is that they all rely on multi factor calibration and some estimation of workload (whether function points or other estimators). Calibration is difficult unless the project is part of a series of similar developments because it relies on data from previous projects and the factors affecting them may not apply to the current project.

Workload estimators become less and less reliable as the project increases in size, complexity and novelty.

An alternative approach is expert judgement usually based on work breakdown structures and domain expertise. Unfortunately expert judgement is biased towards over optimism for two reasons. Firstly oversimplification syndrome affects the estimate, and secondly there is often pressure to minimise the estimate to meet management or marketing expectations (which are even more heavily biased by over simplification syndrome). Textbooks on costing often suggest that managers use "expert assessment". This involves asking three experts to estimate the expected cost of a project, then using the average or median value of the three estimates as the cost predictor. It is proposed here that the following formula is used[2]:

$$Estimate^{Highest} \chi \lambda^2$$

where λ is a factor between 1 and 10 dependant on the risks identified in Chap. 3 and referred to in point 7.32(a) above

This may prove to be overly pessimistic, but has the virtue of taking account of oversimplification syndrome and combating pressure to conform to external expectations. If the cost of the project appears too high, action should be taken to reduce the scope of the project rather than placing pressure on the cost estimator to reduce the estimate.

(f) Plan Deployment Strategy

If the deployment phase is not managed correctly, it can result in considerable damage to both the reputation and the finances of an organisation [6]. Deployment of the whole of a large system in one shot, the so called "big bang" approach is a high risk strategy. Agile processes recommend small, frequent, incremental upgrades as new functionality becomes available. Where there is little risk to the live system from each upgrade, and the installation process is relatively simple, this can be a successful strategy. For mission critical systems there is always a risk that even an apparently small change can have considerable repercussions on the system. Too many, too frequent changes can introduce instability and risk into the system. An appropriate balance must be struck.

Alternative approaches include piloting the new system in a small geographic area or part of the organisation or introducing new features over a period of time and monitoring acceptability. Another option is parallel running of the new system and the old. This can be costly and care needs to be taken that any changes affecting the old system during the parallel running are reflected in the new system.

(g) Checklist of hidden costs

Whetever the implementation strategy, the feedback effects of deployment need to be recognised. Baxter and Sommerville [3] identify two elements of systems

---

[2]There is no empirical evidence to support this formula. It would be an interesting project to see how it performed in practice compared to existing cost models. Of course, as with all cost models, determining the criteria for success would be paramount. This model does however have the virtue of simplicity.

design in socio-technical systems; the "systems development" and "the change process". The "change process" refers to the fact that the deployment of a new IT system inevitably results in disruption to work practices, personal relationships and a variety of other social aspects of work. These need to be taken into account if the technological changes are to deliver the advantages they promised. There can be major costs associated with manging these change processes. A contextualised checklist would be one tool for supporting the deployment task. It would help to plan the changes required rather than post hoc reacting to the consequences of implementation.

The task of managing the repercussions of deployment in the application domain environment is often seen as the client's responsibility, and certainly the client has a major role to play in planning the change, but the development organisation needs to recognise its responsibility too. This goes beyond just providing training on the system and a help file. The developer has a responsibility to support the broader impact. This also represents an opportunity for developers and implementation staff to improve the system and potentially identify some of new opportunities for future development.

7.3.3 Staff Selection, Development and Relationships

(a) Emphasis on communication skills in selection

One of the main themes throughout this book is that effective communications between people in different work and organisational cultures is essential for successful SSD. The section in this book in Chap. 4 on communications skills expounds some theoretical understand of interpersonal and intergroup communication. Human communication at the level required for SSD is more sophisticated than normally required. Some people are better at empathic communication than others and take more interest in wanting to communicate than others. Traditionally employers have employed software systems developers for their technical skills rather than their interpersonal skills. This exposition suggests that this balance needs to change. Communications are more than a question of being able to talk to a wide range of people. Good communications skills include such skills as active listening, preparedness to ask searching questions, coping with negativity and challenging authority and received wisdom. "Ability to work in a team" includes manging conflict, lucidity, and offering support to colleagues as well as openness to cooperative working. These are skills that have not been greatly emphasised in the past and are generally not explicitly expressed or sought during recruitment. Finding people with the necessary skills may be challenging. It is important however to know what to look for.

(b) Communication skills workshops

As with any other skill, communications skills can be enhanced through education and training if people are prepared to work at them. In a traditional software engineering culture, staff members may not be particularly committed enhancing their softer skills. There are also ethical considerations to be considered. Developing ones soft skills is closely allied to developing self-awareness and being open to self-exploration. Staff should not be coerced into participating in such activities when they can affect their lives outside of work as well as in it. On the other hand, being able to work effectively with fellow workers is important, and when that work is intricately connected to interpersonal communications, it becomes necessary to enhance skills in this area.

Management training programmes are well versed in providing training courses that include communication skills, and many of these would be appropriate for software systems development staff. However the level of acceptance amongst software systems development staff of the value of such courses may be lower than say amongst management trainees. Some cultural change may be required to improve acceptance.

Dimensions of Team Dynamics (DOTD, see Appendix A) is a framework to help to enhance team communications by exploring team members' perceptions of each other as co-workers in a supportive and structured manner. In this way, differences between team members' can be explored and intra-team communications enhanced without undermining staff members' personal boundaries. Belbin's self-perception inventory [4] can be used in a similar way to explore preferred team roles. In many SSD organisations, very little formal effort is undertaken to enhance team working. Given the nature of the SSD task, this deficiency should be addressed.

(c) Developer direct engagement with stakeholders

Vision workshops are a form of developer engagement with stakeholders and consequently face the problems associated with stakeholder engagement. This level of engagement needs to be negotiated between client and provider. This apparently straightforward proposal is however fraught with practical, logistical and political problems. Agile methodology recommend a representative user becomes part of the development team, but how representative is the representative? An expert user is probably too valuable to the commissioning organisation to allow her/him to have a sabbatical with the software development team. Occasional meetings might be possible, but attendance at the daily scrum meeting for example is unlikely.

On the other hand, development staff on the customer's site can be intrusive and disruptive. Furthermore, developers talking to end users may be seen as seditious by some organisations. Clearly these problems need to be the subject of negotiations between the systems developers and the client organisation. Technology such as conference calling, email and blogs could alleviate some of the logistical difficulties. Some means of ongoing dialogue between stakeholders and developers aimed at reducing the cognitive gap between the application domain and the development domain should be seen as a priority for the development organisation if they wish to achieve customer satisfaction.

(d) "Vision" workshops

Traditionally in SSD organisations a common understanding of the product to be developed has been achieved using various tools such as use cases, data flow diagrams, entity relationships and so on. As abstract models, they are well adapted to defining what is definable, but cannot identify what has not been included in the model. In some ways the precision of these models obscures the fact that they have excluded some potentially vital information. Abstract models of the product lack the sensitivity of human communication and they are very poor at recording quality requirements. Stakeholders, who are unlikely to have particular expertise in interpreting these abstract models will be unlikely to be able to identify what data has been lost.

Vision workshops are a way of addressing these deficiencies. They would be positioned at a higher level of abstraction than say use cases, filling in the lost information from use cases. Ideally they would include stakeholders and developers and avoid formal notations, using instead rich pictures and rough sketches. All participants would have the opportunity to ask questions and make suggestions giving developers the opportunity to create their own vision of the product and compare their vision with other members of the development team and with stakeholders.

The meeting should be facilitated by an experienced facilitator who could observe participants and ensure everyone has the opportunity to participate whatever their status in the group and help to identify differences in interpretation. The role of the facilitator is critical in equalising power differences between group members and ensure that everyone is able to contribute effectively and constructively. When differences in interpretation occur, they should be applauded as they identify ambiguities which need to be resolved. Thus differing interpretations become drivers of better understanding.

The vision is not static. As developers become more familiar with the intricacies of the requirement, more details emerge and need to be resolved. Stakeholders will reinterpret their own requirements as tacit knowledge becomes explicit, and as they build their understanding of what is being proposed and what might be possible. Further vision workshops should therefore be held on a regular basis during the development to monitor the inevitable changes in the vision. This is not a precise science, but whenever a question is raised such as "should we do this in this way or that in that way?" it might prompt the need for the next vision workshop.

Vision workshops will increase the cost of the development, but also help to plan for the deployment and thus reduce that cost. By helping to ensure that all developers share a common vision with stakeholders, vision workshops should also reduce the cost of rework later in the process and increase stakeholder satisfaction with the finished product.

(e) Egalitarian approach to design decisions

Often a chief designer, team leader or even "Scrum Master" is, or acquires responsibility for making major architecture and design decisions regarding the project. Brooks argued forcefully that this was the correct organisational structure in his essay on "The Surgical Team" [7].

There are at least three problems with this approach. The first is that it places all the responsibility for the system design on the surgeon. This will, of course, pretty much ensure a single common vision as only one person will be driving that vision. Differences will however arise and potentially be more difficult to resolve as they are likely to occur later in the process as fewer opportunities will have arisen for them to emerge earlier. With less discussion amongst team members, there is less probability that that vision generated by the surgeon will be the correct one. There are fewer checks and balances to question the vision. This approach may well be suitable for scientific projects or operating system development where the scope for multiple visions is limited, but where there are multiple, divergent, competing stakeholders, it places a large burden on the shoulders of one person to get every decision right.

The second problem is that this approach limits the opportunity for other members of the development team to contribute to the design. In doing so, it reduces the responsibility of other team members for the design thereby reducing their sense of responsibility towards the project and potentially their commitment as well. This negative side effect could result in errors being missed.

Similarly, reducing the involvement of less senior team members in decision making also reduces their engagement with leadership and the development of those skills.

Finally, limiting the opportunities of the rest of the team to contribute ideas will reduce their opportunities to gain experience in decision making. So, whilst the surgical team might work in the short term, it is not sustainability in the longer run.

A fourth potential problem might be that the rest of the team become demotivated and begin to feel disrespected because their potential contribution is undervalued. This can lead to lower productivity and opportunities for doing things better being missed.

An alternative approach is greater inclusivity, recognising the contribution all team members can make. Sharing the responsibility for the productive effort more evenly, offers a better prospect that the software system produced will meet user expectations. A system developed using a more diverse group within the development team provides greater opportunity to challenge and refine the vision of the product.

This approach is dependent upon an inclusive and supportive team culture, and this may well conflict with the prevailing culture. Many organisations may advocate inclusivity without taking the necessary steps to encourage it. The vision workshops play an important role is developing an egalitarian culture within the development team as would communications workshops. Team management also has an important role to play by encouraging open communications and ensuring congruence between the avowed culture and managerial behaviour.

7.3.4   Changes Arising from the Relationship Between Theory and Practice

(a) Management training in group process and group facilitation

The manager's role in a Theory Y organisation is a good deal more sophisticated than in a Theory X organisation. This is one reason why the Theory X style of management is appealing. The Theory X manager is in charge, tells her/his subordinates what to do and they do it or suffer the consequences. At least this is the case in principle. The humanistic school of management would argue that management control is an illusion and fails to utilise the talent available amongst the workforce. Contingency Theory suggests for non-routine production processes such as SSD, Theory X is a poor option because expertise resides with the worker rather than the manager, so the worker needs to be afforded independence of thought and, to a large extent, action.

The Theory Y manager has to manage with the (preferably positive) cooperation of staff. She/he uses influence rather than coercion. The argument presented here however takes the management role beyond Theory Y. The SSD manager is someone who facilitates team discussion, observes the group process and supports cooperative working and decision making. These are skills few managers will acquire as a matter of course. Many managers would not recognise their need for such skills. Managers would therefore require training to be able to work in this way. There are courses providing this type of training. Those offered by The Tavistock Institute for example explore group dynamics. Some coaching courses include group facilitation. Other providers are available who approach the problem of group facilitation from different theoretical orientations.

Lack of management expertise is a barrier to the adoption of an SSD approach that would need to be addressed. The prevailing culture within an organisation will determine how much of a barrier adopting an SSD approach might be.

(b) Less emphasis on quality process improvement and more on supporting quality processes

There has been a great deal of momentum behind the drive towards quality process definition and standards as a way to deliver quality products through software process improvement (SPI). This movement has been less well received by practitioners as it tends towards increased bureaucracy without necessarily delivering higher quality products. The link between quality processes and quality products in SSD has never been proven, and even when correlation has been shown, causation has been questioned.

Open systems theory suggests that the link between process definition and product quality can, at best, be tenuous as the feedback from lower level, undocumented processes always has the potential to disrupt the documented procedure. Effort expended on more and more rigorous process definition therefore is being expended in an attempt to try and protect against an unknown assailant who may strike at an unforeseeable time in an unpredictable way. Finer and finer grained process definition suffers from the law of diminishing returns. The more definition and the more detailed that definition, the less useful it becomes. A more productive approach is to try to capture previous experience as war stories and guidelines rather than rigid procedure. So when a similar situation arises, there is a collective knowledge set that can be referred to that can be adapted as necessary to meet the needs of the current situation.[3] Providing an expert knowledge database could prove to be a better investment than further expenditure on process improvement.

(c) More time and resource spent on understanding the external environment and feedback from the system to the environment.

Checkland [10] with his background in systems thinking was amongst the first to suggest that understanding the operational environment was a crucial step towards developing systems that stakeholders wanted. Time spent in this activity is well spent. Unfortunately, this can be a costly activity in time and resources during which it appears that little progress is being made. Soft Systems Methodology (SSM) has not achieved the recognition that Agile has. Although based on open systems theory, SSM is methodologically based rather than theory driven, so although the virtues of SSM may be clear, it has been difficult to persuade software systems commissioners to support the activity. In the absence of strong empirical evidence or a widely accepted theoretical model, increasing timescales for questionable benefit is a hard case to make. There is little doubt that the SSD approach will be confronted with the same hurdle despite providing a theoretical foundation.

Similarly to the up-front processes of SSM, the instinct to drive down costs and squeeze timescales reduces the effort available to ensure that post deployment activities are managed. Introducing a new software system will result in substantial changes in the wider environment. Planning the implementation, deployment and post deployment process [3] will both help to ensure greater acceptance of the system and offer the opportunity to consider how the client organisation can best benefit from the potential opportunities the new system might provide. Currently SSD organisations consider their work done when the system is handed over. Recognising that the post-deployment phase as an

---

[3]Rosen [28] satirised the excessive use of procedures in his spoof defect analysis report on the Y2K bug.

integral part of the development process would provide a service most commissioning organisations are likely to appreciate as well as offering up new business opportunities.

There is little doubt that the front end and the back end of the development process have been considered the poor relations of software development. SSD organisations truly committed to quality may wish to reconsider these priorities.

(d) Problem to be understood from multiple stakeholder perspectives
The concept of understanding the problem from the point of view of multiple stakeholders is well recognised, but the analysis here puts this issue front and centre. Both functional and non-functional requirements need to be considered and conflicting requirements resolved.

The problem in the past has often been gaining access to those stakeholders who have low status in the client organisation, but have great influence on the acceptance of the product. Often their views and knowledge have been subordinated to the commissioning stakeholder; after all he who pays the piper calls the tune. From a SSD point of view however, the new development needs to be understood from an end users perspective. Stakeholders should include those people indirectly affected by introduction of changed systems. This might be, say a warehouse picker who receives instructions from the system. Politics and prejudice often preclude asking for information from such groups. Software systems developers need to try to overcome such restrictions.

(e) Contract Management ~ Sharing risk
In general, there are two forms of procurement contract for SSD; "time and materials" (T&M) and "fixed price". In fixed price contracts, the commissioning organisation agrees a specific price for the system. If the problems are greater than envisioned, or the project takes longer than agreed, the commissioner still only pays the agreed sum. Sometimes failure to deliver on time incurs additional penalties. In this situation, the developer carries all the project risk. A reasonable supplier will factor this into their cost calculation and include a substantial contingency factor into the pricing of the system. This might be up to three times the expected cost. (Noting the costing formula in point "i". Above, this may actually be too conservative.)

In SSD projects, fixed price contracts often lead to conflict between the developer and the commissioner. They are based on an agreed set of requirements and will not include requirements that emerge during the development process. The developer will argue that these are new and/or changed requirements. The commissioner will argue that the "changed" requirements are neither new nor changed; the developer just didn't understand the requirement in the first place. The developer actually usually has the upper hand in this argument. If the developer pulls out of the agreement, it would leave the commissioning organisation, possibly having spent considerable time and money developing the specification, without a supplier and having to start all over again with a new supplier. The so called "fixed price" therefore becomes much more variable than originally envisaged.

Some suppliers have been known to take advantage of this situation by charging excessively for every minor change however difficult it is to implement.

In a T&M contract, it is the commissioner that carries the risk because if the project takes longer than predicted, the cost will increase. The developer in this case will likely quote a much lower cost. However this can lead to reputational damage if the final cost is far greater than the original estimate due to emerging requirements.

Both these approaches have contributed to the very poor reputation of the software systems development industry.

In SSD, it is inevitable that requirements will change. The level of volatility will depend upon those risk factors identified in Chap. 3. It would be reasonable therefore to agree a pricing structure based upon these factors and share the cost and the risk accordingly, rather than reach an agreement based on the fiction of a frozen requirements specification. Continuing with the assumption that requirements can be pre-determined and therefore the cost of a development can be predicted with any accuracy can only lead to further reputational damage. As has been noted, the Agile approach of developing small increments and, presumably paying on delivery, is a way of hiding the eventual cost. It is also likely to lead to additional costs. Early architectural decisions have to be reworked to accommodate later requirements increasing the amount of work required. Commissioning organisations must decide if this is an acceptable trade off depending on their circumstances.

7.3.5 Curriculum Changes Arising from the Theory

This is not the place to design a full academic programme on software systems development, although there has been sufficient theoretical input identified here to satisfy the QAA subject benchmark requirements for either an undergraduate or post graduate degree in SSD. Such a degree would, along with retaining some of the existing practical aspects of a qualification in computing such as programming, database design and web development, also include open systems theory, group theory, ethnography and culture, management organisation and theory. One of the potential benefits of such a programme would be to appeal to a more diverse set of students. In particular it would be hoped that this type of course would attract a more equal gender balance as it would emphasise the "softer" skills over the more traditional technical skills. Clearly, there are many more things for an HEI to consider, but, when bearing in mind the question of professionalising the IT industry (see below), such a course could play a significant role.

Regardless of whether a complete academic programme were to be considered, the arguments within this book would point towards a number of changes in existing curricula, namely:

(a) A greater emphasis on theoretical and practical communication skills such as listening skills, interpersonal and intra-team communications and cooperative team work
(b) A module on requirements elicitation
(c) Changes to software engineering modules to distinguish between models, methodologies and methods, more emphasis on non-functional requirements, the inclusion of soft systems methodologies and managing emergent requirements.
(d) The inclusion of open systems theory in the programme.

Whist it is likely that some of these suggestions have already been incorporated in some higher education programmes, they are not common. Their more general inclusion with a higher profile would help to address some of the difficulties student are confronted with when they graduate and start work. These changes would also support the advancement of SSD in general by enculturating the next generation of workers with the attitudes, values and skills necessary to improve software systems quality.

7.4   Future Research

It would be presumptuous to suggest that researchers in SSD should stop what they are doing and turn their attention to researching this new paradigm of software systems development as a human communications process, but the identification of the limitations of the software engineering paradigm should give researchers some pause for thought. Many of the topics covered in this book are well known, but the dominance of the software engineering concept has driven research into method and tools rather than theoretical constructs and models. This alternative paradigm offers the opportunity to consider other areas of research in SSD which may prove worthwhile. Some of the current gaps in research include:

(a) The effects of personal insecurity on systems development
(b) Requirements elicitation from non-technical stakeholders
(c) Exception and non-functional use cases
(d) The environmental effects of SSD introduction
(e) Pair designing
(f) Factors affecting requirements volatility
(g) Managing SSD staff

(h) Risk based project costing.

The proposition made in this book that software systems development is a unique human activity resulting from software's determinacy and intangibility is clearly open to challenge. Furthermore, that this should make any difference to the processes and procedures used to develop it is also debateable. Other academic disciplines have thrived on controversies of this nature. It is hoped that the arguments presented in this book will at least spark a more vigorous discussion regarding the nature of software systems and the processes involved in software systems development.

7.5 Professionalisation of Software Systems Development

For many years organisations such as the British Computer Society and I.E.E.E have advocated the professionalisation of the IT industry by which they mean that employees in the industry should possess an appropriate qualification in computing or IT before they are allowed to practice in the profession, in the same way that doctors, lawyers or engineers are restricted. This has failed to happen. There are no restrictions on who can enter the occupation of computing at any level or within any sub-discipline within the field. This is problematic because if software systems are to become more reliable, both in terms of operation and development process, it needs a development community that understands the special peculiarities of the discipline. This book has argued that SSD is a unique occupation (contrary to the views of Rönkkö et al. [27]) and hence worthy of academic investigation on that basis. It follows therefore that, if the consequences of not having specialist expertise are serious enough to warrant exclusion to the profession of non-specialists, then exclusionary privileges should be awarded.

Clearly the consequences of SSD failure can be very serious, but this, in itself, is insufficient. An occupation must be able to demonstrate that it also possesses a unique body of knowledge that practitioners must possess. Software engineering has failed to do this.

An explanation of this failure can be found within the ideas discussed in the discipline of the "sociology of the professions". One of the preeminent proponents of this discipline is Abbot [1].

Abbot (ibid.) proposed a model of professional jurisdiction; by which he meant how professions gain and maintain authority over work in an occupation in the eyes of government, the public and other professions. His model suggests that professions achieve this status through a process of "Diagnosis", "Inference" and "Treatment". Diagnosis describes how problem domains are categorised and colligated (structured/described). Inference is the theoretical underpinning of the discipline, or rather the epistemology (accepted ways of thinking) about problems. It connects diagnosis to treatment for complex problems faced by the domain. Inference confers the right to theorise because the theoriser must have knowledge of the theoretical base.

Any profession has rules dictating when a professional must resort to complex inference. (op. cit. p. 51)

The theoretical base must be the unique domain of the "professional"[4] practitioner.

Treatment concerns the ways to solve the problem.[5] To date, computing has focussed on treatment to the detriment of diagnosis and inference. Treatment includes tool development, languages, methodologies and methods, as well as standards and procedures. This emphasis has resulted from the confusion between models and methodologies discussed in Chap. 1 and a paucity of models on which to base inference.

"Inference" (a distinct and unique body of knowledge) is important to defend the subject from jurisdictional claims by other professions and to prevent erosion of professional status created by alternative approaches to problem solution. If limited or no theory exists, there is nothing to exclude untrained people from entering the occupation. Abbot argues that professions gain jurisdiction over their work by establishing when judgement is required to solve complex problems. Jamous and Peloille [17] describe this as the "indetermination/technicality ratio". If solutions can be determined simply by the application of techniques and little judgement is required, the indeterminacy ratio is low. When expert knowledge is required to determine an action, the ratio is high. This occurs in "non-routine" occupations [25].

If theory exists, but is not unique to the discipline, it makes it possible for other academic domains to say "We already do that. Your discipline offers nothing new." Examples of this happening can be seen in business schools offering degrees in ecommerce and maths schools providing degrees in operational design.

Computing represents a recent challenger to a jurisdictional claim over sociotechnical solutions. This claim is challenged by previously existing authorities such as electrical engineers, creative designers, mathematicians and business consultants. Without articulating a unique theoretical position that can be intellectually and rigorously defended, computing has no grounds on which to pursue its claim.

Typical software systems curricula [11, 14, 18, 20, 26] address the "what" and the "how" of subject areas rather than the "why" of the problem domain. Take for example computer systems architecture. The curriculum covers what architectures exist and how they work, rather than why one might choose one architecture rather than another? Furthermore, choosing between architectures does not require a unique body of knowledge. For example, a business economist might equally be qualified to make the choice. Another example might be software engineering. There is some theory to suggest that complexity in programs should be avoided, but this theory derives from cognitive psychology, not from computing theory, and it not an obligatory topic in computing courses, so not essential knowledge. Computing courses teach how to program using modularity or object orientation; in other words, how

---

[4]Professional in this context means more than simply being paid. Refer to Abbot [1]. for arguments relating to professionalism.

[5]Abbot contends that the relationship between inference and treatment is, in practice, not necessarily as close as professionals would like to believe (or make believe). This does not detract from the necessity to maintain the inferential base.

to solve a problem, not the theoretical components of problem constructs. An analysis of the IT curricula would reveal that the drawer labelled "unique computing theory" would be pretty bare; certainly compared to academic disciplines that have achieved exclusive entry to the occupation. In computing what is offered is a series of treatments. The principles underlying inferential thinking are limited.

It can be argued that a justifiable jurisdictional claim could be lodged on the combination of Brooks' "No Silver Bullet" paper [8] identifying four attributes of software (intangibility, malleability, complexity and "conformability" and Dijkstra [12] fifth property "determinacy" as discussed in Chap. 2. These unique combination of properties result in complex patterns of inferences that require expert knowledge.

The challenge for computing departments is to develop general theory which describes this process sufficiently to connect the treatments to diagnosis using inference. Offering treatments that cannot be substantiated by underlying theory, whether these be object orientated approaches or software process improvement, have little credibility however fashionable they become, because it is not possible to predict if they will or will not be effective with any certainty.

Theory from other academic domains may offer potential perspectives that are helpful, but they need to be considered with reference to how the properties of software affect production. Software systems development offers the basis for a unique intellectual jurisdictional claim. If the inferential framework is not applied, catastrophic failure [21, 22] can occur. The strength of this claim requires the development of diagnostic processes (requirements elicitation) and the inferences (systems architectures) that derive from the uniqueness of SSD.

Exemplars of the type of understanding required might be the relationship between reliability, security and usability in this context of a complex, intangible, determinant artefact. Another possibility might be reconstruing SDLC as a state model, rather than a stage model and the inferences resulting from this for the development process. Diagnosis might result in, say a combination of SSM with Agile development methods. Dependent on the context, other treatments might be recommended. Only an expert software systems developer would possess the expert knowledge to make an appropriate recommendation. Knowing what factors to consider could well be grounds for a legitimate jurisdictional claim. This is very different from the current situation when a project manager has few guidelines and no rules on which to base a judgement.

A third line of enquiry might be modelling the interrelationship between the social-technical and the socio-dynamic aspects of the software systems development process. The theory that currently exists is insufficient and insufficiently coherently articulated to provide computing professionals with jurisdiction over work in computing.

Jurisdiction is awarded by governments, the public or the work place on the grounds of exclusivity of knowledge. Professional status and the exclusive right to operate in an occupational domain is the badge of jurisdiction. Software Engineering's focus on tools (treatment) in the absence of theory (inference) undermines the profession's claim to professional status and hence jurisdiction. Computing departments and computing curricula therefore need to refocus on developing and teaching theory rather than on how to implement a database or program a game. In turn, this will help to defend computing departments from jurisdictional claims over computing from, for example, psychology, business and engineering technology departments.

This is not the first call for the development of theory in computing. A call emerged from the International Conference on Software Engineering 2000 [13]. Sommerville [30] made a similar plea. Glass in a series of articles [15] seems to endorse this call and McBride [23] also suggests the need for such theory. The theories articulated here present an embryonic body of knowledge. Further and possibly different theory will be required to achieve exclusivity.

7.6   Last Words

This book has striven to demonstrate that

(a)   Software systems development is a unique human activity and therefore should be studied as a unique phenomenon.
(b)   Current approaches to software systems development do not adequately account for the uniqueness of SSD
(c)   Applying ideas from other academic domains provides a better understanding of the process and points towards a new SSD paradigm.

The theories and ideas adopted from other disciplines have been discussed in limited depth in order to concentrate on the specific matters of interest to readers of this book. Some of the subtleties have consequently been overlooked and the nuances between arguments within these disciplines glossed over. It is recognised that more detailed exploration of some of these ideas could result in different conclusions being reached. It is quite possible that current practice and research for example in the field of neuroscience could result in more interesting conjectures.

Two aphorisms come to mind

• A little knowledge is a dangerous thing
• Fools rush in where angels fear to tread.

This book has been written with these aphorisms in mind, but it cannot be denied that the possibility of falling foul of them is a distinct possibility. This would be a price worth paying if the ideas presented here prompt further discussion, closer inspection or improved models. It may be that some of these ideas cannot be substantiated, others may not prove to be as useful as hoped. However, the process of discussing them is, of itself, valuable.

There is too little theory regarding software systems development and hence too little knowledge to support practical decision making. This needs to change if SSD is to emerge into a mature discipline. The inadequacies with the current dominant paradigm are too evident for it to provide a reliable basis on which to progress. This alternative may prove to be equally fallible, but, if its rejection comes as the result of intellectual debate and empirical evidence, it will have made a useful contribution to the discussion.

7.7 Discussion Questions

1. Section 7.2 of this chapter identifies five questions concerning the factors affecting communications between the application domain and the development domain. Construct an outline research plan to investigate one of these questions.
2. Would it be possible to develop a generic model or to develop some guidelines on sufficiency of process detail required for software systems development to begin in view of the infinitely recursive nature of real world systems?
3. If requirements elicitation is a socio-technical activity, what generic skills does a requirements analyst require most, and why?
4. What are the similarities and differences between Dimensions of Team Dynamics (DoTD, see Appendix A) and Belbin's Self Perception Inventory? How useful are each of these tools for software systems development teams?
5. This book suggests that software process improvement offers a poor return on investment in terms of delivering real product quality. Is this a valid criticism of SPI?
6. Section 7.4 of this chapter identifies 8 potential areas for researchers to investigate. If you were to be responsible for allocating research funding, which of these projects (if any) would you prioritise and why?
7. Is pursuing exclusivity in access to work in the field of software systems development a valid aspiration and if so why/why not? Is it achievable?
8. Do the software attributes of intangibility, malleability, complexity, conformity and determinacy make the activity of software systems development unique as is argued in this book? If so are the differences between software systems and other human artefacts sufficient to warrant specialised study in SSD? If not, what can be learnt from the development processes of those other, similar products to improve the success rates of software systems?

References

1. Abbot A (1988) The system of professions. University of Chicago Press, Chicago
2. Al-Kilidar H et al (2005) Evaluation of effects of pair work on quality of designs. In: Australian software engineering conference. IEEE, Brisbane Australia
3. Baxter G, Sommerville I (2011) Socio-technical systems: from design to systems engineering. Interact Comput 23(1):4–17
4. Belbin RM (1981) Management teams: why they succeed or fail. Heinemann, London
5. Boehm BW, Papaccio PN (1998) Understanding and controlling software costs. IEEE Trans Softw Eng 14(10):1462–1477

6. Bourn J (2003) Unlocking the past: the 1901 census online. N. A. Office. HMG. HC 1259 Session 2002–2003, London
7. Brooks F Jr (1995) The surgical team. The mythical man month. In: Brooks F Jr (ed) Reading, Addison Wesley, pp 29–37
8. Brooks F Jr (1987) No silver bullet: essence and accidents of software engineering. Computer
9. Canfora G et al (2006) Performances of pair designing on software evolution: a controlled experiment. In: Conference on software maintenance and reengineering (CSMR'06). IEEE, Bari, Italy
10. Checkland P (1999) Systems thinking, systems practice. Wiley, Chichester
11. Davis GB et al (1991) IS '97 curriculum report, ACM 1–94
12. Dijkstra EW (1989) On the cruelty of really teaching computer science. Commun ACM 32(12):1398–1404
13. Easterbrook S et al (2000) Beg borrow and steal workshop. In: International conference on software engineering, Limerick
14. Ford G (1991) The SEI undergraduate curriculum in software engineering. In: 22nd SIGCSE technical symposium on computer science education (SIGCSE '91), ACM SIGCSE Bulletin
15. Glass RL (1998–2009) Loyal opposition. IEEE Softw
16. Glinz M (2007) On non-functional requirements. In: 15th IEEE international requirements engineering conference (RE 2007). India Habitat Centre, New Delhi IEEE Computer Soc, pp 21–26
17. Jamous H, Peloille B (1970) Professions or self-perpetuating systems? changes in the French university-hospital system. Professions and Professionalization. vol 3, J. A. Jackson. Cambridge, Cambridge at the University Press, pp 111–152
18. Joint Task Force on Computing Curricula (2001) Computing curricula 2001 computer science. IEEE Comput Soc ACM
19. Kazman R et al (2000) ATAM: method for architecture evaluation. Carnegie-Mellon University Pittsburgh, Defense Technical Information Center, p 81
20. Liberal Arts Computer Science Consortium (2007) A 2007 model for a liberal arts degree in computer science. ACM J Educ Resour Comput 7(2):1–33
21. Leveson N (1993) An investigation of Therac-25 accidents. IEEE Comput 26(7):18–41
22. Lions JL (1996) ARIANE 5 Flight 501 Failure Paris, European Space Agency
23. McBride N (2007) Letter to the professors. Retrieved 20/05/2007, 2007
24. Menzies-Lyth I (1959) The functioning of social systems as a defence against anxiety. Containing anxiety in institutions. I. Menzies-Lyth. Free Association Press, London, pp 43–85
25. Perrow C (1967) A framework for comparative analysis of organizations. Am Soc Rev 32(2):194–208
26. QAA (2007) Honours degree benchmark statement (for Computing), from http://www.qaa.ac.uk/academicinfrastructure/benchmark/statements/computing07.pdf
27. Rönkkö M et al (2010) The case for software business as a research discipline. In: Tyrväinen P, Jansen S, Cusumano MA (eds) International conference of software business (ICSOB). Springer, Jyväskylä, Finland, pp 205–210
28. Rosen CCH (1997) PLUNGE D.A.: a case study. ACM Sigsoft Softw Eng Notes 22(2):82–83
29. Rosen CCH (2003) 10 impossible things to do before breakfast. Softw Eng Notes
30. Sommerville I (2003) Key note. Empirical assessment of software engineering, Keele, Saffs. Keele University, UK
31. Stowell F, Welch C (2012) The manager's guide to systems practice. Wiley, Chichester UK
32. Verner J et al (2008) What factors lead to software project failure? In: Second international conference on research challenges in information science. IEEE, Marrakech, Morocco

Appendix A
Dimensions of Team Dynamics

An Instrument for Facilitating Group Observation and Enhancing Team Effectiveness

Introduction

As a manager, it is often difficult to work out why a perfectly capable team of people is not achieving the results expected. Many teams seem to be able to work well, without excelling. No one individual is necessarily underperforming; they all seem to work well, but it is evident that as a team they are capable of even more. An intervention is necessary, but it is not obvious what that might be. It maybe that team members get along ok with each other, but it still seems a little flat. What can be done about it?

It could be that there is something not quite right with the group dynamic. An expert in group analysis or organisational psychology, or team culture might be able to fathom it out, but that might take a long time and be costly. Spending that, given the circumstances couldn't be justified and still may not get to the bottom of the problem. In any case, the likelihood is that a consultant would come in, observe one or two inefficient practices, write a report, cost a lot of money and leave without solving the underlying problem, that is the quality of intra-team communications.

Dimensions of Team Dynamics (DoTD) provides a way of addressing this problem by providing a tool to support organisational learning. DoTD is an observational tool that provides a model and a common language that encourages intra-group dialogue.

Derived from theories of group dynamics that suggest unconscious interpersonal processes affect task achievement, DoTD supports the raising of user's own awareness of the group process. It provides a way to discuss team dynamics and how the socio-dynamic relationships within the team affect the group process without threatening the social fabric of the team. The hidden, intrinsic strengths and weaknesses of the team can be identified, appropriate action can be agreed and the outcomes monitored in a safe and unthreatening way.

© Springer Nature Switzerland AG 2020
C. Rosen, *Guide to Software Systems Development*,
https://doi.org/10.1007/978-3-030-39730-2

DoTD works because it provides a structure for asking questions about what is happening within a team rather than offering magic solutions or silver bullets. It is designed to facilitate thought and discussion and promote open and honest dialogue between team members rather than the diagnosis of problems. The team itself can do that. The philosophy of DoTD is that there are no right or wrong answers, only what works for the group. The team (including managers and supervisors) is in the best position to understand how the group's dynamics and unvoiced concerns affect the team's effectiveness. DoTD gives voice to those concerns.

What is the DoTD Approach?

DoTD explores a team's interpersonal and intra-group dynamics using seven dimensions:

1. Valency of vision
2. Leadership and initiative taking
3. Structure and flexibility
4. Group or self motivation
5. Task or social orientation
6. Acceptance of responsibility
7. Self belief.

These dimensions emerged from empirical observations of teams in both commercial and educational settings [7]. The model is a practical application of those findings based on obscure[1] group psychology and socio-dynamic theory. In effect DoTD provides a language that all team members can use and understand. This provides a safe environment in which sometimes strained relationships can be explored.

Teams, and relationships within teams are defined, not so much by what team members say to each other, but by what they are not able or prepared to say to each other. The anxiety these unexpressed feelings generate can often dissipate a team's energy; meeting targets, but not excelling. DoTD works because it is non-judgemental. It does not attribute right or wrong. It simply provides a mechanism for explaining why something is happening. It allows team members to explore and express their differences in perception of each other and to get a sense of how other team members perceive them without feeling angry or resentful. It treats all team members as equals providing the opportunity for team members to express themselves openly and freely. So the DoTD instrument provides a safe medium for managers and group members to exchange ideas and promote a group's cohesion.

---

[1]DoTD is based on the Freudian concepts of transference and counter-transference [5], and Bion's Basic Assumption Theory [3].

DoTD describes 7 dimensions of team dynamics. The dimensions are:

	Dimension name	Dimension polarities
1	Valency of vision	Clarity, consistency and potency
2	Leadership and initiative taking	Leadership/initiative taking v concordance/passivity
3	Structure and flexibility	Desire for structure v desire for flexibility
4	Group or self-reliance	Group orientation v individual orientation
5	Task or social orientation	Task orientation v social orientation
6	Acceptance of responsibility	Acceptance of responsibility v Laissez Faire
7	Self-belief	Confidence in ability v fear of failure

The following section provides brief descriptions of each of the seven dimensions:

Valency of Vision

Valency of vision is different from the other dimensions as it is a team level attribute rather than an intra-team attribute. One of the key success factors for any project is that the group share a common vision of what is to be achieved. Vision is more than just to stated objectives. It encomposses all the attributes of the project. This is generally recognised as important, but vision is ephemeral. It is difficult to pin down. The vision is an abstract concept that lives in the minds of each team member, and is different for each team member. But how different is it?

Part of the difficulty in answering this question is that the vision keeps changing. It is in constant flux. One minute it seems clear, the next moment a minor change in perceptual focus throws it up in the air again. This fluidity is a problem in its own right because how can a team member know that they are doing the right thing? It also makes it difficult for team members to challenge each other's concept of the vision because it is not clear exactly what is being challenged. Vision is difficult to articulate. No one wants to appear stupid for asking questions about something everyone else appears to think is obvious, so everyone assumes that everyone else agrees on the vision. Significant differences go undetected. The Valency of Vision dimension challenges the assumption that everyone agrees on the vision.

Valency of vision has three attributes[2]:

• Consistency:	Is the vision is always changing? How much is it changing? The consistency attribute asks how quickly it is changing.
• Clarity:	How well define is the vision? Is what the project is trying to achieve clear and obvious or is it a bit fuzzy?
• Potency:	How forcefully are team members holding to their understanding of the vision? Are team members fully committed to the vision or are there doubts about the vision?

---

[2]On the DoTD instrument "consistency", "clarity" and "potency" are given a value between 1 and 10; 1 being the lowest and 10 the highest.

These three attributes allow the group to express a personal opinion regarding the commonality of vision. If any of the attributes are scored low it would indicate that something needs to be addressed. If they are high for some team members, but low for others, it might indicate a rift in the group which could be explored further. Each team member may have a different perception of each of the three attributes. It is their perception of the three attributes that is important. Agreement on these three attributes would indicate a healthy group environment, even if team members actually hold different visions. A large level of disagreement would indicate something to investigate.

Team members may well differ in their understanding of what the team is expected to achieve. This may not only be a source of conflict within the team, but also engender a level of anxiety amongst team members. Anxiety can lead to team members becoming defensive and undermine the team's capacity to work together.

Evaluating shared vision therefore is also a proxy measure of how well the team is communicating with each other. Understanding this dimension therefore offers powerful insight into the group process.

Leadership and Initiative Taking

Leadership has long been recognised as an important attribute in management theory and many books have been written on different aspects of the subject.

The concept of leadership is intimately associated with ideas of authority and power, and is often only applied to senior members of a team. Here however, by associating leadership with initiative taking, it can be disassociated from hierarchical and assumed power. All members of a team can take initiatives based on their own judgement. How comfortable they are to act on their ideas or to suggest changes is a measure of how supported and trusted they feel. A high self score would indicate a degree of personal security and acceptance in the team. Identifying another team member as being low in leadership and initiative taking may indicate that that person might not be fully accepted into the team.

Leadership and initiative taking is contrasted with concordance. This is the idea that someone may feel more comfortable being given work to do rather than suggesting change. Where concordance is a self-perception this may indicate a personal preference and indicate a degree of contentment. On the other hand, it may indicate a lack of assertiveness that could be alleviated with better support. Where it is other people's perception in may indicate a level of exclusion from the group.

Two problems can arise when people take initiatives beyond their authority. Firstly, it might divert a person away from higher priority work and waste resources on activities for which they have little authority and therefore find harder to achieve. Secondly, leadership can be used to depower and exclude other group members. This can be extremely damaging to the group as a whole and result in wasted resources.

Alternatively, if too few team members are prepared to act on their own initiative, opportunities may be missed. Initiative taking may be blocked due to anxiety about the acceptability of the initiative, or as a result of passivity and non-engagement with the objectives of the group. Understanding where members of the group are on this dimension can help to unlock untapped dynamism in the group.

This instrument treats leadership and initiative taking as the same thing differentiated only by the persons position in the group. Recognising who is capable and prepared to take initiatives and who is more comfortable being given more direction helps a team recognise the talents the team possesses. Leadership/initiative taking can be equated to the "Shaper" role identified by Belbin [2]; concordance may be more akin to "company worker/implementer". As Belbin observed, both roles are valuable in a team.

Structure and Flexibility

Structure and flexibility are mutually contradictory phenomena. The more structure something has, the less flexibility is possible. Flexible organisations and people are able to respond quickly to changes in circumstance. However, a lack of structure can lead to insecurity and anxiety that militates against taking initiatives and risk. People may express a desire for both more structure and more flexibility without being aware of the contradiction. This is a fundamental dilemma with which organisations and managers must struggle. Some team members may like more structure, whilst others may want more freedom. Quality assurance procedures and other bureaucratic processes may also affect the team's ability to respond appropriately to changes in circumstance. Recognising each person's needs in regard to structure and flexibility enables a manager to establish the most productive regime for that person. Differences in perception between how team members see other team members and how those team members feel about themselves could indicate opportunities might be being missed due to a team member being over restricted or under supported.

Group or Self-Reliance

Some people feel more comfortable working with other people and bouncing ideas around, whereas others prefer to work by themselves and find their own inspiration. For the former, working with a group of introverts (as she/he might see them) can be soul destroying. For the latter, being "forced" to join in can be a nightmare. A team that understands and respects each other's preferences will be a comfortable place to work, this is rarely discussed in the work place. Team members' perceptions of other team members may be ill conceived. Having the opportunity to discuss people's preferences openly is a means of correcting misconceptions and creating a more harmonious workplace.

DoTD provides an opportunity to discuss team members' preferences and accommodate them where possible. Team cohesion does not equate so much to everyone joining in, but to everyone contributing. Providing the opportunity for each member to contribute in the way they feel most comfortable is likely to be more productive than pressuring them to conform to a mode of interaction that does not suit them.

A cohesive team is clearly desirable, but too much cohesion can result in a collusive atmosphere where dissent is felt to be unacceptable. This can lead to "group think" [6]. An absence of divergent thinking can also result in opportunities being missed. Too great a need to work with other people may lead to low productivity as individuals could neglect their own work and indulge in displacement activity. Knowing the balance in the team therefore is extremely useful.

Task or Social Orientation

Task orientation versus people orientation has, for a long time, been at the forefront of thinking about how groups of people work together [1, 4]. Similar to group orientation versus individual orientation, how people prefer to work with other people is a matter of personal preference.

This dimension refers to whether team members tend to focus on the task set and are therefore less inclined towards developing relationships within the team, and those that feel working with other people helps them complete the task. In software systems development (SSD), being able to communicate and work cooperatively with others is essential, but the evidence suggests that SSD attracts people who are more task orientated. This dimension therefore is valuable for seeing what the balance is in the team.

More than any other of the dimensions, this dimension appears to be context specific. In this respect it is related to the structure versus flexibility dimension. People who are more flexible are likely to shift between task and social orientation more than those who tend towards wanting greater structure. It could be therefore that when team members evaluate other team members, their observations are based on an unrepresentative snapshot. If team members are perceived as say, task oriented, but they see themselves as socially oriented, it could be a sign that that team member is under pressure. If many of the team see themselves as task oriented, it may indicate limited communication and sharing in the team. Team cohesion depends upon a certain amount of social interaction, so lack of social interaction may be a problem. The level of social interaction however may be culturally determined. The correct level therefore needs to be sensitive to the prevailing culture.

The balance between task and social activities seems to be an important indicator of the effectiveness of the group, and a measure of the health of relationships between group members.

It is worth noting that there may not actually be a contradiction between these two dimensions. It is possible that great teams both get the job done and have a good time and care for each other.

Acceptance of Responsibility

There is great potential for confusion with the concept of responsibility. The word responsibility is used in a number of senses.

- Feeling responsible for something or someone differs from being responsible for it or them.
- A person may be ascribed responsibility without the capability of affecting what happens, or what somebody else does.
- Someone wanting to be seen as acting responsibly, that is capable, of doing something.
- Having a sense of personal responsibility towards someone or something which may, or may not, relate to that person's ability to affect the outcome.

The usage here however, is much narrower than these other senses. It is whether or not a person accepts responsibility for her/his own feelings and actions.

Acceptance of personal responsibility in the sense of this dimension only applies when the person could, if they chose, affect the outcome. Feeling responsible for something one cannot influence can be quite corrosive. It can engender feelings of powerlessness and lower self-confidence if the person feels that they should be able to change something but cannot achieve that change. However, taking responsibility for something can ensure that something is done about it.

The other end of this spectrum is a laissez faire attitude. Some people are able to get on with the job and not let distractions worry them. On the other hand, there may be occasions when it may be possible to intervene, but because what is happening is not strictly their responsibility, they leave it to someone else to deal with.

This dimension can engender strong emotions, and is therefore the most sensitive of all the dimensions. It is possible that team members might perceive someone who takes responsibility for everything as overly dominant. Alternatively, someone who is too laid back can be seen as irresponsible. Both perceptions can result in frustration and resentment. Lack of acceptance of responsibility can lead to defensive reactions, by offloading responsibility onto others or blaming others for not acting if problems result from lack of action. This can cause a great deal of tension in a group and reduce the level of trust and openness of interpersonal communications. In a software development team this can lead to errors creeping into the product.

Managers and supervisors can become particularly critical of team members if they feel that a team member has not taken responsibility when the manager believes they should have. This is a defensive reaction to the manager's sense of powerless-ness. Managers may feel (and may be held responsible for) the success or failure of the team, but also feel they have insufficient authority to influence team behaviour. Managers who are, or feel they are under pressure may blame team members (possi-bly a particular team member) for failures and even resort to bullying and harassment. A manager needs considerable insight into their own feelings and behaviour to fully appreciate their own role within this dimension. It causes difficulty when a manager is unaware of their influence over a team. This can be difficult for the team to address. In these circumstances it may be necessary for someone outside the team to facilitate a resolution.

Where blaming is common, it is often a sign that the organisation and members of it are under stress.

Acceptance of personal responsibility does not exclude finding scapegoats, but the more comfortable a person feels with the responsibilities they carry, the less likely they are to feel the need to blame other people.

It may help to reduce any tension relating to this dimension to discuss what team members understand by this dimension. It is always good practice to use specific examples when giving feedback to others, and is particularly useful when team members discuss this dimension with each other.

Self Belief

Confidence is a key factor in decision making. During the life of a project, it is necessary for each individual in the group to make many decisions, and the level of confidence that they have in their ability to make those decisions will influence whether or not they decide to undertake the task. Belief in one's own ability should be contrasted with actual competence as judged by others. Belief in competence is a question of self-perception and is subject to the complexity of the concept of self-perception. Self-perception is influenced by the perception of others and therefore reflects some aspects of intra-group relationships.

The principle effect of lack of self-confidence is to limit the activities that a person is prepared to undertake. Sometimes this leads to procrastination (starting block nerves) when the activity is delayed, or slow to get off the ground. Fear of failure can be greater if the person also fears they will be criticised if they are not seen to be successful. Perception of criticism is sufficient to undermine a person's confidence, even if actual criticisms have not been openly expressed. Indeed, unspoken criticism can be more toxic than open criticism. Lack of confidence can restrict what a group is able of achieving even when there is no obvious reason for team members to doubt their own ability. Lack of self-belief can be directly related to the valency of vision dimension. If team members are unclear about the vision it may well undermine their self-belief.

It is possible that a person may be, or appears to possess, confidence in their ability that is not justified by their actual ability. Some people may attempt tasks for which they are not capable. How managers and supervisors respond to this situation can influence the ability of the team to achieve its potential in the longer term.

In some respects, this dimension brings managers closer to their parental role in the group than any of the other dimensions, and therefore closer to the emotional life of the team. Team members are at their most vulnerable when their capability is challenged and therefore may well re-enact (at an emotional level) long standing patterns of behaviour with authority figures such as managers. Managers can be sucked into the team member's pattern of behaviour if they are unable to recognise this dynamic, reacting to the dynamic rather than with understanding and empathy. As with the acceptance of responsibility dimension, managers need self-awareness to respond appropriately to team members' behaviour.

In summary, this dimension can identify a potential source of anxiety within members of the team that can limit the team's effectiveness. Mangers need to work sensitively if they are to realise untapped potential within their team.

How to Use DoTD

DoTD can be used in one of two ways; by a manager/supervisor as an observational tool or as a vehicle to improve communication within the team.[3]

As a way of improving communication, managers can use DoTD to help identify areas of concern or miscommunication within the team. Each team member is given the instrument to use to evaluate themselves and the other members of the team.[4] These results can then be used to facilitate a group discussion; identifying similarities and differences between group members' perceptions of themselves and each other. The instrument is then evaluated and the observations used to prompt discussion between team members.

Evaluation is interpretive, not descriptive. It is intended to enhance communications between team members and identify perceived problem areas. It does not measure the scale of a problem or describe the problem. An observation is only a problem if team members consider it to be a problem. The instrument provides the vehicle for communication, but the group members themselves needs to describe the actual problem.

DoTD is a two stage process. The first stage is completing the forms and analysing them.

During the analysis, the patterns to look for are:

- Levels and levels of agreement on the "Valency of Vision" dimension.
- High levels of agreement/disagreement and patterns of response across the team for each dimension.
- Differences between team members' assessment of a team member on a dimension and a team member's own perception on that dimension.
- Lack of discrimination between a team member's self rating and that of their rating of other team members. (This could indicate a team member's inability or unwillingness to relate to other team members as individuals.)
- Patterns of response by a team member across dimension in respect to other team members.

Team members can look for patterns in their own responses and reflect on what they feel is important to them in terms of their attitudes to other team members.

---

[3] Agreement to participate from team members should be sought before the exercise begins and the level of confidentiality decided. For example are team members' names going to be shared?

[4] On the instrument, team member 1 for example should be the same team member throughout the instrument. Participants can either replace "member 1" with their initials or keep names on a separate sheet not to be handed in. If members' names are withheld, this could limit the level of evaluation possible.

The second stage is a team meeting (or a series of team meetings). The team meeting should be facilitated. This could be by the team manager or by an external facilitator if funding allows. At this stage the facilitator will be looking for:

- Themes emerging during discussions (concerns, anxieties, regrets, satisfactions).
- Scapegoating of any given team member (i.e. consistently being blamed or criticised)
- Subgroups within the group (gender divide, age divide, etc.)
- Differences in attitudes and values
- Strong expressions of sentiments (raised voices, faster interaction)

and

- encouraging all team members to contribute
- observing patterns in the communication
- identifying themes
- reflecting back these observations to the team members.

Managers can do the evaluation of the forms themselves looking for patterns to identify the potential strengths and weaknesses in a team dynamic and decide how an intervention might play out. Used in this way, the DoTD instrument provides a structured approach to the manager's observations and can quickly identify problem areas without disrupting the functioning of the team.

The objective of the team meeting can vary. Examples might be:

- Identifying potential bottlenecks in communication
- Encourage more open communication
- Consider the culture within the team
- Explore hidden tensions within the team.

The intention of the framework is to provide a common language that all can use to encourage group cohesion and understanding; helping to resolve hidden conflicts and perceptual differences.

An ideal outcome of this approach would be that team members engage in an ongoing dialogue between themselves that sustains a growing awareness of how they can best work with each other.

"Valency of Vision" is split into three attributes. Each attribute is given a value between 1 and 10. The rest of the form is completed simply by marking a cross for each dimension between the two polarities (e.g. between group orientation and personal orientation) and for each team member (including the team member completing the form as "self"). One of the team members can/should[5] be the team manager/supervisor. The instrument can be used to see if there are similarities or differences between team members regarding each dimension, between each team member's perceptions of others and between other team member's perceptions and self.

---

[5]The instrument can be used in a so called 360° fashion. That is managers and supervisors can be included amongst team members.

Differences and similarities can be used to spark a discussion about team member's perceptions. Managers may ask questions of themselves about how their observations affect the motivation of the team as a whole and of individual members of the team. Is there evidence explaining how the team constrains its own achievement? Are there imbalances in the team that have or could lead to (covert or evident) conflict? An example might be that the majority of the team are highly task oriented, and therefore little consideration is given to the team's processes, or that most of the team are socially oriented, and one person is self-oriented. This might help to explain relationships in the team, or why there is resistance to some management initiatives.

The instrument can provide some very rich data, but this data must be interpreted in the context of the team and the organisational culture that surrounds the team. Managers can identify clear patterns which can help them to manage the team more effectively. When the whole team completes the instrument and it is used to initiate a group discussion, the results can be even more successful. Team members can compare differences in their perceptions of the team and of other team members. They can use the instrument to highlight issues that would be difficult to raise in everyday interactions. The instrument can help team members give feedback to each other. How the instrument is used is determined by the appropriateness within the organisational culture. What is acceptable? What can be challenged? The DoTD can help to raise issues and challenge assumptions that cannot be broached in other ways.

How does DoTD Compare to other Approaches?

There are many other approaches to making teams more effective. Many of these approaches are used in a therapeutic context rather than a work context. In the therapeutic context participants have signed up to the treatment. No such contract exists in the work context. There is a boundary between therapy and staff development that should be respected. DoTD is intended to support this boundary, but the facilitator needs to be aware if this boundary is being approached.

DoTD shares most in common with the Belbin self perception inventory [2]. However, whereas Belbin is most concerned with team formation and task allocation, DoTD's focus is on the ongoing group. It is not always easy to select an ideal group or change the membership of it when things are not quite right. Working with the existing team membership enables every team member to achieve their own potential rather than side lining underachievers as often happens. Different people may have different capabilities and talents, but in the most effective teams all work with each other to bring out the best in each. DoTD provides a mechanism for enabling this to happen.

DoTD is "epistemological", "non-orthogonal" and "non-judgemental". Epistemological in this context means that each person using the instrument will have their own interpretation of meaning of each dimension. Non-orthogonal refers to the fact that the dimensions interact and affect each other and cannot be totally disassociated from each other. These two attributes of this approach provide a mechanism for encouraging dialogue. There can be no right or wrong as each person's perception is as valid as everyone else's. Users of the framework will construe their own understanding of the model and apply it accordingly. Thus the model provides a structure for facilitating users constructions of their own conceptual models of the socio-dynamic relationships within the team. It provides a more structured approach to understanding the effects of team socio-dynamics and a way of achieving a common understanding using generic concepts.

Non-orthogonality implies that the dimensions should be seen as a network of interdependent associations that interact with each other rather than being independent variables conducive to objective analysis or measurement. For example, a person who takes an initiative might be seen as acting on behalf of the team. In this example, there would be a perceived interaction between initiative taking and team orientation. Similarly, a task oriented person might be socially isolated. In this case, the interaction would be between task orientation and individual orientation.

The non-judgemental aspect of the model enables mutual, non-blaming feedback to be shared. For example, being task oriented, in itself, is neither good nor bad. It may be problematic if a task oriented team member concentrates on the task to the extent that they fail to communicate with other people in the team. It may be an asset if everyone in the team knows what has to be done and just needs to get on and do it. This applies equally to all seven dimensions. The objective of the model is to establish whether a team is functioning at its maximum effectiveness, rather than assess 'good' or 'bad' behaviour. The same behaviour might be effective in one context, and detrimental in another.

The dimensions are a means of analysing a social system. As such the dimensions interact with each other in the same way that elements within a system interact with each other. For example, task orientation may limit the scope of a person's conceptual vision, and may lead one person to expect other people to provide resources and information deemed outside the self-defined scope of their responsibility. Having chosen a passive role for themselves, they might criticise other people if the expected resources are not provided. Appreciating interconnectivities of this type is an objective of the analysis rather than a distraction from it. The interactions between dimensions help to understand how the system works as a system rather than focussing attention on individual members of the system.

Every team operates within its own self-created paradigm. Within this world there are self imposed injunctions and constraints that constrict the effectiveness of the team. This instrument can help to identify the constraints that prevent the team achieving its full potential in a non-threatening and mutually supportive manner.

References

1. Bales RF (1958) Task roles and social roles in problem solving groups. In: Maccoby EE, Newcomb TM, Henry Holt HEL (eds) Readings in social psychology, pp 437–447
2. Belbin RM (1981) Management teams: why they succeed or fail. Heinemann, London
3. Bion WR (1961) Experiences in groups. Routledge, London
4. Forsyth DR (1983) Group dynamics. Pacific Grove, California
5. Freud S (1950) Fragment of an analysis of a case of hysteria. Collected papers, vol III, pp 13–145. Hogarth and Institute of Psychoanalysis, London
6. Janis I (1971) Groupthink. Psychol Today, 43–76
7. Rosen CCH (2008) The influence of interpersonal and intra-group factors on the software development process. Computer Science. Keele University, Staffordshire UK

Appendix B
Dimensions of Team Dynamics Observation Sheet

© Springer Nature Switzerland AG 2020
C. Rosen, *Guide to Software Systems Development*,
https://doi.org/10.1007/978-3-030-39730-2

Valency of Vision

Score between 1 and 10
(1 low 10 high)

Clarity   Consistency   Potency

Leadership / Initiative taking

How prepared is each member of the team to take a leadership role or suggest initiatives?

Concordance

Is the team member happier to agree to the work they are given than to suggest changes to it?

	1	2	3	4	5	6	7	8	9	10
Self										
Member 2										
Member 3										
Member 4										
Member 5										
Member 6										
Member 7										
Member 8										
Member 9										
Member 10										
Group Overall										

Desire for Structure

How much does each member of the team prefer team structure, team roles and team hierarchy to be formal?

Desire for Flexibility

How much does each member of the team prefer team organisation and roles to be flexible?

	1	2	3	4	5	6	7	8	9	10
Self										
Member 2										
Member 3										
Member 4										
Member 5										
Member 6										
Member 7										
Member 8										
Member 9										
Member 10										
Group Overall										

Group Orientation

How much does each member of the team like to work closely with other team members?

	1	2	3	4	5	6	7	8	9	10
Self										
Member 2										
Member 3										
Member 4										
Member 5										
Member 6										
Member 7										
Member 8										
Member 9										
Member 10										
Group Overall										

Personal Orientation

How much does each team member prefer to work by themselves, reducing their interaction with other team members?

	1	2	3	4	5	6	7	8	9	10
Self										
Member 2										
Member 3										
Member 4										
Member 5										
Member 6										
Member 7										
Member 8										
Member 9										
Member 10										
Group Overall										

Task Orientation

How much does each team member prefer to get on with the job and see social interaction as a diversion from work?

	1	2	3	4	5	6	7	8	9	10
Self										
Member 2										
Member 3										
Member 4										
Member 5										
Member 6										
Member 7										
Member 8										
Member 9										
Member 10										
Group Overall										

Social Orientation

How much does each member of the team enjoy social activities at work and / or outside work time?

	1	2	3	4	5	6	7	8	9	10
Self										
Member 2										
Member 3										
Member 4										
Member 5										
Member 6										
Member 7										
Member 8										
Member 9										
Member 10										
Group Overall										

Acceptance of Responsibility

How much does each team member accept responsibility for making sure the whole project makes progress?

	1	2	3	4	5	6	7	8	9	10
Self										
Member 2										
Member 3										
Member 4										
Member 5										
Member 6										
Member 7										
Member 8										
Member 9										
Member 10										
Group Overall										

Laissez Faire

How much would each team member prefer to just let things be if its not their responsibility?

	1	2	3	4	5	6	7	8	9	10
Self										
Member 2										
Member 3										
Member 4										
Member 5										
Member 6										
Member 7										
Member 8										
Member 9										
Member 10										
Group Overall										

Confidence in Ability

How confident do you think each team member is that they can do the work assigned to them?

	1	2	3	4	5	6	7	8	9	10
Self										
Member 2										
Member 3										
Member 4										
Member 5										
Member 6										
Member 7										
Member 8										
Member 9										
Member 10										
Group Overall										

Fear of Failure

How worried do you think each member of the team is that the project might fail?

	1	2	3	4	5	6	7	8	9	10
Self										
Member 2										
Member 3										
Member 4										
Member 5										
Member 6										
Member 7										
Member 8										
Member 9										
Member 10										
Group Overall										

Optional Comments about using this form

How well did you understand the questions / categories?

How easy / difficult was it to complete the form?

What did you think about the layout of the form?

Would you suggest any changes to the form?

Appendix C
Exercise: The Click and Collect Catalogue Company

Instructions for Excrcise Leaders

The Click and Collect Catalogue Company[6,7] (CCCC) is a role play exercise designed to help students appreciate the problems that can occur in communications between developers and stakeholders and between different groups within the development team. It take approximately 2–3 hours to run, but can be split into $2 \times 1\frac{1}{2}$ hours sessions although these timings can be adjusted to suit the time available and the enthusiasm of the students. It is suitable for both undergraduate and post graduate students. Students do not need any specialist knowledge of computing.

The exercise consists of 6 groups or roles

- Systems Architects
- Development Team Managers
- Development Team Members
- Users
- Consultants
- Directors.

The students are required to prepare to present their brief at the first meeting. The minimum number of students required is 12 students, 2 students allocated to each role, although it may be possible to run the exercise with 6 Master's students at the cost of losing some of the interaction and team dynamics. The maximum recommended is 96.

---

[6]This scenario is entirely fictitious. Any resemblance to any existing organisation whether in name, similarity of function or operation is coincidental and is not intended to represent them in any way.

[7]Adapted from an original concept in Aggressive Retailers Inc. by Richard Manicom Cases in Management Information Systems.

© Springer Nature Switzerland AG 2020
C. Rosen, *Guide to Software Systems Development*,
https://doi.org/10.1007/978-3-030-39730-2

The exercise is conducted in the format of 2 meetings at which all students attend in their ascribed role. The instructor acts as chair of the meetings.

The role of the Chair is to:

1. Invite each role to present their briefing in turn. (It is not necessary for all team members to be involved in the presentation.)
2. Keep time. (both during the presentations and during the preparation time)
3. Ask questions if she/he feels that certain information has not come to light. (It does not matter if the question is answered correctly, or even if it is not answered at all. It is possible that one of the other groups may raise the issue and the Chair can always ask a role to recheck their information. Sometimes some information is lost in the ether at no detriment to the exercise. Sometimes incorrect information adds to the interest of the exercise. Sometimes information is added that is not in the scenarios. All this is perfectly acceptable.)
4. Take notes on the salient points of each presentation.
5. Invite the students to ask questions of the presenting group.
6. Summarise the findings at the end of each meeting.

Each group is given some information about a software systems development project. The information is tailored to the knowledge and concerns pertinent to their role. The information is sometimes the same as another role, sometimes subtlety different depending on how that role might interpret it. Some roles have more information than others.

Running the Exercise

1. Select a period for the exercise either 10 weeks before the Spring peak sales period or 10 weeks before the Autumn peak sales period.
2. Divide the class amongst the 6 roles. Try and keep the groups roughly equal size. (It is a good idea to put students together who do not normally work with each other.)
3. Arrange the class so that students in the same role are sitting together, preferably so that they can work together across a table.
4. Give each student a copy of the briefing for that role.
5. Tell the class that each group has some different information about the project and that they will be presenting the information they have to the rest of the project team.
6. Give the groups 20 min or so to prepare an approximately 5 min presentation of their information. (N.b. It's useful to check that each team understands their brief and knows what they need to present to the rest of the class.)

Each role should present their information in the following order.

1. Strategists
2. Project managers
3. Developers
4. User groups
5. Consultants
6. Directors

7. At the end of each group's presentation ask the other groups of students if they have any questions. If no questions come forward, it might be worth asking for clarification of one or two points from the chair.
8. At the end of all the presentations the Chair should summarise the findings. (The exercise is designed to demonstrate the over optimism of the development managers and the misunderstandings and miscommunications that can occur between participant groups.) This is the end of the 1st meeting.
9. In their groups the students should prepare for the second meeting by identifying remedial actions the CCCC could take to help to rectify the situation. Say 20 min.
10. The purpose of the 2nd meeting is to receive the groups' suggestions and discuss the options.
11. The exercise is completed by a class discussion on learning points from the exercise.

N.b. Approximately 62% of work has been completed in 12 months leaving 38% to do in 8 weeks with 26 development staff (i.e. approx. 460 weeks work required with 200 work weeks effort available.) Project completion is therefore around 8 weeks late with current resources. Consultants should be advised to do these calculations. This information should be withheld from other groups of students.

Although this exercise is purely fictitious, all the details originate from real case studies and demonstrate what can happen in SSD projects.

Overview

The Click and Collect Catalogue Company[8,9] (CCCC) began life as a mail order catalogue sales company after the 2nd World War. It started to open retail outlets where people could browse their catalogue and buy products in the 1980s. It now has 300 retail outlets in towns and cities around the UK, Northern Ireland and the Irish Republic. Its head offices are in Manchester where it has a central warehousing facility. The IT system has grown up haphazardly over the years. New systems have been added as and when they were needed to keep the business going, but without any overall strategy so each system operates more or less independently of each other. Currently there are 5 different IT systems.

1. A warehouse management system—controls stock levels in the warehouse, allocates storage space, and provides buyers with information on suppliers. (WMS)
2. An ordering system with a web front end used by both customers and retail assistants in the retail outlets. (CCCCIT)
3. A distribution management system—organises distribution to the retail outlets and direct to on-line customers. (DMS)
4. Local retail outlet stock management and sales recording system—records sales and tracks stock levels in each of the retail outlets. (LOCATE)
5. Financial management system—manages all head office functions and salaries. (FMS)

All these systems run on hardware originally bought in the late 1980s that is located in the basement of the head office. It is maintained by a small group of in-house IT staff and a software development team that provides 1st and 2nd line support, upgrades equipment when required and develops in-house programs for all the systems at the request of department managers. Much of the hardware has been upgraded over the years, but recently the IT budget has been squeezed. Users are beginning to complain that transaction response times are unacceptably long. And it is not unknown for systems to crash when user demand peaks. IT team managers have been warning that the servers are overdue for replacement and that greater resilience is required against catastrophic failure.

The warehouse too has now reached its full capacity and machinery, some of which dates back to the 1990s, is out of date. It is struggling to meet current demand and has to be replaced in the very near future.

On the advice of external consultants a decision was taken by the board 18 months ago to move to a distributed warehousing system. Initially this will be one warehouse

---

[8]This scenario is entirely fictitious. Any resemblance to any existing organisation whether in name, similarity of function or operation is coincidental and is not intended to represent them in any way.
[9]Adapted from an original concept in Aggressive Retailers Inc. by Richard Manicom Cases in Management Information Systems.

in the North and one in the South. New, mechanised pickers and conveyor belts will be installed at the same time. This will involve the replacement of the WMS system.

Distribution to and from the new warehouses will have to change, so the DMS system will also have to be changed. The task of specifying the new systems was given to a small team of in-house systems architects. Their report, publish 14 months ago, advised that, as so much of the current software would have to change anyway, it would be a good opportunity to revise the CCCCIT and LOCATE systems as well so that they became fully integrated with WMS and DMS. FMS was not included in the plan. In support of their plan they produced an outline systems architecture showing how the four systems would be integrated with the new warehouses. The new system has become known as the Distributed Processing System (DPS).

Approval of the scheme was given 12 months ago.

The warehouse modernisation program calls for the installation of complex systems of conveyor belts, robot forklift trucks as well as driver driven forklift trucks with on-board, on-line terminals that will receive instructions from the DPS. Storage space will be optimised by the system by matching quantity and size of product to storage bin capacity. Incoming product will be directed to the closest available bin with sufficient capacity.

All decisions as to what to ship to which warehouse or to the retail outlet will be based on sales reports and data analytics generated by the replacement for the LOCATE system. The subsystem intended to replace WMS will need to be specially written to integrate with the APIs provided by the warehouse equipment suppliers.

The project is being developed in-house by a team consisting of some of the original in-house team, contractors and two or three new recruits. It is managed by a small team of software development managers.

The implementation plan calls for shutting down the existing warehouse for two weeks while stock is transferred to the new warehouses. Timing of the move is critical to avoid the two peak sales periods in spring and autumn. Final system testing, integration and full scale operational testing is also planned for this period.

The development management team have recently informed the board member with special responsibility for IT that at the current rate of progress there is no chance of the DPS will be ready on time. System testing which should start next week will have to be deferred because there is "quite a lot of programming still to be done." If the cutover date is not achieved it will have to wait until after the next peak sales period.

Strategists' and Architect's Briefing Paper

The Click and Collect Catalogue Company[10,11] (CCCC) began life as a mail order catalogue sales company after the 2nd World War. It started to open retail outlets where people could browse their catalogue and buy products in the 1980s. It now has 300 retail outlets in towns and cities around the UK, Northern Ireland and the Irish Republic. Its head offices are in Manchester where it has a central warehousing facility. The IT system has grown up haphazardly over the years. New systems have been added as and when they were needed to keep the business going, but without any overall strategy so each system operates more or less independently of each other. Currently there are 5 different IT systems.

1. A warehouse management system—controls stock levels in the warehouse, allocates storage space, and provides buyers with information on suppliers. (WMS)
2. An ordering system with a web front end used by both customers and retail assistants in the retail outlets. (CCCCIT)
3. A distribution management system—organises distribution to the retail outlets and direct to on-line customers. (DMS)
4. Local retail outlet stock management and sales recording system—records sales and tracks stock levels in each of the retail outlets. (LOCATE)
5. Financial management system—manages all head office functions and salaries. (FMS)

All these systems run on hardware originally bought in the late 1980s that is located in the basement of the head office. It is maintained by a small group of in-house IT staff and a software development team that provides 1st and 2nd line support, upgrades equipment when required and develops in-house programs for all the systems at the request of department managers. Much of the hardware has been upgraded over the years, but recently the IT budget has been squeezed. Users are beginning to complain that transaction response times are unacceptably long. It is not unknown for systems to crash when user demand peaks. IT team managers have been warning that the servers are overdue for replacement and that greater resilience is required against catastrophic failure.

The warehouse too has now reached its full capacity and machinery, some of which dates back to the 1990s, is out of date. It is struggling to meet current demand and has to be replaced in the very near future.

On the advice of external consultants a decision was taken by the board 18 months ago to move to a distributed warehousing system. Initially this will be one warehouse in the North and one in the South. New, mechanised pickers and conveyor belts will be installed at the same time. This will involve the replacement of the WMS system.

Your department, The Department of Strategic Information Systems (DSIS) was asked to investigate the options for improving the company's information

---

[10]This scenario is entirely fictitious. Any resemblance to any existing organisation whether in name, similarity of function or operation is coincidental and is not intended to represent them in any way.

[11]Adapted from an original concept in Aggressive Retailers Inc. by Richard Manicom Cases in Management Information Systems.

and goods distribution systems. Your report was produced 14 months ago. Your recommendations are outlined below:

1. It would not be sufficient to simply replace WMS as DMS was designed to support only one distribution point. Therefore DMS would also have to be replaced.
2. Data from CCCCIT and LOCATE was currently incompatible with WMS. This meant that output files from CCCCIT and LOCATE were being produced on a weekly basis, passed through in-house written data conversion programs and then sent to buyers who used their own end user developed database to reorder supplies. This was inefficient, prone to error and caused considerable delays in reordering which sometimes resulted in sales being lost due to the unavailability of stock.
3. It was recommended therefore that WMS, DMS, CCCCIT and LOCATE all be integrated into a new system to be called The DPS.
4. All the IT systems currently used by CCCC are located in the basement of head office. Whilst nightly backups of the systems are taken and stored in a secure location, in the event of catastrophic failure it would take at least 5 days to restore systems assuming suitable hardware could be sourced. In the current economic climate this would probably result in company failure. DPS should therefore either be run on duel distributed systems or using a Software as a Service (SaaS) provider. As the current hardware configurations were unable to accommodate demands on the system, more processing capability would, in any case be needed. Initially this should be used to develop the DPS.
5. The warehouses systems providers supply state of the art robot pickers, forklifts, and conveyor belts as well as driver driven forklift trucks equipped with on-board terminals that could receive directions from the DPS. DPS would however have to conform to the APIs (Application Interfaces) provided with the hardware.
6. Distribution to retail outlets and direct to on-line customers would be handled by the DPS.
7. DPS would include an AI (artificial intelligence) system that would analyse sales data, stock levels etc. and reorder product automatically using predictive analytics. This will reduce delays and staffing levels. Data from the current systems that would need to be imported into DPS to enable this function would, in any case, be required to support DPS' distribution functions.
8. As new technologies such as payment systems and product tracking mechanisms were being introduced on a regular basis, it was recommended that all external interfaces for DPS should be compatible with emerging Internet of Things (IoT) international standards.
9. The strategy has incorporated a potential for handling an increase in volumes of up to 100% over a three year period.

Since producing your report the following has been noted:

1. The delivery of the new processing capacity that had been recommended had been delayed because financial terms could not be agreed.
2. Discussions on the international standard for IoT systems were currently at draft level and subject to change.

3. Some of the interfaces with the warehousing hardware have been enhanced during the last twelve months to provide more flexibility and the architects have recommended that adjustments be made to DPS to take advantage of these.
4. A database component of DPS was to be provided by a third party supplier. DSIS did not consider the supplier chosen to be the best system available, and indeed has some deficiencies, but the supplier had offered some generous concessions for using it. The supplier had also suggested a collaborative venture which would enable DPS to be marketed to other firms in retail distribution. This arrangement could prove very lucrative. The supplier also promised as much free support as was required to get the product working.

A schematic of the proposed system is given at the end of this briefing.

Two weeks ago, the board member with special responsibility for IT held a meeting with the development team managers who told him that they thought the project was hitting problems and might not be ready in time. So a series of meetings consisting of all the departments concerned with the development, the board and a group of consultants called in to evaluate the progress of the project, have been called. The agenda for the meetings are included below.

Agenda for Meeting 1

Objectives:

1. To ensure all departments are fully informed about the DPS project.
2. To assess the current situation on the project.

Agenda:

1. Identify the risks involved in the current plan.
2. Determine the prospects of successful completion of the plan.
3. Determine the prospects for the effective operation of the completed system.
4. A.O.B (Any other Business).

Agenda for Meeting 2

Objective:

Establish a plan of action to resolve any issues arising from meeting 1.

Agenda:

1. Determine what mistakes have been made.
2. Establish an action plan for completion and implementation of DPS.
3. Identify how similar problems can be avoided in the future.
4. A.O.B.

The DPS System

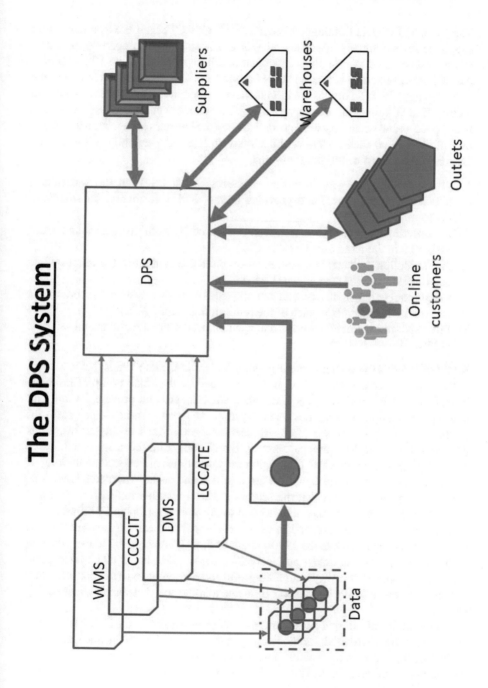

Project Management Team Briefing Paper

The Click and Collect Catalogue Company[12,13] (CCCC) began life as a mail order catalogue sales company after the 2nd World War. It started to open retail outlets where people could browse their catalogue and buy products in the 1980s. It now has 300 retail outlets in towns and cities around the UK, Northern Ireland and the Irish Republic. Its head offices are in Manchester where it has a central warehousing facility. The IT system has grown up haphazardly over the years. New systems have been added as and when they were needed to keep the business going, but without any overall strategy so each system operates more or less independently of each other. Currently there are 5 different IT systems.

1. A warehouse management system—controls stock levels in the warehouse, allocates storage space, and provides buyers with information on suppliers. (WMS)
2. An ordering system with a web front end used by both customers and retail assistants in the retail outlets. (CCCCIT)
3. A distribution management system—organises distribution to the retail outlets and direct to on-line customers. (DMS)
4. Local retail outlet stock management and sales recording system—records sales and tracks stock levels in each of the retail outlets. (LOCATE)
5. Financial management system—manages all head office functions and salaries. (FMS)

All these systems run on hardware originally bought in the late 1980s that is located in the basement of the head office. It is maintained by the small group of in-house IT staff and software developers that your team manages and provide 1st and 2nd line support, equipment upgrades when required and develop in-house programs for all the systems at the request of department managers. Much of the hardware has been upgraded over the years, but recently the IT budget has been squeezed. Users are beginning to complain that transaction response times are unacceptably long. It is not unknown for systems to crash when user demand peaks. Your team have been warning company directors that the servers are well overdue for replacement and that greater resilience is desperately needed to prevent catastrophic IT failure.

The warehouse too is apparently close to reaching its full capacity and machinery, some of which dates back to the 1990s, is out of date. It is struggling to meet current demand. This is causing delays and increasing the workload on the IT systems and must be replaced in the very near future. On the advice of external consultants a decision was taken by the board some time ago to move to a distributed warehousing system.

On the advice of external consultants a decision was taken by the board 18 months ago to move to a distributed warehousing system. Initially this will be one warehouse in the North and one in the South. New, mechanised pickers and conveyor belts will be installed at the same time. This will involve the replacement of the WMS system.

---

[12] This scenario is entirely fictitious. Any resemblance to any existing organisation whether in name, similarity of function or operation is coincidental and is not intended to represent them in any way.

[13] Adapted from an original concept in Aggressive Retailers Inc. by Richard Manicom Cases in Management Information Systems.

Distribution to and from the new warehouses will have to change, so the DMS system will also have to be changed. The task of specifying the new systems was given to the in-house systems architects. Their report, publish 14 months ago, advised that, as so much of the current software would have to change anyway, it would be a good opportunity to revise the CCCCIT and LOCATE systems as well so that they became fully integrated with WMS and DMS. FMS was not included in the plan. In support of their plan they produced an outline systems architecture showing how the four systems would be integrated with the new warehouses. The new system has become known as the Distributed Processing System (DPS).

Approval of the scheme was given 12 months ago.

The warehouse modernisation program calls for the installation of complex systems of conveyor belts, robot forklift trucks as well as driver driven forklift trucks with on-board, on-line terminals that will receive instructions from the DPS. Storage space will be optimised by the system by matching quantity and size of product to storage bin capacity. Incoming product will be directed to the closest available bin with sufficient capacity.

DPS will control what to ship to which warehouse and the retail outlets based on real time sales reports and data analytics. DPS functions need to be written to integrate the APIs provided by the warehouse equipment supplier with DPS.

The project is being developed by your project staff, a few specialist contractors and two or three new recruits. Your team is managing the whole project.

The implementation plan requires the existing warehouse to be shut down for a two week period while DPS is installed and tested on the new servers. Timing of the installation has been planned to avoid the two peak sales periods in spring and autumn. Final systems testing, integration and full scale operational testing of the new servers will also take place in this two week period. The new warehouse hardware must also be installed, tested and integrated with DPS.

Your team recently reported to the Board that development progress had been slower than expected due to the reasons presented below.

The DPS project is a 25–30 person in-house development team which has been drawn from various parts of the company and includes 8 freelance contract staff with specialist skills. It is managed by your team.

System testing which should start next week will have to be deferred because there is quite a lot of programming still to be done. If the cutover date is not achieved it will have to wait until after the next peak sales season has passed.

Reasons for this are:

1. Poor development systems availability which has affected productivity.
2. The systems architects have insisted on certain features (in particular the use of a specific database application) which have increased the development costs and do not seem to be totally necessary.
3. Users have made repeated requests for additional features.
4. The team have been informed that not all the stores will have access to new payment and tracking system when DPS is introduced so additional interfaces

have been developed to provide tracking information and support for old style payment systems.

5. Software for monitoring and controlling the robot pickers in the warehouse was not included in the original specification. This is a new requirement and has added extra cost and time.

Once the new warehouse equipment is installed it will not be possible to ship merchandise to the retail outlets until the whole combination of the new warehouse equipment and the DPS are working properly. Tension between the user group and the IT department have been growing as fears that the DPS will not ready on time grow and it will affect sales. Sales team bonuses are dependent on meeting targets, and these users are already trying to blame the development team for the delays.

An assessment of the current position is that the project is running two weeks late as a result of the poor availability of the development system. Further delay could be cause if more development time is lost as a result of the poor systems availability.

Further points to note:

1. A project plan has been produced on a whiteboard in the senior manager's office. It show the two week slippage from the original plan.
2. The development team have an expert on how the current system works who used to be responsible for its maintenance.
3. Three of the team have attended university level courses on managing inventories, heuristic algorithms and AI.
4. Three weeks ago, after a rather testy meeting between the department's managers and the director responsible for IT, external consultants were called in to evaluate the project. They have been nosing around, asking questions and distracting the development team from their work. They have not yet reported any findings.
5. Further distraction has been caused by an audit demanded by the quality management team who are looking at development processes.
6. The detailed specifications of the warehouse hardware APIs have not yet been provided despite repeated requests, but sufficient information has been gleaned from on-line specs and manuals to develop dummy modules to handle the interface. These will be amended on the fly as the specs become available.
7. Two or three meetings have been held between the development team and the merchandising and sales teams. The DP department is satisfied that it is fully aware of the users' requirements and have kept users fully informed of developments. Minutes of these meetings weren't kept.
8. Two meetings between the director responsible for IT and DP managers have been held. Further resources, particularly more staff and a dedicated development system were requested. He said he would look into it, but no more funding has been made available.
9. Managers are being put under very great pressure to get the project finished.

The project team consists of:

ProjectManagers   3
Programming Supervisors   1

Database Senior Analysts	1
Database Analysts	2
Analysts	1
Senior Programmers	4
Programmers	4
Junior Programmers	5
Contract Programmers	8
Systems Architects	0 (currently active on the project)
Project Controllers	0 (The programming supervisor acts as the project controller for the programmers.)

The work completed so far is as follows:

Work months Used	190
Current Staff	29
Databases Module Designed	14 of 20
Program Modules Designed	47 of 62
Program Modules Written	42 of 62
Program Modules Unit Tested	32 of 62
Program Modules Signed Off	28 of 62

Agenda for Meeting 1

Objectives:

1. To ensure all departments are fully informed about the DPS project.
2. To assess the current situation on the project.

Agenda:

1. Identify the risks involved in the current plan.
2. Determine the prospects of successful completion of the plan.
3. Determine the prospects for the effective operation of the completed system.
4. A.O.B (Any other business).

Agenda for Meeting 2

Objective:

Establish a plan of action to resolve any issues arising from meeting 1.

Agenda:

1. Determine what mistakes have been made.
2. Establish an action plan for completion and implementation of DPS.
3. Identify how similar problems can be avoided in the future.
4. A.O.B.

Development Management Team Briefing Paper

The Click and Collect Catalogue Company[14,15] (CCCC) began life as a mail order catalogue sales company after the 2nd World War. It started to open retail outlets where people could browse the catalogue and buy products in the 1980s. It now has 300 retail outlets in towns and cities around the UK, Northern Ireland and the Irish Republic. Its head offices are in Manchester where it has a central warehousing facility. The IT system has grown up haphazardly over the years. New systems have been added as and when they were needed but files must be transferred between LOCATE and WMS on a daily basis. Each system operates more or less independently of each other. Currently there are 5 different IT systems.

1. A warehouse management system—controls stock levels in the warehouse, allocates storage space, and provides buyers with information on suppliers. (WMS)
2. An ordering system with a web front end used by both customers and retail assistants in the retail outlets. (CCCCIT)
3. A distribution management system—organises distribution to the retail outlets and direct to on-line customers. (DMS)
4. Local retail outlet stock management and sales recording system—records sales and tracks stock levels in each of the retail outlets. (LOCATE)
5. Financial management system—manages all head office functions and salaries. (FMS)

All these systems run on hardware originally bought in the late 1980s that is located in the basement of the head office. You maintain them and provide 1st and 2nd line support, equipment upgrades when required and develop new software for all the systems when required. Much of the hardware has been upgraded over the years, but recently the IT budget has been squeezed. Users are constantly complaining that transaction response times are dreadful. It is common for systems to crash when user demand peaks. It has not helped that the software for DPS (the new replacement system) is being developed on the same servers that provide the real time support for the current systems. IT team managers have been warning that the servers need to be replaced and that greater resilience is required to avoid unrecoverable, catastrophic IT systems failure.

Your team started work on DPS, 12 months or so ago. It is due for handover in 6 weeks time, but there is no chance this deadline will be met. Much of the code still needs to be written and not much testing has been completed.

The implementation plan will require the existing warehouse to be shut down for two weeks to install DPS. Final system testing, integration and full scale operational testing will take place during this period.

---

[14]This scenario is entirely fictitious. Any resemblance to any existing organisation whether in name, similarity of function or operation is coincidental and is not intended to represent them in any way.

[15]Adapted from an original concept in Aggressive Retailers Inc. by Richard Manicom Cases in Management Information Systems.

The development management team told the board member responsible for IT that, at the current rate of progress, there is no chance that the DPS will be ready on time. System testing which should start next week will have to be deferred because there is still tons of programming and module testing to be done.

The main problems are that:

1. The system DPS is being developed on hardware that crashes at least once a week. It takes at least 30 minutes for a complete reload. At other times it runs so slowly that it can take an hour to run a compilation that would normally only take seconds. Reloads to install upgrades have to be done overnight because other users are using the system. This means that it is only possible to run one system test per day. All of this is very frustrating and has reduced development progress to a crawl.
2. The systems architects have insisted on particular features (such as the use of a specific database application) that have increased the development costs and seems completely unnecessary. They have also insisted that the interfaces with payment systems comply with ISO Internet of Things standards, but these keep changing so the software has had to be rewritten two or three times.
3. Users have made repeated requests for additional features such as information on supplier delivery times to be included in the knowledge database and real time currency conversion.
4. The team have been informed that not all the stores will have access to new payment and tracking system when DPS is introduced so additional interfaces have been developed to provide tracking information and support for old style payment systems.
5. Software interfaces for monitoring and controlling the robot pickers in the warehouse was not included in the original specification. This is a new requirement and has resulted in extra cost and time.

The new warehouse hardware is dependent on DPS as is the new warehouse. It is felt that the distribution and sales departments are scoring points over the development team, crying wolf over the 2 week delay in shutting down the warehouse and claiming that it will affect sales badly if DPS is not ready on time.

There is currently a 2 week delay in delivering DPS. More realistically this is likely to be 3 or even 4 weeks. Concern exists that any more down time could cause further delays.

Further points to note:

1. The project plan which is on a whiteboard in the senior manager's office isn't always accessible as when she has a meeting in there, no one else can get in. It shows a two week slippage from the original plan, but is a mess and very difficult to read.

2. The development team does have expertise on the current systems. One of the developers has been responsible for maintaining them for several years and knows the code inside out.

3. Three of the team have attended university level courses on managing inventories, heuristic algorithms and AI so know how to implement the data analytics requirements.

4. External consultants have been nosing around, asking questions and causing a nuisance. Nobody knows what they're supposed to be doing.

5. The development team are also being expected to prepare for a quality audit due in six weeks time.

6. The detailed specifications of the warehouse hardware APIs have not yet been provided despite repeated requests. Information has been gleaned from on-line specs and manuals. Dummy modules to handle the interface have been developed. No one knows for sure whether these will work until the final specs arrive and they're tested with the actual hardware.

7. Two or three meetings have been held between the DP department and user representatives including merchandising, sales and logistics. Your team is satisfied that it is fully aware of all the users' requirements and has kept users fully informed of developments despite the constant calls for changes from the user group. It was not thought necessary to keep minutes of these meetings.

8. Projectmanagers are asking development staff to work more and more overtime. Some staff are beginning to feel exhausted and a culture of bullying and harassment seems to be growing.

The project team consists of:

ProjectManagers	3
Programming Supervisors	1
Database Senior Analysts	1
Database Analysts	2
Analysts	1
Senior Programmers	4
Programmers	4
Junior Programmers	5
Contract Programmers	8
Systems Architects	0 (currently active)
Project Controllers	0 (The programming supervisor acts as the project controller for the programmers.)

The work completed so far is as follows:

Work months Used	190
Current Staff	29

Databases Module Designed   14 of 20
Program Modules Designed   47 of 62
Program Modules Written   42 of 62
Program Modules Unit Tested   32 of 62
Program Modules Signed Off   28 of 62

Agenda for Meeting 1

Objectives:

1. To ensure all departments are fully informed about the DPS project.
2. To assess the current situation on the project.

Agenda:

1. Identify the risks involved in the current plan.
2. Determine the prospects of successful completion of the plan.
3. Determine the prospects for the effective operation of the completed system.
4. A.O.B (Any other Business).

Agenda for Meeting 2

Objective:
   Establish a plan of action to resolve any issues arising from meeting 1.

Agenda:

1. Determine what mistakes have been made.
2. Establish an action plan for completion and implementation of DPS.
3. Identify how similar problems can be avoided in the future.
4. A.O.B.

User Group Briefing Paper

The Click and Collect Catalogue Company[16,17] (CCCC) began life as a mail order catalogue sales company after the 2nd World War. It started to open retail outlets where people could browse their catalogue and buy products in the 1980s. It now has 300 retail outlets in towns and cities around the UK, Northern Ireland and the Irish Republic. Its head offices are in Manchester where it has a central warehousing facility. The IT system has grown up haphazardly over the years. New systems have been added as and when they were needed to keep the business going, but without any overall strategy so each system operates more or less independently of each other. Currently there are 5 different IT systems.

1. A warehouse management system—controls stock levels in the warehouse, allocates storage space, and provides buyers with information on suppliers. (WMS)
2. An ordering system with a web front end used by both customers and retail assistants in the retail outlets. (CCCCIT)
3. A distribution management system—organises distribution to the retail outlets and direct to on-line customers. (DMS)
4. Local retail outlet stock management and sales recording system—records sales and tracks stock levels in each of the retail outlets. (LOCATE)
5. Financial management system—manages all head office functions and salaries. (FMS)

The warehouse has now reached its full capacity and machinery, some of which dates back to the 1990s, is out of date. It is struggling to meet current demand and clearly has to be replaced in the very near future.

On the advice of external consultants a decision was taken by the board 18 months ago to move to a distributed warehousing system. Initially this will be one warehouse in the North and one in the South. New, mechanised pickers and conveyor belts will be installed at the same time. This will involve the replacement of the IT systems with one integrated systems known as DPS.

The implementation plan calls for shutting down the existing warehouse for two weeks while stock is transferred to the new warehouses and the new system installed. Timing of the move is critical to avoid the two peak sales periods in spring and autumn. Final system testing, integration and full scale operational testing is also planned for this period. The next peak is due to begin in 8 weeks time.

At a recent meeting with the board member with special responsibility for IT your group who represent all the probable user of the system such as purchasing, sales and distribution/logistics departments expressed concern about the new system. Your main worries are:

---

[16]This scenario is entirely fictitious. Any resemblance to any existing organisation whether in name, similarity of function or operation is coincidental and is not intended to represent them in any way.

[17]Adapted from an original concept in Aggressive Retailers Inc. by Richard Manicom Cases in Management Information Systems.

1. Critical information concerning the project is being withheld. Through working level contacts with the development team you have heard that the DPS project would probably be late, but the DP department were not saying how late. This made it difficult to analyse the impact on the business since the entire modernisation of the warehouse was dependent upon the DPS.

2. With regard to the functions to be provided by the new system, the DP staff had listened carefully to the objectives the users were trying to accomplish, but had been quite guarded on how these objectives were to be achieved. Many of the tasks staff thought that they would continue to undertake now appear to have been incorporated into the new system (such as seasonal shipping adjustments, purchasing agreements and so on). Users were unclear how the system would do this. Your group have been told that an all singing and dancing AI system is being implemented to do this. However, the DP staff doing the development apparently had only recently been on relatively low level quantitative analysis courses. They thought they knew what they were doing but it was far from clear that the programmers understood all the complexities and subtleties of supplier relations. For example, it was sometimes better to a pay slightly higher price in the short term to guarantee long term consistent supply. Prices could always be negotiated down later. How was the AI going to deal with this?

3. Users have serious concerns about how the cutover was to be handled from the existing system to the DPS since this would occur at the same time as the new warehousing equipment was to be installed. You have been told simply that this had been taken care of.

4. One user in merchandising who was responsible for keeping the existing system running was concerned that all the changes that had been made over the years to the current system were not been carried forward into the new system. The changes had been applied by maintenance staff and it was not clear that the development team were aware of all the modifications. Not all the changes had been documented. Also, there were a number of end user developments that were now in standard use. How were these being incorporated into the new system?

5. Another user was concerned that the senior analyst had not really understood how the existing systems had worked. For example, special promotions could be offered to customers by staff in the retail outlets. These were often last minute deals to get rid of surplus stock. How would the new system manage these? The development staff seemed to think users are nit picking, but the business depends on how these thinks work.

6. General concern was expressed that the developers did not understand the criticality of peak periods. 80% of annual sales were made in these two periods. Any delay would not only lose sales in the short term, but could mean losing major accounts forever. Sales staff had got the impression that the DP staff thought that all sales were to the public, but over the last couple of years CCCC had been building up client accounts. These now accounted for 25% of all sales. If these customers were not satisfied, particularly in the run up to, and during the peak period, CCCC would be in serious trouble.

7. Marketing and sales staff salaries were dependent on bonuses earned for meeting targets set each year. They were very unhappy that they were facing large cuts in income because the DP staff couldn't do their jobs properly.
8. No one had spoken to any of the users about how their jobs might change (or even if they would have jobs at all) once the new system had been implemented. This was a real worry.

Agenda for Meeting 1

Objectives:

1. To ensure all departments are fully informed about the DPS project.
2. To assess the current situation on the project.

Agenda:

1. Identify the risks involved in the current plan.
2. Determine the prospects of successful completion of the plan.
3. Determine the prospects for the effective operation of the completed system.
4. A.O.B.

Agenda for Meeting 2

Objective:
   Establish a plan of action to resolve any issues arising from meeting 1.

Agenda:

1. Determine what mistakes have been made.
2. Establish an action plan for completion and implementation of DPS.
3. Identify how similar problems can be avoided in the future.
4. A.O.B.

Consultants' Briefing Paper

The Click and Collect Catalogue Company[18],[19] (CCCC) began life as a mail order catalogue sales company after the 2nd World War. It started to open retail outlets where people could browse their catalogue and buy products in the 1980s. It now has 300 retail outlets in towns and cities around the UK, Northern Ireland and the Irish Republic. Its head offices are in Manchester where it has a central warehousing facility. The IT system has grown up haphazardly over the years. New systems have been added as and when they were needed to keep the business going, but without any overall strategy so each system operates more or less independently of each other. Currently there are 5 different IT systems.

1. A warehouse management system—controls stock levels in the warehouse, allocates storage space, and provides buyers with information on suppliers. (WMS)
2. An ordering system with a web front end used by both customers and retail assistants in the retail outlets. (CCCCIT)
3. A distribution management system—organises distribution to the retail outlets and direct to on-line customers. (DMS)
4. Local retail outlet stock management and sales recording system—records sales and tracks stock levels in each of the retail outlets. (LOCATE)
5. Financial management system—manages all head office functions and salaries. (FMS)

All these systems run on hardware originally bought in the late 1980s that is located in the basement of the head office. It is maintained by a small group of in-house IT staff and a software development team that provides 1st and 2nd line support, upgrades equipment when required and develops in-house programs for all the systems at the request of department managers. Much of the hardware has been upgraded over the years, but recently the IT budget has been squeezed. Users are beginning to complain that transaction response times are unacceptably long. And it is not unknown for systems to crash when user demand peaks. IT team managers have been warning that the servers are overdue for replacement and that greater resilience is required against catastrophic failure.

The warehouse too has now reached its full capacity and machinery, some of which dates back to the 1990s, is out of date. It is struggling to meet current demand and has to be replaced in the very near future.

On the advice of external consultants a decision was taken by the board 18 months ago to move to a distributed warehousing system. Initially this will be one warehouse in the North and one in the South. New, mechanised pickers and conveyor belts will be installed at the same time. This will involve the replacement of the WMS system.

---

[18]This scenario is entirely fictitious. Any resemblance to any existing organisation whether in name, similarity of function or operation is coincidental and is not intended to represent them in any way.

[19]Adapted from an original concept in Aggressive Retailers Inc. by Richard Manicom Cases in Management Information Systems.

Distribution to and from the new warehouses will have to change, so the DMS system will also have to be changed. The task of specifying the new systems was given to a small team of in-house systems architects. Their report, publish 14 months ago, advised that, as so much of the current software would have to change anyway, it would be a good opportunity to revise the CCCCIT and LOCATE systems as well so that they became fully integrated with WMS and DMS. FMS was not included in the plan. In support of their plan they produced an outline systems architecture showing how the four systems would be integrated with the new warehouses. The new system has become known as the Distributed Processing System (DPS).

Approval of the scheme was given 12 months ago.

The warehouse modernisation program calls for the installation of complex systems of conveyor belts, robot forklift trucks as well as driver driven forklift trucks with on-board, on-line terminals that will receive instructions from the DPS. Storage space will be optimised by the system by matching quantity and size of product to storage bin capacity. Incoming product will be directed to the closest available bin with sufficient capacity.

All decisions as to what to ship to which warehouse or to the retail outlet will be based on sales reports and data analytics generated by the replacement for the LOCATE system. The subsystem intended to replace WMS will need to be specially written to integrate with the APIs provided by the warehouse equipment suppliers.

The project is being developed in-house by a team consisting of some of the original in-house team, contractors and two or three new recruits. It is managed by a small team of software development managers.

The implementation plan calls for shutting down the existing warehouse for two weeks while stock is transferred to the new warehouses and the new IT system installed. Timing of the move is critical to avoid the two peak sales periods in spring and autumn. Final system testing, integration and full scale operational testing is also planned for this period.

The development management team have recently informed the board member with special responsibility for IT that at the current rate of progress there is little chance of the DPS will be ready on time. System testing which should start next week will have to be deferred because there is "quite a lot of programming still to be done." If the cutover date is not achieved it will have to wait until after the next peak period. As a result, your consultancy firm was called in to review the whole project. You will be asked to present your report towards the end of the first meeting (see below).

Preliminary Report

Project Overview

The objectives of the Distributed Processing System (DPS) project is to extend the functionality of the current distribution system in the following ways:

1. Replace the WMS, CCCCIT, DMS and LOCATE systems with one integrated system capable of providing direct access to the following real time information:
   a. warehouse inventory levels
   b. stock levels in the stores
   c. outstanding delivery requests between the warehouse and stores
   d. outstanding purchase requests from suppliers required by the warehouse.

2. Replace the main inventory control mechanism of the existing system with new logic that will automatically replenish stores' stocks from the warehouse based on sales reported from on-line and in stores data. Together with seasonal demand history and data analytics this will automate repurchasing to a large extend and provide expert information to human purchasers where necessary.

3. Provide on-line information to the warehouse operators that will determine inventory picking for, and assembly of, shipments to stores as driven by the new replenishment algorithms outlined above. The on-line access will be implemented coincident with the new warehousing equipment which will provide stock location identifiers appropriate to the new warehousing system.

4. Improved logic in generating stock storage and picking instructions that will optimise space utilisation, the movement of robotic trucks and conveyor belt systems and efficiency of distribution.

5. The new system will be compatible with:

   a. Automatic warehousing hardware
   b. On-line purchasing
   c. Internet of Things International standards.

6. Implementation of new database structure to provide data structures appropriate to the new information.

7. Conversion of existing database files to the new structure.

8. Support on-line communications with driver driven fork trucks in the warehouse.

Project Plan

Original Budget	250 work months
Planned start	Current date minus 12 months
Planned Completion	Current date plus 8 weeks
Actual Start	Current date minus 9 months.

Current Status

Work months Used	190
Current Staff	29
Databases Module Designed	14 of 20
Program Modules Designed	47 of 62
Program Modules Written	42 of 62
Program Modules Unit Tested	32 of 62
Program Modules Signed Off	28 of 62

Current Staff Assignments

ProjectManagers	3
Programming Supervisors	1
Database Senior Analysts	1
Database Analysts	2
Analysts	1
Senior Programmers	4
Programmers	4
Junior Programmers	5
Contract Programmers	8
Systems Architects	0 (currently active)
Project Controllers	0 (The programming supervisor acts as the project controller for the programmers.)

N.b. Work remaining appears to be considerably greater in the 8 weeks remaining than the resources available. This needs to be calculated.

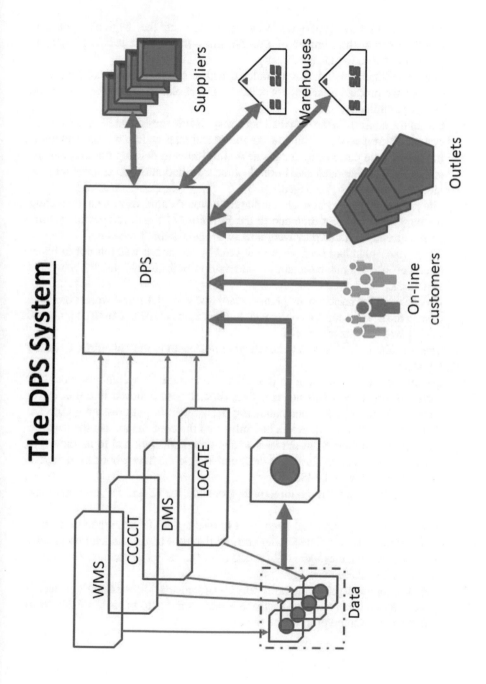

Comments on Project Management

1. The programming supervisor was appointed at the beginning of last month because the number of programmers had grown too large for the projectmanagers to manage directly.
2. The projectmanagers felt that too much time had been spent on database design because the product used was not suitable. The choice had been dictated by the systems architects.
3. One of the analysts in the team had been responsible for maintaining the current system. He was an expert on how the merchandising system worked and knew the appropriate philosophy for the new algorithms to develop the data analytics and knowledge database. Several other staff had attended courses on how inventories should be managed.
4. The project management team felt that they would come very close to meeting the target, but had lost time due to the fallibility of the development system. They currently felt that they were now two weeks behind schedule.
5. The cutover plan had been given low priority so far but was felt not to be an issue because the database analyst understood both the old and the new data structures.
6. No one from the project management team had visited the new warehouse sites or seen the new automated equipment, but had read details of it in trade journals. A visit was felt unnecessary.
7. The consultants had sensed some negative responses to their enquiries from the DP staff.
8. The project management team did not believed that the warehouse would be closed down if DPS was not ready on time. It was believed that this was a tactic being used by the merchandising department to put pressure on the DP department. However, directors had informed the consultants that the lease on the current warehouse ran out in 8 weeks time and stock had to be moved to the new sites. The new sites were designed around the new robotic systems and would not work with DMS.
9. Two meetings between the director responsible for IT and DP managers had been held.
10. Two or three meetings had been held between the DP department and user group representatives. The DP department believed that it had kept users fully informed and that they were fully aware of the users' requirements. There were no minutes of these meetings.
11. The development plan was on a whiteboard in the DP manager's office. It showed a two week slippage on the original plan due to the system shutdown which had prevented progress on the development.

12. Consultant's estimate is that barely half the resources required to complete the work on time are available. (Actual calculation of resources required and projected completion date can be done using project data above.)

Agenda for Meeting 1

Objectives:

1. To ensure all departments are fully informed about the DPS project.
2. To assess the current situation on the project.

Agenda:

1. Identify the risks involved in the current plan.
2. Determine the prospects of successful completion of the plan.
3. Determine the prospects for the effective operation of the completed system.
4. A.O.B.

Agenda for Meeting 2

Objective:
   Establish a plan of action to resolve any issues arising from meeting 1.

Agenda:

1. Determine what mistakes have been made.
2. Establish an action plan for completion and implementation of DPS.
3. Identify how similar problems can be avoided in the future.
4. A.O.B.

Directors' Briefing Paper

The Click and Collect Catalogue Company[20,21] (CCCC) began life as a mail order catalogue sales company after the 2nd World War. It started to open retail outlets where people could browse their catalogue and buy products in the 1980s. It now has 300 retail outlets in towns and cities around the UK, Northern Ireland and the Irish Republic. Its head offices are in Manchester where it has a central warehousing facility.

Competition in the catalogue trading market has become fierce in the last 5 years, and although CCCC has successfully doubled the volume of sales, margins have been halved. The company struggled to survive the 2008 financial crash and had to borrow heavily to keep going. The squeeze on margins and the sluggish UK economy has meant that the company has not been able to reduce the level of debt as it had hoped. Consequently, the cost of further borrowing for the company is relatively high. The cost of servicing this historic debt has meant that although CCCC has made an operating profit in each of the last two years, it has suffered accumulated losses of £0.5m over the same period. This has resulted in a number of cost cutting exercises and reduced investment in new equipment.

A market analysts report suggested that by specialising in corporate clients rather than retail and investing in logistics, CCCC could beat the market. They are well placed to do this as they have been cultivating this side of the business for the last 3 or 4 years and have a good reputation for delivery. Margins will remain tight however and the only way to boost profit will be to increase volumes. The next 2 peak sales periods will be critical for the company's future.

Just over 18 months ago the Board recognised that something had to be done. The warehouse was reaching full capacity and the machinery, some of which dates back to the 1990s, is out of date. It is struggling to meet current demand and has to be replaced in the very near future. The IT systems too was creaking and experts in the company suggested something radical had to be done with it. External consultants were bought in to advise the company. They advised a move towards a distributed warehousing system, upgrade of the warehouse management hardware to modern robot controlled systems and to replace the warehouse management computer system. The company's own IT strategists and architects were given the task of advising how this could be done, and produced their report 14 months ago.

The IT strategists reported that it would be possible to increase throughput at reduced cost by:

1. Integrating all the current IT systems into one new system
2. Manage the new warehouse machinery with the new system
3. Add an artificial intelligence component that would be able to

---

[20]This scenario is entirely fictitious. Any resemblance to any existing organisation whether in name, similarity of function or operation is coincidental and is not intended to represent them in any way.

[21]Adapted from an original concept in Aggressive Retailers Inc. by Richard Manicom Cases in Management Information Systems.

a. provide much better real time reports on business activity
b. speed up deliveries
c. optimise warehouse storage capacity.

The new system would be known as the DPS (Distributed Processing System).

This report was approved 12 months ago and work began. However the investment costs have seriously stretched the finances of the company. The costs have risen from the original estimate of £1.2m to a current spend of £2m and an expectation that a further £1/2m will be needed. This drain on resources is causing serious cash flow difficulties. The banks have agreed to support CCCC for a further 3 months but have threatened to foreclose if the trading position shows no signs of improving by then. DPS has to begin to show a return on investment by then. The lease on the current warehouse runs out in 8 weeks time and cannot be extended.

The board member with special responsibility for finance who also has responsibility for IT recently held a meeting with the development managers who told him that they thought the project was hitting problems and might not be ready in time. Having previously heard rumours that all was not well he called in external consultants three weeks ago to examine the situation. Development managers expressed unease with this decision. The consultant's verbal report will be available at the coming project meeting.

The IT director also held a meeting with a group representing the system's intended users. They expressed the following concerns:

1. The users felt that they were being kept in the dark by the development team managers. They knew from working level contacts that the DPS project would probably be late, but the DP department were taking no official stand on how late. This made it difficult for them to analyse the impact on the business since the entire modernisation of the warehouse was dependent upon the DPS.
2. The DP staff had taken account of user requirements but were not very forthcoming on how these requirements were to be provided. DP staff also seemed to be adding additional features off their own bat that the users thought were not strictly necessary.
3. The users had concerns about how the cutover was to be handled from the existing system to the DPS since this would occur at the same time as the new warehousing equipment was to be installed. The implementation plan called for shutting down the entire warehouse for two weeks during the run up to the next peak sales period. During this time the new equipment must be installed, tested and integrated with the DPS.
4. The users were not sure how changes made to the old system would be carried forward.
5. The users weren't sure that DP staff really understood how the existing system worked.

A series of meetings has been called of all the parties involved in the project. The agendas for the meetings is below.

Agenda for Meeting 1

Objectives:

1. To ensure all departments are fully informed about the DPS project.
2. To assess the current situation on the project.

Agenda:

1. Identify the risks involved in the current plan.
2. Determine the prospects of successful completion of the plan.
3. Determine the prospects for the effective operation of the completed system.
4. A.O.B.

Agenda for Meeting 2

Objective:
   Establish a plan of action to resolve any issues arising from meeting 1.

Agenda:

1. Determine what mistakes have been made.
2. Establish an action plan for completion and implementation of DPS.
3. Identify how similar problems can be avoided in the future.
4. A.O.B.

Index

© Springer Nature Switzerland AG 2020
C. Rosen, *Guide to Software Systems Development*,
https://doi.org/10.1007/978-3-030-39730-2

Printed in the United States
by Baker & Taylor Publisher Services